Movement for Change

Evangelicals and Social Transformation

Editor: David Hilborn

The Evangelical Alliance Commission on Unity and Truth
among Evangelicals

(ACUTE)

British Library Cataloguing in Publication Data
A catalogue record for this book is available from the British Library

ISBN 1–84227–275-6

Typeset by the Editor
and printed and bound in Great Britain by
Nottingham Alpha Graphics

Contents

The Temple Addresses

Afterword

Contributors

David Hilborn (Editor) is Head of Theology at the Evangelical Alliance UK. In this role, he runs the Alliance's Commission on Unity and Truth among Evangelicals (ACUTE). ACUTE has published a number of books in conjunction with Paternoster Press, and he has been closely involved in their production. He edited *Faith, Hope and Homosexuality* (1998), *The Nature of Hell* (2000) and *'Toronto' in Perspective* (2001), co-edited *God and the Generations* (2002), and contributed to *Evangelicalism and the Orthodox Church* (2002) and *Faith, Health and Prosperity* (2003). With Ian Randall, he co-authored the first full-length history of the Alliance, *One Body in Christ* (2001). In his own right, he has published books and articles on theology and culture, ethics, liturgy and the development of Evangelicalism. His 1997 book, *Picking Up the Pieces* (Hodder & Stoughton) has been influential in helping Evangelicals and others to understand and engage with postmodernity. He holds degrees from the Universities of Oxford (MA) and Nottingham (BA, PhD). His doctoral thesis, on theological language, was supervised by the Revd Prof Anthony Thiselton. Alongside his academic work, he pastored United Reformed Church congregations in Nottinghamshire and central London before joining the Church of England. He currently serves as Assistant Curate at St Mary's, Acton, in West London. He is also an Associate Research Fellow of the London School of Theology (formerly the London Bible College).

Joel Edwards is General Director of the Evangelical Alliance (UK). After emigrating to Britain as a child from Jamaica, he grew up in North London, attending a local congregation of the New Testament Church of God. He read theology at the London Bible College (now the London School of Theology) and, on graduating, worked for ten years as an officer in the Inner London Probation Service. After ordination and service as a Pastor in Mile End New Testament Church of God, in 1988 he was appointed Director of the West Indian Evangelical Alliance (latterly the African-Caribbean Evangelical Alliance). In 1992 he became UK Director of the Evangelical Alliance, and in 1997 succeeded Clive Calver as General Director. As well as appearing regularly on radio and television, he is the author of *Lord, Make Us One - But Not All the Same! Seeking Unity in Diversity* (London: Hodder & Stoughton, 1999) and *Cradle, Cross and Empty Tomb* (Hodder & Stoughton, 2001). He is an executive member of the New Testament Church of God and continues to serve their Mile End congregation as Associate Pastor.

David Bebbington is Professor of History at the University of Stirling. He was an undergraduate at Jesus College, Cambridge and commenced his doctorate there before completing it as a Research Fellow of Fitzwilliam College in 1975. He began teaching history at Stirling in 1976. He since has also taught at the University of Alabama, at Regent College, Vancouver, at Notre Dame University, Indiana, at the University of Pretoria, South Africa, and at Baylor University, Texas. He is the author of *Patterns in History* (IVP, 1979), *The Nonconformist Conscience* (Allen & Unwin, 1982), *Evangelicalism in Modern Britain* (Unwin Hyman, 1989), *William Ewart Gladstone: Faith and Politics in Modern Britain* (Eerdmans, 1993) and *Holiness in Nineteenth-Century England* (Paternoster, 2000). He has edited *The Baptists in Scotland* (Baptist Union of Scotland, 1988) and *The Gospel in the World: International Baptist Studies* (Paternoster, 2002). In addition, he has co-edited with Mark Noll and George Rawlyk *Evangelicalism: Comparative Studies of Popular Protestantism in North America, the British Isles and Beyond, 1700-1990* (Oxford, 1994), with Roger Swift *Gladstone Centenary Essays* (Liverpool, 2000), and with Timothy Larsen *Modern Christianity and Cultural Aspirations* (Sheffield Academic Press, 2003). He has recently returned to the subject of Gladstone, producing *The Mind of Gladstone* (Oxford, 2004), a volume on the theological, classical and political thought of the four times Liberal Prime Minister.

John Wolffe is Professor of Religious History at the Open University. After graduating from the University of Oxford (MA, DPhil), he taught history at the University of York before joining the O.U. as Lecturer in Religious Studies in 1990. He then served as Sub-Dean (Research and Quality Assurance) of the Faculty of Arts from 1994 to 1997 and as Head of the Department of Religious Studies from 1998 to 2001. He currently chairs a course on Evangelicals, Women and Community in Nineteenth century Britain, and will soon chair another on Conflict, Conversion and Co-existence in Religion. His research is concentrated on interactions between religion and national identity in the North Atlantic world since the late eighteenth century, and he has a particular interest in Evangelicalism. Future plans include an international survey of Evangelicalism between the 1790s and the 1850s, and a major project on William Wilberforce. His publications include *The Protestant Crusade in Great Britain 1829-1860* (Clarendon Press, 1991); *God and Greater Britain: Religion and National Life in Britain and Ireland 1843-1945* (Routledge, 1994); *Evangelical Faith and Public Zeal: Evangelicals and Society in Britain, 1780-1990*, (ed. SPCK, 1995); *Great Deaths: Grieving, Religion, and Nationhood in Victorian and Edwardian Britain* (British Academy/Oxford University Press, 2000), and *Yorkshire Returns of the 1851 Census of Religious Worship: Volume 1: Introduction, City of York and East Riding*, Borthwick Texts and Calendars 25 (University of York, 2000).

Keith Warrington is Director of Postgraduate Studies and Lecturer in New Testament Studies and Greek at Regents Theological College, Nantwich, Cheshire. Prior to this, he served with Operation Mobilisation in Europe, co-founded and pastored a church on Merseyside, and then pastored a church in Derbyshire. His postgraduate degrees were based on an exegesis of James 5:13-18 (MPhil), and on the healings and exorcisms of Jesus and contemporary healing praxis (PhD). He is the editor of the *Journal of European Pentecostal Theological Association* and is also an editor of the *Studies in Charismatic and Pentecostal Issues* series (Paternoster Press). He has written and edited a number of books and articles, including *Pentecostal Perspectives* (Paternoster, 1998) *Jesus the Healer: Paradigm or Phenomenon?* (Paternoster, 2000) and *God and Us: A Life-Changing Adventure* (Scripture Union, 2004). He is currently preparing two more volumes for publication: *The Spirit in the New Testament and the Christian* (Hendrickson, 2004) and *Healing and Suffering: Biblical and Pastoral Reflections* (Paternoster, 2004). He serves on ACUTE, the Theological Commission of the Evangelical Alliance.

Graham McFarlane is Deputy Director of Research and Senior Lecturer in Systematic Theology at the London School of Theology (formerly London Bible College). He did both undergraduate and post-graduate work at the London Bible College (BA, MA) before completing a doctorate on Edward Irving's Christology under the late Professor Colin Gunton at King's College, London. His publications include *Christ and the Spirit: The Doctrine of the Incarnation According to Edward Irving* (Paternoster, 1996); *Edward Irving: The Trinitarian Face of God* (St. Andrew Press, 1996); *Why Do You Believe What You Believe about the Holy Spirit?* (Paternoster, 1998), and *Why Do You Believe What You Believe about Jesus?* (Paternoster, 2000).

Anna Robbins is Director of Training and Lecturer in Theology and Contemporary Culture at the London School of Theology (formerly the London Bible College). A Canadian, she took degrees at the Universities of Carelton (BA) and Acadia (MA, MRE) before completing a PhD under Professor Alan Sell at the University of Wales, Aberystwyth - published as *Methods in the Madness: Methodological Diversity in Twentieth-Century Christian Social Ethics* (Paternoster, 2004). She edited and contributed to *Christian Life and Today's World* (Scripture Union, 2002), and has also contributed to *Full of the Holy Spirit and Faith* (ed. Scott Dunham, Gaspereau Press, 1997), *P.T. Forsyth: Theologian for the New Millennium* (ed. Alan Sell, URC, 2000) and *Matrix Revelations* (ed. Steve Couch, Damaris, 2003). Her special interests include ethics and theological method.

John Coffey is Reader in Early Modern British History at the University of Leicester. A graduate of Cambridge University (MA, PhD), his publications include *Politics, Religion and the British Revolutions: The Mind of Samuel Rutherford* (CUP, 1997); *Persecution and Toleration in Protestant England, 1558–1689* (Longman, 2000); 'Democracy and popular religion: Moody and Sankey's mission to Britain, 1873–75', in E.F. Biagini (ed.), *Citizenship and*

Community: Liberals, Radicals and Collective Identities in the British Isles, 1865–1931 (CUP, 1996); 'Samuel Rutherford and the political thought of the Scottish Covenanters' in J. Young (ed.) *Celtic Dimensions of the British Civil Wars* (John Donald, 1997), and 'Puritanism and liberty revisited: the case for toleration in the English Revolution', *Historical Journal*, 41:4 (1998). He acts as an adviser to the Jubilee Centre in Cambridge.

Joe Kapolyo is Principal of All Nations Christian College in Ware, Hertfordshire. Before taking up this post in 2001, he had been a tutor at the college. Prior to that, he was Principal of the Theological College of Central Africa at Ndola in his native Zambia, and served as Pastor of Central Baptist Church, Harare, Zimbabwe between 1991-94. He holds degrees from the London Bible College (BA), the University of London (MA) and the University of Aberdeen (MTh). He is a member of the Accrediting Council for Theological Education in Africa (ACTEA) and is currently preparing a book on 'The Human Condition' for The Global Christian Library - a new set of publications aimed at theological students and church leaders in the developing world, the Series Editor for which is John Stott.

James Jones has been Bishop of Liverpool since 1998. After studying at Exeter University and going on to qualify as a teacher, he trained for the Church of England ministry at Wycliffe Hall, Oxford and served as Curate of Christ Church with Emmanuel, Clifton. He was then Vicar of Emmanuel, South Croydon before being appointed Bishop of Hull in 1994. During his time in Liverpool, he has contributed increasingly to debates on social ethics, and in 2002 published *The Moral Leader* (IVP, with Andrew Goddard). As part of this commitment, he has taken a special interest in the theology of the environment - an issue explored in his most recent book, *Jesus and the Earth* (SPCK, 2003). He chairs the Government's New Deal for Communities programme in Liverpool, the North West Constitutional Convention, and the Board of an inner city faith-based City Academy. He also chairs the Council of Wycliffe Hall.

Jim Wallis is Editor-in-Chief of *Sojourners* magazine in Washington, D.C. and founder of Call to Renewal, a national federation of faith-based organizations working to overcome poverty and revitalize American politics. He has been a visiting Fellow at the Center for the Study of Values in Public Life at Harvard Divinity School and now teaches a course on 'Faith, Politics, and Society' for the Kennedy School of Government at Harvard University. He travels extensively, giving more than two hundred talks each year, and is a frequent commentator on American National Public Radio. His many publications include *Call to Conversion* (Lion, 1982); *The New Radical* (Lion 1983); *Agenda for Biblical People* (Triangle, 1986); *The Soul of Politics* (Zondervan, 1995); *Who Speaks for God? An Alternative to the Religious Right - A Politics* *of Compassion, Community and Civility* (Bantam Dell, 1997), and *Faith Works: Lessons on Spirituality and Social Action* (SPCK, 2002).

Lord Carey of Clifton was the 103rd Archbishop of Canterbury, holding office between 1991 and his retirement in 2002. After service in the RAF, he studied divinity at King's College, London and was Curate at St Mary's, Islington from 1962-66. He then lectured at Oak Hill Theological College in London and St John's College, Nottingham, during which time he was awarded his doctorate. In 1975, he returned to parish ministry, leading a major renovation and mission outreach as Vicar of St Nicholas, Durham - an experience he wrote about in the book *Church in the Marketplace* (Kingsway, 1984). He returned to the ministerial education sphere as Principal of Trinity Theological College, Bristol between 1982 and 1987. He was then appointed Bishop of Bath and Wells and served there until his call to Canterbury. His time as Archbishop was marked by the decision to allow women to be ordained to the priesthood in the Church of England, by the Decade of Evangelism, by the 1998 Lambeth Conference of bishops, and by increased tensions on the issue of homosexuality. His books include *I Believe in Man* (Hodder & Stoughton, 1977), *The Meeting of the Waters: A Balanced Contribution to the Ecumenical Debate* (Hodder & Stoughton, 1985), *The Great God Robbery* (Collins, 1989), *I Believe* (SPCK, 1991), *The Gate of Glory* (Hodder and Stoughton, 1992), *Sharing a Vision* (DLT, 1993) and *Canterbury Letters to the Future* (Kingsway, 1999). His memoirs are due to be published in mid-2004.

Martyn Eden is Director of Strategic Development at the Evangelical Alliance UK. Part of his brief involves oversight of the Alliance's theological and public affairs work, and he has been instrumental in shaping the Alliance's commitment to inspiring Evangelicals to become a Movement for Change at the heart of British civic and community life. Before joining the Alliance he was Dean of the London Institute of Contemporary Christianity and Director of Research and Publications for Christian Impact. Earlier, he had been Principal Lecturer in Public and Social Administration at Southampton Institute for Higher Education. With Ernest Lucas he wrote *Being Transformed* (Marshalls, 1988). He also edited *Britain on the Brink* (Crossway, 1983) and (with David Wells) *The Gospel in the Modern World: A Tribute to John Stott* (IVP, 1993).

Preface

The majority of the papers collected together in this book are drawn from a consultation held at Oak Hill Theological College on 9th-10th July 2002. The consultation was organized by ACUTE - the Evangelical Alliance (UK) Commission on Unity and Truth among Evangelicals. ACUTE, which I direct in my capacity as Head of Theology at the Alliance, comprises some twenty theologians and Christian leaders. Over the past few years, it has sought to define the nature of evangelical unity and witness, and to reflect on controversial issues which have in one way or another challenged that unity and witness. ACUTE's publications have included *Faith, Hope and Homosexuality* (1998), *The Nature of Hell* (2000), *'Toronto' in Perspective* (2001), *Evangelicalism and the Orthodox Church* (2001), *One Body in Christ: The History and Significance of the Evangelical Alliance* (2001), *God and the Generations: Youth, Age and the Church Today* (2002), and *Faith, Health and Prosperity* (2003). In addition to this publication work, both ACUTE and the Theology Department have provided advice and support to the membership, staff and councils of the Alliance, as well as representing evangelical theological concerns more generally within the academic world, the church, the media and wider society.

In 1999, the Directors of the Alliance undertook to address the social transformation agenda which might lie ahead for British Evangelicals in the new millennium. Aware of the significant changes wrought over the previous three decades or so by secularization, multiculturalism and pluralism, and conscious of the major civic and ecclesiastical realignments which had ensued, the Directors resolved to focus the Alliance on the task of encouraging Evangelicals to become a 'Movement for Change' in the public life of the United Kingdom.

While very aware of the breakdown in the so-called 'Post-War Consensus' in politics and social life, and of the severe decline in UK church attendance since the 1960s, the Directors noted that the same period had seen a rise in the number and impact of more issue-specific social movements - movements now characteristically referred to as 'Non-Governmental Organizations', or 'NGOs'. The Directors realized that in many ways the Evangelical Alliance had functioned as an 'NGO' since its formation in 1846 - leading or brokering campaigns on religious liberty, poverty, alcohol abuse, pornography, unemployment, crime and the like.[1] Yet they also saw that whereas for most its

---

[1] For more detail on this record of social involvement, see Ian Randall and David Hilborn, *One Body in Christ: The History and Significance of the Evangelical Alliance* (Carlisle: Paternoster, 2001), 71-102.

history the EA had operated within the relatively amenable context of 'Christendom' - that is, within a culture significantly shaped and institutionalized along Christian lines and according to Judaeo-Christian values - it was now having to operate within a 'post-Christendom' setting where such values attracted less natural support from the state, from lawmakers, from civic authorities, from journalists and broadcasters, and from the population at large. As a 21st century NGO, the Directors realized that the Alliance would have more explicitly to uphold the positive aspects of Britain's Judaeo-Christian heritage, lest these be submerged by the rising tide of relativistic postmodern 'tolerance' and 'diversity'. At the same time, however, they understood that the Alliance would be obliged increasingly to make its case, issue by issue, within an expanding forum of interest-groups, lobbies and 'faith-communities'. While this new situation appeared in many ways to be a daunting one, the Directors took inspiration from the work of Robert Bellah and others, which suggested that social movements represented by as little as 2% of an entire population could, with clear vision, efficient organisation and skilled campaigning, profoundly influence the cultural ethos and social policy of a nation.[2]

In September 2000, the Movement for Change initiative was endorsed by the Alliance's Council of Management. Initial groundwork and research was then undertaken, leading to major presentations on Movement for Change themes at the Alliance's National Assembly of Evangelicals in Cardiff in November 2001. At the same event, a special booklet drafted by an EA staff team including Joel Edwards, Martyn Eden, Mannie Stewart, Gill Troup and myself was circulated under the title *Uniting for Change*. Later the same month, the first in a new series of annual lectures on civic mission - the 'Temple Addresses' - was given by the Bishop of Liverpool, the Rt Revd James Jones at the Inner Temple Hall in London. At the same time, an ambitious mission project called Face Values was formulated to combine established models of evangelism with social transformation initiatives which bore out the Movement for Change ethos. This was launched in the spring of 2002, and culminated in a national media campaign in the autumn. Alongside the characteristic evangelical activism of Movement for Change, two important steps were taken to provide proper reflection on it. The first of these occurred in March 2002, when a Strategic Consultative Forum was convened to look more closely at both secular and religious models of social transformation, and to examine which might be relevant to the Alliance's aims and purposes. The second was the Oak Hill ACUTE consultation on which this present book is based.

---

[2] Robert Bellah, 'Civil Religion: The Sacred and the Political in American Life' (A Conversation with Sam Keen)', *Psychology Today*, 9/8, January 1976, 58-65. For a more detailed scholarly overview of the impact of campaigning organizations on wider society, see Hank Johnston and Bert Klandermans (eds.), *Social Movements and Culture* (London: UCL Press, 1995).

Chaired by Professor David Wright, the consultation featured five of the eight main papers included here: those by David Bebbington, John Wolffe, Anna Robbins, Joe Kapolyo and myself. Graham McFarlane was also scheduled to speak, but had to withdraw unavoidably at late notice; the paper he was due to have delivered is included in this volume. After each presentation, formal responses were made by two representatives from the Jubilee Centre in Cambridge: John Coffey and John Ashcroft. In its advisory work with various civic bodies, in its social regeneration projects and in its establishment of the Relationships Foundation, the Jubilee Centre has been a pioneer in evangelical social transformation, and it seemed appropriate to invite John Coffey to expand on the helpful insights he offered at the consultation. The resultant essay also appears here, as does a new paper by Keith Warrington, who serves on ACUTE. The consultation ended with a plenary session convened by Martyn Eden, who, as Director of Strategic Development at the Alliance, is responsible for the day-to-day management and progress of Movement for Change. His Afterword for this book reflects several of the issues discussed during that plenary, and considers how the Evangelical Alliance, and Evangelicalism in Britain, might move forward in civic and social transformation. Joel Edwards, the General Director of the Alliance, has been a passionate advocate of the Movement for Change agenda from the beginning, and is its highest profile spokesperson. As well as attending the Oak Hill meeting and contributing vitally to the discussions which took place there, his Foreword gives a helpful insight into the genesis of the Alliance's thinking in this area. Finally, given the interrelationship between Movement for Change and the Temple Address, it is good to be able to include here the texts not only of James Jones' inaugural lecture from 2001, but also of those from 2002 and 2003 - respectively given by Jim Wallis and Lord Carey. While these texts are inevitably more rhetorical and less 'academic' than the main papers, they offer valuable insights which complement this book's concerns. The reader will notice that Lord Carey addresses the subject of hope, which was the Alliance's first nominated annual 'theme' of Movement for Change. The theme chosen for 2004 is 'trust', and for 2005, 'respect'.

Given the Evangelical Alliance (UK)'s main sphere of operation, most of the material collected here focuses, appropriately enough, on social transformation in Britain. Having said this, the close historical ties between British and North American Evangelicalism are reflected in the papers contributed by David Bebbington, Anna Robbins and Graham McFarlane, while Joe Kapolyo's analysis of social development in Africa serves as a reminder of the increasing globalization of mission, and my own and John Coffey's analyses of the relationship between church and state in evangelical and Protestant thought draw on instructive examples from overseas.

David Bebbington's *Evangelicalism in Modern Britain* is widely recognized as the definitive work on the subject, and here he applies his extensive knowledge of evangelical social engagement since the eighteenth century to draw instructive contrasts between enduring and sometimes justified public perceptions of Evangelicals as 'censorious, power-loving and hypocritical', and their otherwise 'long and honourable record' of care for the poor and dispossessed. Seeing salutary lessons in this for Evangelicals today, he suggests that they will have to temper their tendency towards 'clamour' on matters of personal morality with a more rounded social theology which balances individual and communal concerns in a biblical way.

Whereas David Bebbington examines the theological motivation and ethos of evangelical social action, John Wolffe explores the mechanisms by which Evangelicals achieved change, including a fascinating comparison of British Evangelicalism's two most famous social reformers, William Wilberforce and Anthony Ashley-Cooper, the seventh Earl of Shaftesbury. Much invoked today by those wishing to re-emphasize evangelical engagement with society, Prof. Wolffe points out that although the culture in which these men operated was significantly different from our own, they can still serve in many ways as exemplars for those looking to transform the world in the name of the gospel.

Keith Warrington casts a biblical scholar's eye over Evangelicalism's historic commitments to social change, and asks provocatively whether they are in fact reflected in the witness of the New Testament and the early Christian community. Although he finds the characteristic emphasis of his own Pentecostal tradition on personal evangelism to be the prior concern of the apostolic churches, he shows that the New Testament does contain the seeds of what would subsequently become a much fuller civic and cultural interaction. Graham McFarlane reviews recent trends in evangelical systematic theology, and demonstrates how leading figures in the field like Stanley Grenz and Miroslav Volf have looked beyond the parameters of evangelical scholarship as such to assimilate models of social, ethical and political trinitarianism developed in the work of Jürgen Moltmann, Stanley Hauerwas, Colin Gunton, Walter Wink, Leonardo Boff and others.

Anna Robbins scrutinizes four models of social transformation which have informed, or which might yet inform, evangelical social theology and ethics. First, she suggests, Evangelicals have sometimes adopted a 'culture war' stance, setting themselves against 'the world', 'liberals', 'secularists' and the like, and steeling themselves to 'fight the good fight'. On occasion, she concedes, such belligerence might have been necessary - even if it has not always presented the gospel in the most attractive terms. She observes, however, that more radical Evangelicals have latterly been influenced by 'Action-Reflection' models, drawing on the thinking of various liberation theologies, and seeking to find a distinctive evangelical response to issues of poverty, feminism, racism and so on. Such 'issue-specific' ethics may well become increasingly prevalent in church and society as a whole, but the challenge for Evangelicals will be to take account of these particular concerns whilst maintaining their historic stress on the systematic, all-encompassing scope of true doctrine. The third and fourth models explored are, writes Dr Robbins, more community-based, comprising Moral Formation and Study-Dialogue Approaches. The first is more localized than the second, and presents various 'communities of virtue' as exemplars to the wider culture; the second is more 'catholic', in that it underlines the importance of an interaction between the academy, the local congregation and the wider church.

Both John Coffey's and my own papers then examine one of the 'sharp ends' of evangelical social theology and ethics - the relationship between Evangelicals and the state. Contrary to certain evangelical stereotypes, Dr Coffey applies his expertise as an historian of the early modern period to show that Evangelicals were in significant ways responsible for the formation of the liberal democratic state. Moreover, he argues that there are many features of this model which Evangelicals will need to preserve, while adopting a more critical stance towards a particular kind of 'late modern' liberalism whose stress on individual autonomy and neglect of 'moral communities' is less amenable to the precepts of the gospel. My own contribution particularizes these concerns in a close analysis of how Protestants and Evangelicals since the Reformation period have dealt with the challenge of Paul's instructions on the state in Romans 13. It culminates in three case studies - of the German church under Hitler, of Baptists in Communist Russia, and of 'concerned Evangelicals' in Apartheid South Africa, and suggests key lessons for evangelical social engagement today. Joe Kapolyo's paper helpfully extends these concerns to the arena of world mission. After reviewing evangelical statements on social concern since the epochal Lausanne Covenant of 1974, he draws on his own experience of development projects in Zambia to remind us that any 'movement for change' by Evangelicals in Britain will now more than ever have global implications.

Great thanks are due to everyone who has contributed to this book, as well as to the thirty-strong group of Alliance staff, ACUTE members and expert speakers who made the Oak Hill consultation such a memorable and productive event. Special thanks must go to my Secretary, Julia Murphy, for all the administrative help she has given in bringing this book to press. As always, my wife, Mia, and my children, Matthew and Alice, have graciously borne my lengthy forays into the study to prepare this latest ACUTE volume for publication. Their love and support is immense and unstinting, and I am forever grateful to them.

It is a privilege to be able to make the creative dialogue and stimulating thought which was on display at the Oak Hill consultation available to a wider audience. I hope it will inspire further positive discussion and, not least, that it will indeed play a part in prompting evangelical and other Christians to become a Movement for Change in contemporary Britain, to the glory and praise of God.

David Hilborn, Advent 2003

Foreword

Joel Edwards

Christianity in Britain is losing ground. Church attendance since the 1960s has plummeted, and the church itself is widely perceived to represent ideas and practices which have become irrelevant. Government and civic institutions as such are becoming more 'neutral' with respect to religion, while at the same time seeking to accommodate a greater diversity of religious traditions and faith communities in an even-handed way. In the process, the UK church is having to come to terms with a relative loss of prestige and public influence.

Of course, the news is not all bad. In some quarters there is significant growth - mostly, indeed, within evangelical congregations. Even where such congregations decline, the loss tends to be slower than in other sectors of the church. This, however, should be cause neither for complacency nor insularity. The divergence of our civic society from the Judaeo-Christian values which have done so much to shape it, and its corresponding embrace of a more secular, relativistic ethos, must be of concern to all Christians. In the long run, it is likely to affect even the most evangelistically successful of fellowships.

Evangelicals should be concerned about the direction of British society because, as Evangelicals, we are defined precisely by our commitment to mission - that is, by our proclamation and demonstration of the gospel not only to individuals, but to the wider world that God has made (Mt. 28:18; Mk. 16:15). A culture which is indifferent, or worse, openly hostile to this gospel will be a hindrance to its spread, and while the New Testament church flourished despite such hostility, it is hardly something that we should actively invite, or seek to promote.

Since 1999, I have been working with my colleagues at the Evangelical Alliance to help our membership take its place at the heart of a 'Movement for Change' in modern-day Britain. Not a reactionary movement looking only to 'change things back' - driven by nostalgia for some imagined 'old-time religion'. Not a triumphalistic movement determined to re-impose Christendom by force. The movement we have in mind is, rather, a movement that will persuade our society - its civic institutions, politicians, legislators and opinion formers, its business leaders and community representatives - to cherish Britain's rich Christian heritage, while at the same time recognizing the relevance of Christian values within the increasingly complex, multicultural sphere that is our public life. It almost goes without saying that we can only hope to do this effectively if we ourselves are seen to be united in love, rather than split over those secondary differences which have so often dogged evangelical witness in the past.

Our culture today is similar in many respects to the pluralistic, spiritually hungry culture which surrounded the first Christians (cf. Acts 17). The numerical growth of other faith groups, and the rise in their influence proportional to Christianity, has encouraged many to adopt a relativistic and even syncretistic approach to religion. Commensurate with this, the 'DIY' spiritualities which have become increasingly popular in recent years show little regard for singular doctrinal convictions or exclusive dogmatic 'labels'. Evangelicals, properly keen as we have been to make specific, rational truth-claims for our faith, must now also develop apologetics oriented to the quest of so many for practical self-authentication. Yet in addition, after the pattern of the apostle Paul, we must be sure to develop a coherent account of our place, and the place of the church as a whole, within our rapidly changing society. That is what Movement for Change is about, and its progress within and beyond the Evangelical Alliance's constituency crucially depends on clear, biblically grounded evangelical theology. For this reason, I was delighted when ACUTE undertook to organize the consultation at Oak Hill College on which this book is based. As one who attended that event, I have many times since gratefully recalled the expert reflections on evangelical social transformation offered there by the historians, ethicists, missiologists, biblical scholars, systematicians and pastors who gave so generously of their time to help us think through the implications of becoming a Movement for Change. Now that David Hilborn has edited these reflections together here, and added valuable extra material relevant to this process, it is good to be able to read them through carefully and follow up the many helpful references which they contain.

I know this book will contribute greatly to the Alliance's shaping of the Movement for Change agenda. My hope is that as we develop that agenda, others will come to see the papers collected here as a valuable resource for understanding and effecting Christian social transformation in Britain today.

1. Evangelicals, Theology and Social Transformation

David Bebbington

During the prohibition era in the United States, a police raid on an illicit saloon was led by 'a large and gloomy gentleman armed with a Bible'. It was a preacher called Elmer Gantry. Pointing at the startled saloon-keeper, he called on the police officers to arrest him. 'I've got you!', he cried. 'You're the kind that teaches young boys to drink - it's you that start them on the road to every hellish vice, to gambling and murder, with your hellish beverages, with your draught of the devil himself!' Gantry had risen from obscure Baptist origins to be the successful pastor of a large urban Methodist church and was cleaning up the town in the name of Christian morality - at the same time as keeping up a string of illicit affairs. He was shortly to be the chief candidate for executive secretary of the National Association for the Purification of Art and the Press, 'affectionately known through all the evangelical world as "the Napap"'.[1] The story is of course fiction, near the culmination of the novel *Elmer Gantry*, published in 1927 by Sinclair Lewis as a trenchant satire on the evangelical world. The book was one of those that, like Lytton Strachey's *Eminent Victorians* (1918) in Britain, fostered a reaction against the Christian manners and morals of a former age. But when all allowance is made for its polemical purpose, it remains a vivid reminder of the enduring popular image of Evangelicals who have taken up world-changing - censorious, power-loving and hypocritical. It may warn us to consider the enterprise of social transformation with caution.

This paper, however, is not concerned with the image of Evangelicals engaging with the problems of their day but with the reality. There is a long and honourable record of efforts by Christians to remedy the defects of society. Over the last two hundred years or so, Evangelicals have often been to the forefront in these campaigns. It is worthwhile scrutinizing the record of the nineteenth and twentieth centuries to discover more about the perils and potential of the enterprise. Although similar patterns could be discovered in America and other lands, this paper is concerned with Britain alone. It falls mainly into two parts. The first part tries to establish a typology of evangelical action on social questions, scrutinizing some of the more salient features that have marked crusades for the improvement of the world beyond the churches. The second looks at the issue from the other end. It examines the degree to

---

[1] Sinclair Lewis, *Elmer Gantry* (London: Jonathan Cape, 1927), 396, 452.

which society has been permeated by Christian standards and asks what role Evangelicals have played in creating them. Finally some questions are asked about the way in which Evangelicals can most fruitfully take part in changing the world. But first of all there needs to be a consideration of the theology that has undergirded these efforts.

A contrast needs to be drawn between evangelical theology relating to this field and that of other Christian groupings. Outside the Roman Catholic Church, which has its own ways of approaching social questions, there have been two other main tendencies in British Christianity during the last two centuries. One is the High Church tradition, stemming largely from the Oxford Movement of the 1830s, that has stressed the doctrines of the church, the sacraments and the ministry. The theological focus of High Churchmen has normally been on the incarnation. Because in Christ God became man, they have argued, the Almighty is concerned with the welfare of the human race. Christians ought to show the same kind of solidarity with suffering humanity that marks the Lord they worship. This, for example, was the burden of the teaching of B. F. Westcott, Bishop of Durham from 1890 to 1901. Putting his teaching into practice, he intervened on behalf of the miners in a strike in his diocese two years after his consecration.[2] One of his books was significantly entitled *The Incarnation and Common Life* (1893). In the twentieth century the best known exponent of this style of social theology was William Temple, Archbishop of Canterbury during the Second World War. His *Christianity and Social Order*, published as a Pelican in 1942, proved deeply influential on post-war reconstruction, giving an impetus to the creation of the Welfare State. Although Temple was also swayed by Reinhold Niebuhr and others, the foundation of his thought is set out in *Christus Veritas* (1924). There philosophical idealism moulded by the Platonic legacy leads up to the claim that the incarnation was an enrichment of the divine life. The taking of humanity into divinity is made the key to understanding and acting in the world. This incarnationalist stance provided a rationale for social concern that was warmly humanitarian.

A second theological tendency in modern Britain has been a more liberal one. Broad Churchmen in the Church of England, sometimes calling themselves Modern Churchmen in the twentieth century, together with broader thinkers in Nonconformity, have had their own approach to social engagement. Although many of them in the later nineteenth century, in the wake of F. D. Maurice, put as much stress on the incarnation as High Churchmen, from the 1890s there were others who began to see the kingdom of God as the theological motif most relevant to the needs of the world. Following the

---

[2] G. F. A. Best, *Bishop Westcott and the Miners* (London: Cambridge University Press, 1967).

German theologian Albrecht Ritschl, they drew a distinction between the church and the kingdom of God, which was altogether larger. It became customary to identify the kingdom with the ideal society that could be brought in by human effort. This was the view, for example, of the Congregationalist Fleming Williams, called 'Flaming Williams' because of his wild rhetoric on behalf of social panaceas. The most scholarly exposition of this point of view was probably to be found in a book by A. E. Garvie, Principal of the Congregationalist New College, London, from 1907 to 1933, called *The Christian Ideal for Human Society* (1930). The basis of his thinking, however, can be found in an earlier work, *The Ritschlian Theology* (1899), a very favourable review of its subject. Garvie was convinced, as he put it in his autobiography, that 'wide-reaching changes in society, especially in the economic system, were an imperative necessity' and that 'the churches were much to blame for their tame acquiescence in [existing] conditions'.[3] There was a sharp cutting edge to the pronouncements of the kingdom advocates, just as there was among those relatively few Evangelicals who took up kingdom theology in the later twentieth century. When the existing state of affairs was compared with an ideal form of society, the glaring contrast demanded action to effect drastic change. Liberal theology was often associated with radical social prescriptions in the twentieth century.

Evangelicals in general have had a very different theological approach to social issues. They, too, have been swayed by their core doctrinal emphases. Evangelicals have stressed the doctrine of the atonement as central to their worldview. The *Evangelical Free Church Catechism*, for instance, issued in 1899 by the National Council of the Evangelical Free Churches, represented a consensus of the views of theologians from each of the main orthodox Nonconformist denominations in England and Wales. What, it asked, did Christ accomplish for us on the cross? 'By offering Himself a sacrifice without blemish unto God', declared the answer, 'He fulfilled the requirements of Divine Holiness, atoned for all our sins, and broke the power of Sin.'[4] The atonement achieved the forgiveness of sins by defeating the principle of sin. Accordingly sin was recognized as the grand enemy of humanity. Furthermore, Evangelicals knew that conversion was designed to be a turning away from sin; and that sanctification was the process whereby actual sin was eliminated, either gradually or suddenly, from human life. Evangelicals might differ over details of theology or points of church order, but all their differences were overlaid by a common belief that the world was impregnated with wickedness from which human beings had to be saved. This conviction coloured their attitude to all the affairs of life. 'At the back of all the world's trouble and

---

[3] A. E. Garvie, *Memories and Meanings of My Life* (London: Allen & Unwin, 1938), 73.
[4] *An Evangelical Free Church Catechism* (London: Thomas Law, [1899]), 10.

economic distress', remarked the Congregational leader J. D. Jones in 1908, 'lay the fact of sin.'[5] This, rather than the incarnation or the kingdom, was the doctrinal orientation that determined the general evangelical understanding of social issues.

Particular individuals, of course, had more precise reasons for social action. William Wilberforce was familiar with the commercial intricacies of the slave trade and his expertise assisted him in the campaign for its abolition. Lord Shaftesbury was aware of the conditions of the common lodging houses of London and that roused him to insist on their regulation. But these were exceptional figures. The evangelical public at large necessarily lacked their specialist knowledge. What the masses in the pews had in common was an awareness of sin. The element in the mind of the rank and file that spurred them to action was consequently a perception of the social evils to be combated. What follows is an analysis of the campaigns that Evangelicals mounted in order to deal with the problems of society. It attempts to show the typical features that have marked them when they have been mobilized to undertake change.

The target of evangelical campaigns, as will be clear from what has already been said, was consistently sin. George Stephen, the chief anti-slavery lecturer in the 1830s, found that he could best rouse evangelical audiences against slavery by branding it 'criminal before God'.[6] Again and again in the rhetoric of subsequent crusades the object of attack was *wickedness*. If ever Evangelicals became convinced that they were responsible for a state of affairs that necessarily entailed sin, and if they possessed the ability to do something to change the state of affairs, they felt bound to act. That belief often carried them into the political arena. Early Methodists were extremely reluctant to enter public affairs because they held that religion was always more important than politics. When, in the 1870s, however, some of them realized that there were laws on the statute book that provided for the health inspection of prostitutes in the vicinity of military and naval bases in order to ensure that the men were not contaminated by contagious diseases, they were outraged. The state was actually condoning sexual promiscuity, an outright sin. Reservations about political action were thrown to the wind. The Wesleyan Methodists turned, as a denomination, into a movement crusading for the abolition of the Contagious Diseases Acts. Henry Fowler, a Wesleyan solicitor who was to become the first Methodist cabinet member, declared that the acts infringed the principle that 'whatever is morally wrong can never be politically right'.[7] It was a slogan that was often to be repeated by subsequent generations of Evangelicals.

---

[5] *Christian World*, 7 May 1908, 22.
[6] George Stephen, *Anti-Slavery Recollections in a Series of Letters addressed to Mrs Beecher Stowe* [1854] (London, 1971), 248.
[7] *Methodist Protest*, 15 February 1876, 16.

Sins, however, could fall into more than one category. The first consisted of obstacles to the gospel. Evangelicals held that human beings need to hear the good news of Jesus Christ. Anything that prevented their access to the gospel was a threat to their salvation that must be hateful to the Almighty. Hence barriers to the spread of the gospel were seen not merely as problems to be overcome but also as devices of the evil one that had to be thrown down. Thus the institution of slavery became the target of evangelical assault in the 1830s because it was seen as inimical to missionary progress in the Caribbean. Slave-owners were harrying missionaries because they suspected that they were fomenting unrest among the slaves. Evangelicals concluded, in the words of the secretary of the Baptist Missionary Society, that 'either slavery or Christianity must fall'.[8] Shortly afterwards, remarkably, evangelical Nonconformists drew the same inference about the Church of England. The unreformed Anglican structures encouraged men to enter the ministry through patronage for the sake of a secure income with minimum duties. In 1833 the Congregationalist Thomas Binney concluded, in memorable phrase, that 'the Church of England damns more souls than it saves'.[9] The established church was an obstacle to the gospel. Although that supposition rapidly ceased to have any plausibility as the Evangelical party in the Church of England increased, it was the original driving force behind the Dissenting movement for disestablishment that took off in the 1830s and 1840s. Perhaps, however, the greatest example of a movement arising from the belief that a barrier to the gospel had to be removed was the temperance crusade. Originally a secular enthusiasm of artisans that was frowned on by the churches as an alternative to the gospel, temperance was taken up by Evangelicals in the last three or four decades of the nineteenth century in church as well as chapel and retained its hold, at least on the chapels, for over a century. The argument that did most to convince them was the case that drunkards were too befuddled in mind to respond to the gospel. If people were weaned off strong drink as adults through coffee houses or warned off it as children by the Band of Hope, then an alcohol-free society would allow full scope to the message of salvation. Whatever prevented conversions must be wrong and so must be put away.

If the first category of evils attacked by Evangelicals consisted of obstacles to the gospel, the second was the battery of substitutes for the gospel. Alternative forms of belief, religious or secular, aroused their ire. The most alarming throughout the nineteenth century and long into the twentieth was the Roman Catholic Church. Associated with memories of past persecution at

---

[8] John Dyer quoted by G. A. Catherall, *William Knibb: Freedom Fighter* ([Chichester:] January, 1972), 6.
[9] R. Tudur Jones, *Congregationalism in England, 1662-1962* (London: Independent Press, 1962), 215.

home and abroad, Rome was a threat to liberty as well as to the faith. The hordes of Irish labourers who arrived in Britain as refugees from the famine of 1845 and subsequent poverty seemed battalions of papal shock troops, and as late as the 1920s the Church of Scotland recommended their deportation back to Ireland. There were successive crises when the evangelical public was roused to agitation against public policy. In 1845 there was an outburst of feeling against Sir Robert Peel's proposal to increase government grants to Maynooth, the Catholic seminary near Dublin; five years later nearly the whole parliamentary session was devoured by the Ecclesiastical Titles Bill, designed to prohibit the adoption by newly appointed Catholic bishops of the titles of existing English sees. There were alarms whenever there were proposals of government grants for Catholic schools, the most famous being in the Edwardian years, when the Baptist leader John Clifford denounced 'Rome on the Rates'. At times even more worrying to Evangelicals, especially to the Anglicans among them, was the progress of ritualism within the Church of England. Liturgical practices copying those of Rome, such as the use of incense and elaborate robes, were resisted by Evangelicals in series of legal battles during the late Victorian years. In 1928 an evangelical agitation managed to engineer in the Commons the defeat of a revised Prayer Book, prepared after protracted negotiation within the Church of England, because it made concessions to Anglo-Catholics. The concern was always to stem the tide of soul-destroying error. Likewise infidelity was resisted, generating, for example, strong evangelical opposition to the admission of Charles Bradlaugh, an avowed unbeliever, into the Commons in the 1880s. On the mission field the foe was paganism: during the nineteenth century there was a sustained evangelical campaign against official sponsorship for the Hindu temples such as that of Juggernaut. Whatever counted as a substitute for the gospel was likely to attract evangelical censure.

Sins in the most usual sense of the word formed the third class of targets of evangelical hostility. Breaches of biblical ethics, especially of the ten commandments, were frequently condemned. Sexual wrongdoing was prominent on the catalogue of wrongdoing. Social purity, as the campaign against sexual vice was called, led to movements for the rehabilitation of prostitutes, especially in the mid-nineteenth century, and to organized demands for the closure of brothels. The representation of sex in pornographic form remained in the 1970s by far the main public issue taken up by Evangelicals. Out of a sample of 160 largely evangelical churches in the Baptist Union, for example, over a period of five years there was discussion or action on world poverty by five, on race relations by eight, on religious education by ten (the second highest figure) but on pornography by as many as forty-seven.[10] The murder of unborn children through abortion became a major preoccupation of evangelical campaigners in the last two decades of the twentieth century, though previously the issue had been largely left to Catholics. Sabbath-breaking was also attacked, so that in the high Victorian years Sunday trains ran at their peril and proposals to open the Crystal Palace on Sundays met a wall of resistance. In the inter-war period there were concerted attempts by Evangelicals to prevent the Sunday opening of cinemas. The law of God, it was felt, had to be maintained, if possible as the law of the land. What Scripture forbade, Evangelicals opposed.

The fact that popular evangelical campaigns have to be analyzed as battles against outright wrongs has important implications. It becomes apparent, to start with, that such crusades cannot properly be called 'humanitarian', the label that historians have traditionally applied to evangelical socio-political attitudes.[11] It is true that the leaders often had a desire to eliminate suffering: Shaftesbury, with his strong sense of aristocratic responsibility for the poor, is a good example. It is also true that anti-slavery in particular was animated by a powerful consciousness of the unity of the human race, stemming from the Enlightenment. The effect of many campaigns was to reduce suffering, but that was not their aim or *raison d'être.* The evangelical public had been aware of the cruelty perpetrated by slave-holders long before the agitation for the termination of slavery. It was only when it became apparent that slavery was incompatible with Christian missions that they rose against it. Inhumanity in itself did not prod their consciences. Nor was the instance of slavery exceptional. In 1842 there was an outburst of indignation in the religious public over conditions in the mining industry that enabled Shaftesbury to promote a bill prohibiting the employment of women and children underground. The cause of the high feeling, far from being disgust at the inhuman treatment of the weak, was shock at the discovery, from a widely publicized illustration in a royal commission report, that male and female children were lowered to work down mine-shafts together half-naked.[12] Fears of sexual immorality were at work. Oppression, whether political or economic, was insufficient to create a sense of outrage, since there had to be the further element of identifiable wrong for which Evangelicals at large felt responsible. A sin was a personal act, not

---

[10] *Signs of Hope: An Examination of the Numerical and Spiritual State of Churches in Membership with the Baptist Union of Great Britain and Ireland* (London: Baptist Union, 1979), xxvi.

[11] E. g. F. J. Klingberg, *The Anti-Slavery Movement in England: A Study in English Humanitarianism* (Yale Historical Publications (Miscellany 17), New Haven, CT, 1926).

[12] Georgina Battiscombe, *Shaftesbury: A Biography of the Seventh Earl* (London: Constable, 1974), 147.

something embedded in the structures of the world. The notion of structural evil, commonplace among present-day theologians, was markedly absent from the thought of the mass of Evangelicals. Only in the case of anti-slavery does the idea seem to have emerged. So resistant to evangelical assaults did American slavery prove that John Dunlop, a Scottish solicitor, identified it as an expression of what he called 'organic sins'.[13] But this was an isolated expression of the opinion that the ordering of the world was in some sense wrong. Evangelicals normally held - at least *en masse* - that political and economic arrangements were fundamentally just. Hence relations of subordination in society were to be accepted. Large-scale changes were not needed for the sake of improving the lot of mankind. Theirs was no blanket humanitarianism or radical social criticism, but rather a number of isolated crusades against particular evils.

Another implication of this analysis concerns the policy that Evangelicals adopted. They regularly supported what may be called a negative solution to the problems they confronted. Their proposals were standardly for the elimination of what was wrong, not for the achievement of some positive alternative. Their campaigns were often explicitly 'anti-', as in the anti-slavery campaign or the anti-Contagious Diseases Acts movement. Unlike recent anti-abortion groups that have labeled themselves 'pro-life' in order to avoid the stigma of negativism, they saw no need to alter their image. Other pressure groups might advocate an innovation, such as votes for women, but evangelical reformers condemned some feature of existing policy. They fell, like the Campaign for Nuclear Disarmament, into the category of protest groups. Their essentially critical stance could in some ways be their strength: it is frequently easier for public authorities, whether local or national, to drop an old policy than to take up a new one. But it also opened the campaigners to the charge of offering no constructive proposals. To this charge Evangelicals had a legitimate reply. Their positive remedy for the defects of the world was the preaching of the gospel. Protest was the other side of the coin from evangelism. Thus in the Festival of Light of the 1970s that objected to permissiveness, supporters were content if their rallies had no effect on society since they constituted a form of witness that might well lead to conversions.[14] The gospel was the complete remedy for the sins of the world, campaigns being merely an auxiliary weapon. It was therefore entirely consistent with their worldview for Evangelicals to be negative in their demands.

---

[13] John Dunlop, *American Slavery: Organic Sins, or the Iniquity of Licensed Injustice* (Edinburgh, 1846), 12, quoted by C. Duncan Rice, 'The Missionary Context of the British Anti-Slavery Movement', in James Walvin, ed., *Slavery and British Society, 1776-1846* (London: MacMillan, 1982), 162.

[14] Roy Wallis and Richard Bland, *Five Years On: Report of a Survey of Participants in the Nationwide Festival of Light in Trafalgar Square, London, on 25 September 1976* (typescript, Stirling, 1977), 42.

Their method followed from their policy. If the authorities were to be impressed by the strength of any movement, protest must be outspoken and widespread. The characteristic technique was therefore the 'agitation' – a word that was introduced into common parlance during the anti-slavery campaign. Paid lecturers ('agitators') or voluntary speakers would address a series of public meetings in an attempt to whip up a maximum pitch of outrage in the audience. The rousing speeches were more like sermons than lectures, but there was often a touch of the theatrical about them as well. William Knibb, a returned Jamaica missionary who in 1832 did more than almost any other man to inflame feeling against slavery, carried around from meeting to meeting a spiked iron collar to brandish in illustration of the punishment meted out to slaves.[15] The grand demonstrations were a spectacular type of entertainment. Frequently they were the scenes for the launching of petitions to parliament or the approval of letters to MPs. Although the vogue for such 'indignation meetings' faded somewhat in the twentieth century with the rise of alternative forms of entertainment, the Trafalgar Square rallies of the Festival of Light were recognizably in the same tradition. Like the marches of witness of the 1990s, the gatherings were designed to display the bond between Christians in the face of a hostile world. Far more attenders at Trafalgar Square in 1976, researchers found, were primarily wanting to demonstrate their solidarity than were concerned to secure effective legislation against immorality or even to protest against Britain's moral decline.[16] Such rallies of the faithful, exciting and enjoyable in themselves, were part and parcel of evangelical agitations.

The manner of evangelical mass movements for change was also distinctive. They displayed a stern moral absolutism, a direct consequence of being directed against sin. Their demands were immutable, sacrosanct, certainly not open to negotiation. Evangelicals engaged in campaigns of this order were assertors of the place of principle in politics. What compromise could there be with wickedness? The resulting intransigence is well illustrated in the United Kingdom Alliance, the chief British pressure group aiming for the prohibition of alcohol that was largely supported by evangelical Nonconformists. When, in 1871, Gladstone's government offered legislation that would restrict the consumption of strong drink but fall short of voluntary local banning of liquor, the organization condemned the proposals outright.[17] No bread, it was felt, was better than half a loaf. There must be no tampering with principle. The same absolutism showed itself over the timing of reform. Change, Evangelicals regularly argued, must come urgently, even immediately. At the same time as

---

[15] Philip Wright, *Knibb 'the Notorious': Slaves' Missionary, 1803-1845* (London: Sidgwick & Jackson, 1973), 126.

[16] Wallis and Bland, *Five Years On*, 34.

[17] Brian Harrison, *Drink and the Victorians: The Temperance Question in England, 1815-1872* (London: Faber & Faber, 1971), 269, 273.

the abolition of slavery became a mass evangelical concern in the early 1830s, the doctrine of immediatism was taken up by the movement.[18] Slavery was wicked; therefore it must be stopped without a moment's delay. Again moral absolutism dictated that evangelical pressure groups vehemently opposed any benefits for participants in the activities they condemned. There should be no reward for wrongdoing. Thus the anti-slavery agitators argued that there must be no financial payments to ex-slaveholders to make up for the loss of their slaves' labour, and the temperance movement resisted compensation to publicans for licences that were withdrawn. Why should the wicked prosper? The rigid moralism of the evangelical campaigns was an unavoidable consequence of their identification of sin as the enemy to be fought.

The evangelical style of engagement with the ills of society has encountered a number of risks. One has been the danger of clamour. A bellicose tone, an inflated rhetoric and exaggerated charges have often marked the campaigns. At the end of the nineteenth century a number of Nonconformist ministers, dedicated to what they deemed Christian goals, fell into this trap. In particular Hugh Price Hughes, the leading Wesleyan activist, habitually engaged in furious tirades against opponents, whether publicans, Catholics or Prime Ministers. A contemporary called him 'a day of Judgment in breeches'.[19] There is a practical disadvantage in clamour, for it stiffens resistance among opponents. Denunciation is also a poor way of making allies, as Hughes found when he tried to enlist the support of the Liberal leader, Lord Rosebery, for one cause after having castigated him for backwardness in another. Rosebery declined, reminding Hughes that his previous statements had been 'distinguished neither by accuracy nor by charity'.[20] Apart from tactical considerations, there is the problem that a hectoring tone is a poor advertisement for Christianity. A militant moralism rarely reflects the meekness, the kindness and the longsuffering commended in Scripture. Few aspects of evangelical religion have done more to deter converts than the stridency of the popular campaigns it has mounted.

Furthermore there has been the danger of diversion from the gospel. It used to be charged that the social gospel was a replacement for the true gospel offered by those who had lost confidence in the supernatural dimension of the authentic variety. A range of scholarship has shown that most social gospellers of the turn of the twentieth century were, on the contrary, loyal to the faith; and many Evangelicals of the more recent past have demonstrated that there is no

---

[18] D. B. Davis, 'The Emergence of Immediatism in British and American Antislavery Thought', *Mississippi Valley Historical Review,* 49, 1962, 209-230.

[19] Arthur Porritt, *The Best I Remember* (London: Cassell, 1922), 60.

[20] D. W. Bebbington, *The Nonconformist Conscience: Chapel and Politics, 1870-1914,* (London: Allen & Unwin, 1982), 52-3.

incompatibility between evangelism and social concern.[21] Yet there may remain a kernel of truth in the old conservative evangelical criticism of social engagement. Enthusiasm for reforming the world can so grasp evangelical communities as to weaken their dedication to basic Christian convictions. Communal energy can be redirected away from spiritual priorities. Many of the chapels that turned to socio-political action around 1900 became so committed to welfare provision and public affairs as to lose their evangelistic edge. R. W. Dale, minister of Carr's Lane Congregational Church, Birmingham, pointed out that the reforming temper, excellent in itself, could sap religious vitality.[22] The twentieth-century decline of the Free Churches does something to justify his case.

There is another snare for Christian discipleship in the crusading style. It is easy to distort the gospel by associating it with a form of law. The adoption of a certain principle or practice, perceived to be a remedy for one of the ills of the world, can become established as a touchstone of Christian obedience. In the 1890s, for example, there were efforts to restrict Methodist church membership to total abstainers.[23] The result of urging this panacea was sharp controversy and division. Although this bout of pressure was resisted, in the twentieth century conservative evangelical circles established their own unwritten code of behaviour. Dancing, smoking and cinema-going were dismissed as worldly practices, unworthy of the devoted believer. Those who liked occasional movies were repelled by the churches where such rules were observed. Temporary applications of Christian principles can be turned into burdensome obligations. Perhaps the greatest service of Martin Luther to the church was to warn against imposing laws where there should be freedom. For want of heeding the Lutheran critique, Evangelicals have sometimes drifted into obscuring the gospel with duties. A certain legalism has taken possession of enthusiastic reformers.

All these perils should not prevent appreciation of the countervailing advantages in the accustomed evangelical approach to social ills. There have been definite achievements through identifying abuses and seeking to end them. The greatest success was probably the abolition of slavery in British dominions in 1833, the result of specifically evangelical pressure on the newly reformed parliament. In an era when the record of bodies on questions of race relations is under constant scrutiny, that triumph of evangelical religion over racial

---

[21] D. [W.] Bebbington, 'The Decline and Resurgence of Evangelical Social Concern, 1918-80', in John Wolffe, ed., *Evangelical Faith and Public Zeal: Evangelicals and Society in Britain, 1780-1980* (London: SPCK, 1995).

[22] A. W. W. Dale, *The Life of the Rev. R. W. Dale of Birmingham* (London, 1898), 648-50.

[23] Bebbington, *Nonconformist Conscience*, 46.

oppression should not be allowed to be forgotten. The Contagious Diseases Acts were suspended in 1883 and repealed three years later, eliminating a serious imposition on women's freedom. And there have been lesser victories in the twentieth century such as the defeat in 1986 of Mrs Thatcher's attempt to deregulate Sunday shop opening hours, the only time her government was vanquished by a sizeable revolt of Conservative backbenchers, though the arrest of the change was to prove only temporary. Evangelicals have injected their characteristic activism into campaigns, such as this one, that otherwise would have been feeble affairs. Their pressure has played its part in adding salt to society so as to slow the decay of Christian standards.

It could also be argued that the evangelical way of undertaking social action has been liberating. The absence of an agreed positive prescription for the ills of society has actually enabled individuals to propose their own ideas in the knowledge that they are not infringing the rulings of higher authority. There is a contrast here with Roman Catholic practice, which in theory at least should conform to papal encyclicals on social affairs from *Rerum Novarum* (1891) onwards. The rulings of the magisterium can inhibit innovations in responses to surrounding problems, as more extreme liberation theologians have discovered to their cost. The contrast with Muslim practice, according to which details of life can be regulated from above by the *sharia*, is even more striking. Evangelicals have held that sin must be avoided, but beyond the limited sphere where wrongs have been identified they have been free to be creative in responding to circumstances. Thus Thomas Chalmers, the evangelical leader in the Church of Scotland, experimented with ways of Christianizing and civilizing the inner cities generated by nineteenth-century urbanization. His practice of concentrated district visitation, when widely imitated, made possible the evangelical penetration of the packed courts of the Victorian city.[24] Because there was no unanimous view of how to act, Chalmers was able to try out his methods and recommend them to others. The evangelical style has permitted flexibility in engaging with the problems of society.

Chalmers's methods of achieving a godly commonwealth point the way to the second part of this paper, an analysis from the other side of the question. Instead of beginning with the Evangelicals and examining their approach to society, we can start with Britain and ask how it came to be as Christian as it did. Callum Brown has claimed in his book *The Death of Christian Britain* (2001) that, before the sudden decay of Christian values in the 1960s, 'the nation's core religious and moral identity' was formed by evangelical religion. From around 1800 to 1963 was 'a last puritan age'.[25] Against previous

---

[24] S. J. Brown, *Thomas Chalmers and the Godly Commonwealth in Scotland* (Oxford: Oxford University Press, 1982), chap. 3.

[25] Callum G. Brown, *The Death of Christian Britain* (London: Routledge, 2001), 1, 9.

sociologists and historians who have supposed that the country was secularized by industrialization and urbanization, Brown holds that mass culture was shaped by evangelical norms during the whole period until the rise of the permissive society heralded its death. Brown's discussion has its weaknesses since it is self-consciously predicated on the theory of postmodernist writers, and especially Michel Foucault, yet it possesses great strengths because it rejects economic determinism and concentrates instead on the experience of lived human beings in their cultural setting. It undoubtedly misrepresents the extent to which women were the exclusive carriers of the predominant values, for work by Linda Wilson has shown the way in which evangelical spirituality united rather than divided the sexes.[26] Brown also exaggerates the persistence of unalloyed evangelical attitudes into the twentieth century, but his estimate that the whole culture was permeated by evangelical assumptions in the mid-nineteenth century has been confirmed by a great deal of recent research, and especially Boyd Hilton's work.[27] The philosopher John Stuart Mill believed in the 1850s that the 'stricter Calvinists and Methodists' were so socially dominant as to put human individuality at risk.[28] British society in the eighteenth century had been notably deficient in Christian virtues, but the high Victorian years were shot through with gospel values. Why was that the case?

One explanation of the success of the evangelical movement in changing its host culture was its own set of characteristics. In the early and middle years of the nineteenth century Evangelicalism was notably faithful to its salient emphases on the Bible, the cross, conversion and activism. Its biblicism consisted primarily in a practical dedication to using the Bible as an inspiration for Christian devotion. Thus Anna Oakden, a well-to-do Wesleyan Methodist from near Uttoxeter in Staffordshire who died in 1856, was said to have been 'assiduous...in reading the Holy Scriptures, making it her object to go through the sacred volume annually'.[29] The Bible was treated unequivocally as the court of appeal in all questions of belief and conduct, giving the movement confidence in the supernatural authority of its message. Evangelicals laid equal stress on the atonement, what one Congregational minister called 'the doctrine of a crucified Saviour'.[30] It was the death of Christ, and not his example, his teaching or even his incarnation, on which Evangelicals loved to dwell. The

---

[26] Linda Wilson, *Constrained by Zeal: Female Spirituality amongst Nonconformists, 1825-1875* (Carlisle: Paternoster, 2000).

[27] Boyd Hilton, *The Age of Atonement: The Influence of Evangelicalism on Economic and Social Thought, 1785-1865* (Oxford: Clarendon Press, 1988).

[28] D. W. Bebbington, *Evangelicalism in Modern Britain: A History from the 1730s to the 1980s* (London: Allen & Unwin, 1989), 106.

[29] *Wesleyan Methodist Magazine*, March 1860, 281.

[30] Alexander Macfadyen, *Life of John Allison Macfadyen* (London: Hodder & Stoughton, 1891), 384-5.

proclamation of Christ's redemption powerfully affected individuals, and even, as Hilton shows, moulded the language in which issues of commercial policy were discussed. Evangelicals urged others to turn from sin to personal faith through conversion, which was often an overwhelming experience. 'Conviction, contrition, wrestling in prayer, and mighty struggling', it was said of a member of the Bible Christian denomination converted in 1859, '- these were the prelude to the happy day when the peace of God first became his blest possession.'[31] Changed lives, multiplied many times over, led to an alteration of the tone of society at large. The fourth characteristic, flowing from the others, was activism. 'To win souls for Christ', ran the motto of the mid-century evangelical Anglican clergyman William Pennefather, 'by all means and by any means'.[32] The zeal to be up and doing was a virtual guarantee of church growth and consequent social penetration. Evangelicals transformed nineteenth-century society by being themselves.

A second reason for the religious tone of Victorian Britain, as Callum Brown stresses, was the battery of media the Evangelicals employed. Predominantly, in the nineteenth century, the media took the form of print. First and foremost was the circulation of the Bible. The British and Foreign Bible Society, founded in 1807, published during its first century no fewer than 186 million Bibles, Testaments and Scripture portions.[33] Colporteurs hawked Bibles for sale round the country; and specialist Bible women took them into the homes of the poor who would not be able or willing to buy a copy themselves. The scriptures were reinforced by an abundance of tracts. The Religious Tract Society had been established even before the Bible Society, in 1799. One of its secretaries, Legh Richmond, was the author of the most celebrated tract of all, *The Dairyman's Daughter* (1809), a simple rustic tale that so touched the hearts of its readers as to enjoy an alleged global circulation of four million by its author's death in 1827.[34] Peter Drummond of Stirling was responsible for setting up a tract depot that deluged the market with innovative variations on the theme. In 1862, for instance, he issued 'Stirling Tracts for Letters' which could be bought at 6d or 8d per dozen for insertion in postal communications.[35] Improving general magazines such as *Chambers's Journal* and *Good Words* were suffused with evangelical principles; periodicals targeting particular

---

[31] W. J. Mitchell, *Brief Biographical Sketches of Bible Christian Ministers and Laymen*, Vol. 1 (J. T. Bigwood: Jersey, 1906), 79.

[32] Robert Braithwaite, *The Life and Letters of the Rev. William Pennefather, B. A.* (London: J. F. Shaw, 1878), viii.

[33] William Canton, *A History of the British and Foreign Bible Society*, Vol. 1 (London: John Murray, 1904), 387.

[34] *The Blackwell Dictionary of Evangelical Biography, 1730-1860*, ed. D. M. Lewis (Oxford: Blackwell, 1995, Vol. 2), 936-7.

[35] Brown, *Death of Christian Britain*, 50.

audiences, such as the *Christian Ladies' Magazine,* also proliferated. There were hugely successful evangelical novelists, among whom Charlotte Elizabeth Tonna, a clergyman's daughter who wrote as Charlotte Elizabeth, was the most eminent of all. Beginning as a children's writer, she proliferated into social novels including *The Wrongs of Women* (1843-4), on the industrial exploitation of her sex.[36] Literature was supplemented by music. Hymn-singing became a popular pastime; and denominational hymn books became almost as common as Bibles. The net effect was to suffuse the popular consciousness with evangelical values. 'Discursive Christianity', in Callum Brown's terminology, became the recognized way in which the society defined itself.

The dissemination of ideas, however, was backed up by actions. Evangelicals practised what they preached by engaging in philanthropy. The earlier nineteenth century was afflicted by some of the ills of industrialization, creating urban squalor and a declining life expectancy for those dwelling in cities. In this milieu Lord Shaftesbury shone. He headed the campaign for restricting the hours worked by industrial employees to tolerable levels; he started ragged schools for the street urchins of London; he pioneered medical boards to combat contagious disease; and he did much more. His tireless efforts on behalf of the weaker members of society were a legend in his lifetime. Yet Shaftesbury was but one of a philanthropic legion who visited the sick, ran orphanages, ladled out soup in hard times or distributed blankets to the poor in winter. Evangelical activism extended beyond concern for souls to care for bodies. There were specialist agencies for prisoners, the blind, the deaf, the handicapped and the elderly.[37] The large number of voluntary associations that were predominantly evangelical in inspiration provided the chief means by which the needs of the age were met. Their annual gatherings, alongside those of the missionary societies, constituted the May Meetings in the Exeter Hall in London, the shop window of the evangelical movement. All this was regarded not as a special mobilization but as the regular work of the Christian, a normal expression of love for one's neighbour. Evangelicals were equally active in meeting the other acutely felt need of the times. Although Scotland had enjoyed a system of publicly provided schools for generations, the nineteenth century opened with England and Wales possessing only a patchy provision of education. The new Sunday schools, however, largely though not exclusively evangelical in inspiration, made one of the greatest contributions to the development of education for the masses. In Manchester in 1834 far more children attended Sunday school than day school.[38] The curriculum, far from

---

[36] *Blackwell Dictionary of Evangelical Biography,* Vol. 2, 1112-14.

[37] Kathleen Heasman, *Evangelicals in Action: An Appraisal of their Social Work in the Victorian Era* (London: Geoffrey Bles, 1962).

[38] A. P. Wadsworth, 'The First Manchester Sunday Schools', in M. W. Flinn and T. C. Smout, eds., *Essays in Social History* (Oxford: Clarendon Press, 1974), 116-17.

being confined to Christian training, included reading and often writing too. Evangelicals provided for the intellectual as well as the physical welfare of the people. One of the chief reasons why their impact was less in the twentieth than in the nineteenth century was that the state was taking over the traditional role of the churches and chapels in supplying charity and schooling.[39] In the earlier period, however, the Evangelicals had been able to spread their influence by deeds as well as words.

A further reason for the success of the evangelical movement in shaping Victorian society was the attitude of the state. Evangelicalism, unlike Catholicism in the France of the second empire or Lutheranism in Sweden throughout the nineteenth century, was a form of religion largely independent of the state. It is true that there was a band of evangelical clergy in the established Church of England from the start of the century and that the Church of Scotland was growingly evangelical at the same time, but the state was ceasing to bestow benefits on public religion. In England there was no more public money for church building after 1824 and in Scotland an application for the same purpose proved fruitless in the following decade. So Evangelicals in the established churches were left to their own resources. Conversely however, Evangelicals outside the establishments, who proliferated during this period, were not suppressed by the state. The tradition of religious toleration had become deep rooted, and when, in 1811, Lord Sidmouth as Home Secretary, proposed to put restrictions on travelling preachers, there was a successful resistance partly orchestrated by Wilberforce.[40] The state did not move against Dissent, and gradually during the Victorian era most of the more grievous disabilities of Dissenters were removed. The working establishment in a European sense had collapsed. The efforts of the Evangelical Alliance to achieve a similar relaxation of the state apparatus on the continent bear testimony to the realization at the time that evangelization depended upon opportunity.[41] The flourishing of religious liberty was a condition of the impact of evangelical religion on Britain.

A final explanation of the phenomenon of evangelical permeation lies in the cultural sphere itself. The intellectual climate of the early nineteenth century, elevating reason, science and observation in the wake of the Enlightenment, was distinctly favourable to the movement. The evangelical worldview was strongly moulded by Enlightenment styles of thinking. Theology, as much as

---

[39] Jeffrey Cox, *The English Churches in a Secular Society: Lambeth, 1870-1930* (New York: Oxford University Press, 1982), chaps 3, 6.

[40] W. R. Ward, *Religion and Society in England, 1790-1850* (London: Batsford, 1972), 54-62.

[41] Ian Randall and David Hilborn, *One Body in Christ: The History and Significance of the Evangelical Alliance* (Carlisle: Paternoster, 2001), chap. 4.

science, was conceived as a rational discipline in which evidences were decisive. 'We are applying', explained Thomas Chalmers, 'the very same principles to a system of theism, that we would do to a system of geology.'[42] Evangelicalism was in harmony with the progressive opinion of the times. Yet as the fresh intellectual fashion of Romanticism, championing will and emotion against the reason and calculation of the Enlightenment, began to spread, initially among the elite, certain Evangelicals began to adapt to this new mood. Edward Irving, a Church of Scotland minister serving in London, led the way by stressing faith against reason, a Romantic spirit against the legacy of the Enlightenment. Doctrinal reformulation, such as the taking up of premillennial teaching about the imminence of the second coming, meant that those with Romantic proclivities were catered for within the evangelical movement. It showed both an accommodation of Christian teaching to the dominant way of thinking at the time and a capacity to adapt to novelties in the intellectual environment. The natural assumptions of large sections of the population were in harmony with the premises of Evangelicalism. So the cultural forces of the times were harnessed for the dissemination of the faith.

For these reasons Britain became notably Christian in the evangelical sense in the Victorian era. Permeation was less than total, especially at the bottom of the social order, and by no means everybody was to be found in church, but the degree of penetration was remarkable even in these respects. In 1851, at the only official census of religion taken in Britain before 2001, roughly 40 per cent of the population was at worship on census Sunday.[43] A variety of evidence suggests that the figure would have been much lower in the previous century; and certainly the equivalent figure at the start of the twenty-first century was only around 8 per cent. It is increasingly appreciated by historians that the middle of the nineteenth century represents a peak of Christianization of the country, at least in modern times. There can be no doubt that the previous growth of Evangelicalism is the chief explanation of the statistics. But the impact went beyond church attenders to influence the whole of British society. Cabinet meetings stopped on Sundays; novels recounted not dissolute behaviour but anguished repentance; and even Karl Marx noticed in the *Communist Manifesto* of 1848 that Evangelicals were at work. Although he interpreted their purpose as 'to secure the continued existence of bourgeois society', Marx recognized that what he called 'organizers of charity, members of societies for the prevention of cruelty to animals, temperance fanatics, hole-

---

[42] Thomas Chalmers, *The Evidence and Authority of the Christian Revelation* (Edinburgh: William Blackwood, 1814), 204.
[43] M. R. Watts, *The Dissenters: Volume II: The Expansion of Evangelical Nonconformity, 1791-1859* (Oxford: Oxford University Press, 1995), 27.

in-the-corner reformers of every imaginable kind' were deeply influential.[44] evangelical religion had changed the life of the nation.

The implications for contemporary evangelical mission cannot be read off directly from the past, but history, as ever, is suggestive. If we take the explanations of the evangelical impact on the Victorians in turn, questions arise about the role of evangelical Christians in the present. In the earlier nineteenth century Evangelicals were confident in their message, based on the Bible and focused on the cross; they aimed for conversions and they were unremittingly activist. Is there a comparable desire today to become immersed in Scripture? Do Evangelicals dwell on the atoning work of Christ? Do they fashion their programmes so as to turn people from darkness to light? And are they prepared to put themselves out through hard work? Again, the evangelical movement of the nineteenth century concentrated on using the media for its purposes. By contrast with the situation in the United States, British Evangelicals have been largely excluded from the airwaves since the emergence of radio and television. Although there have been efforts to remedy the position in the recent past, have they done enough to enter this field? Are they considering alternative forms of communication, visual as well as literary? Are they willing to finance them? In the early nineteenth century, Evangelicals were to the fore in philanthropy and education, but many of their successors retreated from charitable work in the twentieth century as a diversion from the gospel. Have they fully grasped their heritage of caring for human need once again? Although many churches have rightly seen the opportunities for mother and toddler groups at the bottom of the educational ladder, have they sufficiently looked for other chances to make provision for the young? The British state has traditionally been tolerant of religious diversity. With the shift away from Christian assumptions in the late twentieth century, are Evangelicals sufficiently aware of the potential pressures from a politically correct state on their openings for evangelism? Recent developments in France and Belgium, where the activities of Evangelicals have been under threat, may herald similar events in Britain. Is the ground being prepared for the defence of religious liberty? And since the alignment of Evangelicals with the cultural trends of the day was once so beneficial, are their successors taking pains to be *au courant* with developments? Are too many Evangelicals inclined to see postmodernism, with its motifs that are awaiting use for cultural penetration, as a threat rather than an opportunity? Conversely, are those who recognize its significance sufficiently aware of the need to continue catering for the large section of the population that is not swayed by postmodernist presuppositions? These and similar questions call for further exploration.

---

[44] Karl Marx and Friedrich Engels, *The Communist Manifesto* (Harmondsworth, Middlesex: Penguin, 1967), 113.

At the opening of the twenty-first century Evangelicals can look back on a long-standing heritage of engagement with the problems of society. On the one hand, they have taken part in campaigns for the correction of the evils in the world around them. Their theology, by contrast with that of others, has led them to make sin their target. They have therefore typically adopted a negative policy, a method of agitation and a manner that rejects compromise. There have been successes, but the attendant clamour, diversion from the gospel and attitude of legalism have constituted serious risks. On the other hand, Britain in the mid-nineteenth century showed signs of the thorough indigenization of Christianity. The country, of course, had its moral blind spots; but its public life and general tone were remarkably shaped by evangelical priorities. By 1852, according to Thomas Binney, then the most prominent Nonconformist minister in London, a portion of society was 'pervaded by the Christian element'.[45] Evangelicals had made an impact through putting their distinctive principles into practice, through sustained use of the media, through meeting felt need, through benefiting from state toleration and through their affinity for contemporary culture. These sustained processes, rather than militant campaigns, were what had transformed the land. Pondering their history may well lead Evangelicals to prefer the slower and less spectacular methods that have reaped such rewards in the past. That is the way to root the gospel in our culture; and it is also the way to avoid imitating Elmer Gantry.

---

[45] Thomas Binney, *Is it Possible to Make the Best of Both Worlds? A Book for Young Men* (London: Nisbet, 1855), 105.

2. Historical Models of Evangelical Social Transformation

John Wolffe

There have of course been many 'movements for change' in Christian history, not least in the history of Evangelicals since the eighteenth century. Indeed to the extent that Evangelicalism has been defined and characterized, as David Bebbington argues, by ongoing activist impulse and emphasis on life-changing conversion, endeavour to change individuals and through them the society in which they are located is of its very essence.[1] More specifically there are numerous instances in which Evangelicals have had a far-reaching historical impact. One might start with the impact of Methodism in early industrial Britain, which, according to an influential line of thought derived from the French historian Elie Halévy, was instrumental in averting revolution. [2] Then there was the role of William Wilberforce and the networks with which he was associated, not only in eventually successful campaigns against colonial slavery, but in promoting religious and moral revival at home.[3] Meanwhile across the Atlantic, Evangelicals played a fundamental role in the era between the Revolution and the Civil War in shaping the society and culture of the new American nation.[4] Nonconformity, with its deep and broad evangelical inspiration, played a key role in the social fabric of Victorian Britain, and also exercised considerable political influence.[5] At this very period Lord Shaftesbury provided a parallel example of substantial evangelical influence on society applied by a politically conservative and socially élitist individual.[6] During the

---

[1] D. W. Bebbington, *Evangelicalism in Modern Britain* (London: Allen & Unwin, 1989), 5-12.

[2] For a survey of the debates see G. W. Olsen (ed.), *Religion and Revolution in Early Industrial England: The Halévy Thesis and its Critics* (Lanham, Md.:University Press of America, 1990).

[3] For an old but still useful account see Ernest Marshall Howse, *Saints in Politics: The 'Clapham Sect' and the Growth of Freedom* (University of Toronto Press, 1952; reprinted London: Allen and Unwin, 1971), and for more recent perspectives, David Hempton 'Evangelicalism and Reform c.1780-1832' in John Wolffe (ed.), *Evangelical Faith and Public Zeal: Evangelicals and Society in Britain 1780-1832* (London: SPCK, 1995), 17-37.

[4] For a recent authoritative survey of this process see Mark A. Noll, *America's God From Jonathan Edwards to Abraham Lincoln* (New York: Oxford University Press, 2002), 161-208.

[5] D. W. Bebbington, *The Nonconformist Conscience: Chapel and Politics 1870-1914* (London: Allen & Unwin, 1982); James Munson, *The Nonconformists: In search of a lost culture* (London: SPCK, 1991).

[6] G. F. A. Best, *Shaftesbury* (London: Batsford, 1964).

twentieth century the capacity of Evangelicals to shape British society might seem to have lessened, although it remained more significant than is acknowledged by secular historians.[7] Undeniably, though, Evangelicalism has remained a major influence in the United States, and, especially in newer Pentecostal and indigenous forms, it has certainly stirred major 'movements for change' in Latin America, Asia and Africa in recent decades.[8]

There is therefore no lack of models and inspiration for evangelical transformation of society. The question immediately arises, however, as to what it is about the historical and social context of early twenty-first century Britain that tends to make Evangelicals subconsciously feel that most if not all of them are variously anachronistic, unrepeatable or culturally inappropriate. Is this feeling sound judgement or mere defeatism, or perhaps a mixture of the two? This is a key point to which we shall return at the end of the chapter.

Initially, though, there will be an examination of historical examples of evangelical social influence exercised through three different kinds of channels: first, the churches themselves, second, prominent individual Christians acting independently of church structures, and, finally, interdenominational and pan-evangelical agencies. Intuitively contemporary Evangelicals tend to look to this final category, of parachurch agencies - whether the Evangelical Alliance itself, the Bible Society, CARE, or mission societies - as the primary source of initiatives in social and cultural transformation. With the distinguished exceptions of the SPG and SPCK - neither of which are primarily evangelical - none of these bodies have a history going back further than the end of the eighteenth century. Many are much more recent. In earlier eras directly church-based and individual initiatives were therefore often the only approaches available. Is contemporary deference to societies, networks, and alliances therefore an historical aberration or rather an appropriate response to a changed environment? This is a further fundamental question that underlies the analysis in this chapter.

A further preliminary is to emphasize that a short survey such as this cannot begin to cover all possible historical models and mechanisms whereby Evangelicals have sought to bring about social transformation. It seems best therefore to focus on some significant examples and trends, with the intent of indicating some preliminary conclusions.

---

[7] David Bebbington, 'The Decline and Resurgence of Evangelical Social Concern 1918-1980', in Wolffe (ed.), *Evangelical Faith and Public Zeal*, 176-197.

[8] John Wolffe, 'Evangelicals and Pentecostals: Indigenizing a Global Gospel', in John Wolffe (ed.), *Global Religious Movements in Regional Context* (Aldershot/Milton Keynes: Ashgate/The Open University, 2002), 13-108; David Martin, *Pentecostalism: The World Their Parish* (Oxford: Blackwell, 2002).

1. Churches

First we shall look at churches as direct agents of social transformation. Part of the inherent mindset of Evangelicals is to see themselves as a committed crusading minority, often at odds with their environment and certainly never satisfied with it. This attitude has been accentuated during the last two generations as organized Christianity has been in numerical retreat, and theological liberalism has been evident among some of its professed leaders. Indeed, as a recent analysis of American Evangelicalism has argued, there is a case for seeing a sense of being embattled as an inherent feature of the evangelical tradition.[9] It is therefore essential to remind ourselves that up to at least the beginning of the twentieth century the institutional churches were central to the social and political fabric of this country. Imagine a world with very few of the social and leisure options available to us today: without cinema, television, telephone, easy transport or any of the secular community support structures we may denigrate but still take for granted. Until the 1870 Education Act elementary education was largely provided and controlled by the churches, and Sunday Schools played a crucial role in giving a rudimentary secular as well as religious education to children unable to attend day schools. The Labour cabinet minister George Lansbury, recalling his youth in the 1860s and 1870s, wrote that there was then 'no social life outside religious organizations'.[10] Echoes of such experience can be found in much more recent times: Joel Edwards has recalled that his local New Testament Church of God in the 1960s was 'the place where you kept alive ... your social centre'.[11] In the nineteenth century, however, a sense of the centrality of church in social life was not a feeling confined to committed Christians.

It was true that the social influence of the state churches was more often directed to the maintenance of stability and the established social order than towards social transformation. Nevertheless even here talented and committed Evangelicals could exercise a considerable social impact, notably in promoting elementary education, and in encouraging moral reform. Early instances of important evangelical Anglican ministries included those of Samuel Walker at Truro in Cornwall from 1746 to 1761 and William Grimshaw at Haworth in Yorkshire from 1742 to 1763.[12] The kind of transition that could take place is most eloquently evoked in George Eliot's short novel, *Janet's Repentance*.

---

[9] Christian Smith, *American Evangelicalism: Embattled and Thriving* (Chicago: Chicago University Press 1998).

[10] George Lansbury, *My Life* (London: Constable & Co., 1928), 29-30.

[11] Quoted Ian Randall and David Hilborn, *One Body in Christ* (Carlisle: Paternoster, 2001), 346.

[12] F. Baker, *William Grimshaw, 1708-1763* (London: Epworth Press 1963); G.C.B. Davies, *The Early Cornish Evangelicals* (London: SPCK, 1951).

This account is all the more telling because it comes from the pen of a woman who by the time of writing in the mid-1850s had emphatically rejected the personal evangelical convictions of her youth. She is describing the impact of Evangelicalism in the 1820 on the town 'Milby', led by the Anglican curate Mr Tryan, a scenario modelled on her childhood recollections of the real-life ministry of an evangelical clergyman, John Edmund Jones, in Nuneaton.

> Evangelicalism had brought into palpable existence and operation in Milby society that idea of duty, that recognition of something to be lived for beyond the mere satisfaction of self, which is to the moral life what the addition of a great central ganglion is to animal life. No man can begin to mould himself on a faith or an idea without rising to a higher order of experience: a principle of subordination, of self-mastery, has been introduced into his nature; he is no longer a mere bundle of impressions, desires and impulses. Whatever might be the weaknesses of the ladies who pruned the luxuriance of their lace and ribbons, cut out garments for the poor, distributed tracts, quoted Scripture, and defined the true Gospel, they had learned this - that there was a divine work to be done in life, a rule of goodness higher than the opinion of their neighbours; and if the notion of heaven in reserve for themselves was a little too prominent, yet the theory of fitness for that heaven consisted in purity of heart, Christ-like compassion, in the subduing of selfish desires.[13]

George Eliot's perception was that in a closely integrated local community such changes of heart and attitude by the evangelical minority inevitably had an impact in bringing about wider social transformation. As she hints, though, the evangelical role in such transformations was not immune from charges of hypocrisy and self-righteousness. Moreover there were certainly cases, as in the long and determined ministry of Francis Close at Cheltenham in the early Victorian years, when the very effectiveness of Evangelicals in changing a community could lead to criticism and backlash from those who felt outward conformity was being imposed upon them.[14]

A particularly interesting example of an evangelical attempt to bring about social transformation based on the local church was associated with the ministry of Thomas Chalmers, the leading Evangelical in the Church of Scotland in the first half of the nineteenth century. Chalmers was converted while Minister of Kilmany, an agricultural parish in Fife, and when he moved to a large slum parish in Glasgow in 1815 he found his model for urban ministry in an idealized vision of mutually supportive rural community. At the

---

[13] G. Eliot, *Scenes of Clerical Life* (Oxford: Oxford University Press, 1985), 227-8.
[14] Michael Hennell, *Sons of the Prophets: Evangelical Leaders of the Victorian Church* (London: SPCK, 1979), 104-21; A. F. Munden, 'Francis Close' in Donald M. Lewis (ed.), *The Blackwell Dictionary of Evangelical Biography 1730-1860* (2 vols., Oxford: Blackwell, 1995), i. 232.

core of his endeavours was evangelism and religious education among the poor, not only as an end in itself, but in order to establish a foundation of shared Christian commitment as a basis for social responsibility. His proposed solution to the extensive poverty and deprivation of the early industrial city was to move away from impersonal systems of aid by the state, municipality or voluntary societies, and to depend rather on the good-neighbourliness of a Christian community. Thus he reinvigorated a structure of elders and deacons in his parish, with responsibility for investigating and relieving cases of need. Their first response was to encourage relatives and neighbours to help, then if that failed to give temporary assistance themselves, and only as a last resort were they to resort to institutionalized sources of funds. Chalmers claimed that such measures made his parish of St John's able to support its own poor in the early 1820s. This assertion is open to considerable question, but the sense that the churches had a duty to support the poor, and that the parish centred on its church could be a self-sufficient and mutually supportive community, became a powerful vision in early Victorian Britain.[15]

Alongside such primarily 'top-down' models of social change associated with the state churches, was a more 'bottom-up' process bound to the great expansion of Methodism and of evangelical Nonconformity in the late eighteenth and early nineteenth centuries. Although Methodism traces its origins back to the conversion of John Wesley in 1738, for much of the rest of the eighteenth century it remained a fairly small-scale movement. At the time of Wesley's death in 1791 there were still only 56,605 members in England. During the next few decades, however, numbers increased exponentially. They almost doubled, to 109,135 in 1806, and more than doubled again, to 267,652, in 1826. In 1851 there were 490,000 Methodists, and numbers continued to climb for the rest of the century, although now doing little more than holding their own as a proportion of population. Nevertheless for much of the second half of the nineteenth century Methodist membership held steady at a proportion of about 4 % of the English figure, comfortably double the 2% that, according to Robert Bellah, is needed to change the quality of a culture. Between the mid-eighteenth and the mid-nineteenth centuries Congregationalist numbers increased from about 15,000 to about 165,000 and Particular Baptists from about 10,000 to about 122,000. Between them these two other predominantly evangelical denominations accounted for a further 2.5% of the adult population.[16]

---

[15] Stewart J. Brown, *Thomas Chalmers and the Godly Commonwealth in Scotland* (Oxford: Oxford University Press, 1982); John Roxborogh, *Thomas Chalmers: Enthusiast for Mission* (Carlisle: Paternoster, 1999).

[16] A. D. Gilbert, *Religion and Society in Industrial England* (London: Longman, 1976), 31-2, 37; Robert Bellah, 'Civil Religion: The Sacred and the Political in American Life (A Conversation with Sam Keen)', *Psychology Today*, 9/8, January 1976, 58-65.

What lies behind these impressive figures is not merely a pattern of church growth that is the envy of any twenty-first century evangelist, but the transformation of many communities. Early Methodism combined a political conservatism with a social radicalism that imbued working-class and poverty-stricken men and women with a sense of their own self-worth in the sight of God and their neighbours.[17] The state churches were slow to respond to the pastoral challenges of a very rapidly expanding population, and very often Methodists and Nonconformists, stirred initially by the work of itinerant revivalist preachers, set up class meetings and chapels in localities poorly served by the Church of England. Revivalism could often strike a ready chord with people who, although unchurched, still shared in a supernaturalist popular culture. In an environment devoid of any other institutional fabric for local civil society, the chapel would quickly become a focus of the community, providing education, mutual support, social interaction and leisure interest as well as spiritual and moral instruction. Such a pattern can be seen occurring across England from Cornish fishing villages to Durham and Northumberland mining settlements.[18] It was even more apparent in the Welsh valleys, and in the Scottish Highlands and Islands, although here denominational and cultural patterns of religious observance developed that were distinct from those operative in England.[19] There is a revealing parallel to be drawn here with the upsurge of Pentecostalism in Latin America since the 1960s, where amidst a similar process of rapid economic and social change new evangelical churches have become an important focus for the building of local community.[20]

Overall levels of church attendance in the nineteenth century are a matter of academic debate, focused around a fascinating, but flawed document, the Census of Religious Worship of 1851.[21] The best-informed estimates would

---

[17] For in-depth analysis of Methodism in its social and political context see David Hempton, *The Religion of the People: Methodism and popular religion c.1750-1900* (London: Routledge, 1996).

[18] David Luker, 'Revivalism in theory and practice: the case of Cornish Methodism', *Journal of Ecclesiastical History*, 37 (1986), 603-19; Robert Moore, *Pitmen, Preachers and Politics: The Effects of Methodism in a Durham Mining Community* (Cambridge, 1974).

[19] E. T. Davies, *Religion in the Industrial Revolution in South Wales* (Cardiff: University of Wales Press, 1965); Allan I. Macinnes, 'Evangelical Protestantism in the nineteenth-century Highlands', in Graham Walker and Tom Gallagher (eds.), *Sermons and Battle Hymns: Protestant Popular Culture in Modern Scotland* (Edinburgh: Edinburgh University Press, 1990), 43-68.

[20] David Martin, *Tongues of Fire: The Explosion of Protestantism in Latin America* (Oxford: Blackwell, 1990).

[21] There is a substantial literature on the Religious Census, including (for an increasing proportion of counties) published transcripts of the original returns for individual

suggest that on Sunday 30 March, when the census was taken, between a third and a half of the total population attended at least one church service. But was the glass half full or half empty? The tendency of commentators since the 1850s has been to dwell on the fact that even at the supposed high-water mark of Victorian Christianity probably more than half of the population did not attend religious worship. Allowance, though, has to be made for a number of factors that would have unavoidably prevented people from attending. Not only were there the very young, the very old, the sick, and those who had to stay at home to look after them, but many for whom, especially in rural areas, a lengthy journey to church on poor roads, on foot, in rainy early spring weather would have dampened even the strongest devotional feelings. Then as now there is evidence that parents of young children attended alternately.[22] And even those whose Sunday attendance might be very infrequent could turn out for occasions such as Watch-Night services, Harvest Festivals and Sunday School anniversaries, as well as for rites of passage, especially weddings and funerals. In the late nineteenth century too active churches and chapels often developed an extensive range of ancillary organizations, such as mothers' meetings, men's gatherings, Girls Friendly Society and Boys Brigade that drew in many who would not necessarily have been regular attenders at Sunday worship. [23]

It is legitimate therefore to infer that some kind of church influence extended itself to a substantial majority of the population of Victorian Britain. The geographical distribution was very uneven though, with mappings of church attendance appearing as a patchwork quilt. Broadly speaking, attendance was higher in the south and east of England than in the north and west. Wales, though, recorded some of the highest figures of all. Attendance tended to be lowest in large cities, especially those that had grown most rapidly in the Industrial Revolution, and highest in market towns and smaller cathedral cities, with rural areas in something of a middle position. Much, though, depended on the social geography and ministry of particular parishes and settlements - was the settlement pattern concentrated or dispersed? Were clergy and ministers overworked and negligent or conscientious and well-supported? Did secular authorities such as village squires or major local employers encourage participation, or where they indifferent to it? Enquiries of this kind are not

---

churches. The most recent overview is K.D.M. Snell and Paul S.Ell, *Rival Jerusalems: The Geography of Victorian Religion* (Cambridge: Cambridge University Press, 2000).

[22] For examples see John Wolffe (ed.), *Yorkshire Returns of the 1851 Census of Religious Worship: Volume 1: Introduction, City of York and East Riding* (York: University of York, 2000), 30-1 (the 'Alternate attendance of Husband and Wife'), 75 ('The bad state of the weather, & of the roads ... often make a material difference in the numbers present').

[23] John Wolffe, *God and Greater Britain: Religion and National Life in Britain and Ireland 1843-1845* (London: Routledge, 1994), 75-97.

merely of local and antiquarian interest, because the indications are that attitudes to organized religion in local areas can become part of a family and community tradition that is transmitted across the generations. A church that is seeking to strengthen its spiritual and social impact in its locality would be well advised to find out whether the longer-term history is one of widespread support and involvement or of indifference and alienation.

The central role of the church in the secular as well as the religious social fabric was a source of tension for Evangelicals, especially those in the Church of England and the Church of Scotland, where the parochial system and constitutional national status implied a pastoral responsibility for everyone in the territorial parish. The outworking of a conversionist theology could lead to evangelical clergy - especially those of a more Calvinist disposition - being accused of neglecting the majority of their parishioners in order to concentrate their attention on a congregation of the converted.[24] Ministry of this kind was also perceived as socially divisive. Such fears help to explain the hostility of many early nineteenth-century Anglican bishops to zealous evangelical incumbents. There was a further tension for evangelicals in the national churches between a sense of primary spiritual allegiance to Christ, and the legal obligations of establishment. These were most dramatically illustrated in the Disruption of the Church of Scotland in 1843, which had its roots in church resistance to the right of patrons, upheld by the secular courts, to appoint ministers who had not been accepted by the congregations they would serve. A very substantial and predominantly evangelical minority seceded to form the Free Church of Scotland. For a few years it seemed a similar movement might follow in the Church of England, at the time of a long drawn out court action between 1847 and 1850 in which the High Church Bishop of Exeter refused to institute an evangelical incumbent because of his allegedly unsound views on baptism. Crucially, however, the eventual verdict of the secular courts in England was in favour of the right of Evangelicals to maintain their position within the Church of England.

For Nonconformists too, the importance of their chapels as secular as well as religious institutions could bring dilemmas. Especially as the high spiritual temperature of early Victorian revivalism tended to recede in the latter part of the century, it became apparent that many were attending as much for social as for spiritual reasons. Evangelical orthodoxy might be troubled by this, but it is surely pertinent to ask whether in the cause of social transformation it was necessarily a 'bad thing'. Do we see the fact that the young D. H. Lawrence was shaped in many ways by the Nottinghamshire Congregational chapel he

---

[24] W. J. Conybeare, 'Church Parties', in Stephen Taylor (ed.), *From Cranmer to Davidson: A Church of England Miscellany* (Woodbridge: Boydell/Church of England Record Society, 1999), 287-90.

attended [25] as illustrative of the social and cultural failure of late nineteenth-century Evangelicalism, or of its success? Such issues seem inescapable in a church-based approach to social transformation: further investigation of historical models will not provide easy answers, but it may well suggest some useful precedents and examples.

2. Individuals

The second model of evangelical social transformation to be explored is the role of individual pioneers. Some aspects of this analysis have already been anticipated. Clearly the church-led transformations discussed above often owed much to individual leaders, usually clergy and ministers, who nonetheless worked through and reshaped church structures. The focus now, however, is rather on the role of individual Christians, usually lay people, whose work was accomplished primarily outside the organization of the institutional church.

There are of course numerous men and women who could be cited here. Due to constraints of space, however, it may well be of greatest interest to concentrate on two of the most deservedly famous examples of evangelical Christians who have brought about far reaching social, moral and political change, William Wilberforce (1759-1833), and Anthony Ashley-Cooper, Earl of Shaftesbury (1881-85).[26] Wilberforce's greatest achievement was the abolition of the slave trade in British ships, a measure enacted by Parliament in 1807, after nearly 20 years of campaigning. Shaftesbury was responsible above all for the limitation of working hours in industry, but promoted numerous other measures of social reform, including improvements to the treatment of the mentally ill and sanitary improvement in Britain's overcrowded and disease-ridden cities. Wilberforce and Shaftesbury are often mentioned in the same breath as examples of past evangelical achievement, but with an undercurrent of depression that implies we will never see their equals in our own generation. It is true that much in the political environment has changed since Shaftesbury's day, and moreover that no church or other organization can guarantee to produce leaders of such outstanding quality. Nevertheless, rather

---

[25] Margaret Masson, 'The Influence of Congregationalism in the First Four Novels of D. H. Lawrence' (Durham PhD thesis, 1988).

[26] The comparison that follows is drawn from evidence in contemporary lives, R. I. and S. Wilberforce, *The Life William Wilberforce* (5 vols., London: John Murray, 1838) and E. Hodder, *The Life and Work of the Seventh Earl of Shaftesbury, KG* (3 vols., London, 1887), and modern biographies, notably John Pollock, *Wilberforce* (London: John Constable, 1977) and G.B.A.M. Finlayson, *The Seventh Earl of Shaftesbury 1801-1885* (London: Eyre Methuen, 1981). For my own biographical surveys of Wilberforce and Shaftesbury see *The Oxford Dictionary of National Biography* (Oxford: Oxford University Press, 2004 (forthcoming).

than simply despair or await the dispensations of providence, it appears constructive to draw out a number of features of the lives and careers of these two men that that may still suggest relevant models for contemporary political and social action:

1. **They were both committed professional politicians.** Wilberforce was first elected to Parliament when barely 21, and sat continuously in the House of Commons until failing health forced his retirement in his mid-60s. Shaftesbury was elected to the Commons at 25, served there, apart from a short gap, until he inherited the title a quarter of a century later, and thereafter made the best of the more limited opportunities offered by the Lords. Both worked extremely hard even when struggling with poor health or increasing age, recognizing that there was no easy way to secure their objectives. Their professionalism as politicians also induced a realism that could lead them to make short term compromises in order to secure intermediate objectives, but ones that could be helpful stepping stones to longer-term ideals.

2. **Both were politicians before they were converted.** Wilberforce's conversion did not come until 1785, when he was already MP for Yorkshire; Shaftesbury's not until the mid-1830s, when he had already held junior government office. It is hard to know how much to make of this point. It may, though, be very significant, both in providing them with inside experience of secular politics, and in stirring a Christian vision for politics that was more sustainable than that of those who came into parliament as already committed Christians, with naïve and unrealistic ambitions that were subsequently dented and trimmed. It also meant that they had already built lasting associations with central secular political figures, such as William Pitt and Lord Palmerston, who remained friends with them even when they found their Christian zeal perplexing. The implication for a present-day evangelical movement for change is an important one, in that it suggests that currently non-Christian politicians could have an important role to play.

3. **Both sacrificed secular political ambition.** Undoubtedly both Wilberforce and Shaftesbury had the ability and the connections to have become Cabinet ministers. Wilberforce, however, early made it clear he was not interested in government office, and Shaftesbury several times turned it down when it was offered to him. The temptation was more insidious because it seemed to provide an opportunity to bring a more Christian tone to government. Like Wilberforce, however, he realized that the integrity of his Christian witness and the consistency of his support for the particular causes he wished to promote could very easily have been seriously compromised by government office.

4. **Both demonstrated conspicuous involvement and integrity with reference to secular political issues.** In 1805 Wilberforce faced an agonizing dilemma over how to vote in the Commons on a motion for the impeachment of Henry Dundas, Viscount Melville, the First Lord of the Admiralty, who was alleged to have condoned the misappropriation of naval funds by a subordinate. Wilberforce was supportive of the government, and above all of the Prime Minister, his friend William Pitt, at a time of national crisis. Nevertheless he spoke and voted against Melville in the belief that this was an essential step in maintaining the incorruptibility of those holding public office. Arguably, the Melville case, a foretaste in some ways of contemporary political sleaze, was a formative moment in establishing the relatively high expectations of public servants in Britain, and Wilberforce's role, as an acknowledged moral arbiter, was crucial. In 1846, Shaftesbury, now convinced like the Prime Minister, Sir Robert Peel, that it was essential to repeal the Corn Laws, resigned his parliamentary seat for Dorset, where his constituents were strongly opposed to repeal. This was a setback to the cause of factory reform because it kept him out of parliament for eighteen months, but he recognized that cause would not be well served if he appeared inconsistent and dishonourable in other aspects of this career.

5. **Neither avoided confrontation, but fought their battles graciously.** A feature of both Wilberforce and Shaftesbury was their ability to retain the respect of fair-minded opponents, because they did not resort to public demonizing or diminishing of those who disagreed with them. Wilberforce was assisted in this respect by great personal charm and sociability.

6. **Both maintained strong personal devotional lives**. This statement may well seem the stuff of pious legend, but it is in fact well supported by the surviving personal manuscript diaries of both men. These are evidence of regular daily devotion and intense self-examination before God. The detail can appear somewhat introspective and spiritually self-indulgent, but the outcomes helped to sustain the integrity and commitment so apparent in their public lives.[27]

7. **Both received strong personal support from others**. Both men were happily married - albeit in Wilberforce's case not until he had already been involved in the anti-slave campaign for a decade – and had large families to which they were devoted. Family life appears to have been an essential balance to the pressures of public roles, and was not neglected. They also

---

[27] Wilberforce's manuscript diaries are at the Bodleian Library in Oxford, and Shaftesbury's at the University of Southampton.

found sources of spiritual counsel and support, Wilberforce from John Newton, the slave ship captain turned clergyman and hymn-writer, and Shaftesbury from Edward Bickersteth, a leading evangelical clergyman and founder of the Evangelical Alliance, and later from Alexander Haldane, proprietor of the *Record* newspaper, an ancestor of the *Church of England Newspaper*.

8. **Both were prepared to address the big issues**. It would have been possible to take a more limited approach to both the slave trade and factory reform questions, seeking modest changes to meet specific Christian and humanitarian concerns, while leaving the fundamentals unchanged. Wilberforce and Shaftesbury were both prepared to accept such minor improvements as interim measures, but they kept their attention firmly on the big vision. Hence they had to face real and prolonged conflict, but they motivated supporters to feel that they were engaged in a struggle that was really worthwhile, and in the long term brought about substantial change.

9. **Both were willing to work with non-Christians**. The anti-slavery campaign and the factory reform movement were both coalitions of diverse forces, in which evangelical Christians were prominent, but not necessarily dominant. In Parliament success eventually depended on bringing together a majority with a whole mixture of motives and agendas.

10. **Conversely, both were prepared to ride out criticism from fellow Christians**. Political realities were not always well understood by those outside parliament, and both men could be perceived as hesitant or lukewarm, when they were simply waiting for the best moment to promote their cause. Similarly their readiness to work with non-Christians could be discomfiting for purists. Nor was there always a united Christian consensus behind the causes they promoted: initially not all Christians were convinced of the sinfulness of slavery; initially, too, some Christian opinion saw any state regulation of working conditions as intrusive. A 'movement for change' has to be ready for criticism in quarters that can sometimes seem uncomfortably close to home.

These ten points would still seem likely to repay careful consideration and application. Certainly they are interesting as a kind of historical benchmark by which to evaluate other instances of social and political action by individual Evangelicals, which were much less effective and therefore now largely forgotten. Very often one can quickly identify a failure or obvious weakness on one of them: for example, a lack of sustained political professionalism, an excessive rigidity of adherence to perceived Christian principle, a refusal to engage in meaningful cooperation with non-Christians, or on the other hand, a readiness to compromise too much, leading to loss of moral authority.[28] The implication for churches, pan-evangelical organizations, and their leaders is that there needs to be a readiness to support without controlling. How many contemporary Christian leaders would have the wisdom and humility shown by John Newton, who readily counselled the young Wilberforce, but described himself as one of the 'little folks' who 'are so distant from the public circle in which you move'?[29] Newton was adamant in urging Wilberforce to stay in public life, and in suggesting the underlying spiritual and biblical principles he should follow, but made no attempt to influence his actual political strategies and tactics, realizing these were outside his own competence.

Another aspect of Wilberforce's career is worthy of note. On several occasions he published books and pamphlets in order to gain a wider public audience for his views. Particularly successful in this respect was his *Practical View of the Prevailing Religious System of Professed Christians in the Higher and Middle Classes in this Country Contrasted with Real Christianity*, published in 1797. It rapidly went through numerous editions and had a wide readership. As its title implies, it was a critique of contemporary nominal Christianity, and an exposition of distinctively evangelical convictions and practice presented as social and political necessities as well as spiritual imperatives. It certainly played an important role in stimulating the spread of Evangelicalism among the early nineteenth-century middle class. Its effectiveness derived in large part from the conviction of its personal testimony and from the fact that it was written by a prominent layman rather than a clergyman who would have had a perceived vested interest in the spread of Christianity. Had Wilberforce been alive two centuries later his chosen medium might well have been a television series rather than a book, but the impact of his work indicates the potential importance of Christian public figures having the time, courage and means for some kind of explicit testimony.

3. Pan-evangelical agencies

There is an inherent and revealing tension in Evangelicalism between the individualistic impulses of its adherents, and the parallel urge to form societies and agencies for a wide range of purposes. Although such organizations were rare until the 1790s, they then began to develop rapidly, with the founding

---

[28] For examples of the pitfalls encountered by other nineteenth-century Evangelicals in public life see the entries in *The Dictionary of Evangelical Biography* for John Campbell Colquhoun (1803-70), James Edward Gordon (1790-1862), Charles Grant (1778-1866) and Edward Miall (1809-81).

[29] Bodleian Library Oxford, MS Wilberforce c. 49, ff 14-15, Newton to Wilberforce, 1 November 1787.

initially of the major mission societies and the Bible Society. A plethora of other societies rapidly followed and by the second quarter of the nineteenth century. Their annual meetings, held in London and concentrated into a few weeks in May, became a kind of highpoint in the upper and middle class evangelical social calendar. They were significant in drawing together Anglicans and Nonconformists in specific common causes at a period when interdenominational tensions were otherwise acute. The London City Mission, founded in 1836, was a particularly good example of how individuals who were at odds with each other on other fronts could still cooperate for an immediate evangelistic purpose.[30] In general a great deal was achieved during the Victorian era at the grass roots by dedicated voluntary effort. It is significant that in the later part of his life Shaftesbury increasingly came to see voluntary societies rather than political action as the best mechanisms for promoting the evangelical cause.

It should be noted that the longer-standing evangelical organizations were predominantly directed towards explicitly religious and evangelistic purposes, although these were construed as including education. Indeed some well-supported organizations, such as the Church Association, which battled against High Church ritualism in the Church of England in the later nineteenth century, had rather narrow and sectarian agendas that later Evangelicals might well regard as at best a diversion of energy from wider and more pressing needs.[31] Societies with what we would now regard as a wider social or moral agenda were comparatively rare, and tended to have a single-issue focus, for example on Sabbath Observance or temperance. The development of organizations with a multi-issue range - such as CARE and the Jubilee Centre - has been primarily a later twentieth-century development. It suggests an awareness that the disjunction between evangelical values and those of the wider society has become sufficiently wide that a holistic rather than piecemeal approach has become necessary. In this respect the Evangelical Alliance's own sense of a changing identity to become an active 'movement for change' fits into a wider historical pattern.

The path to pan-evangelical cooperation has, however, been one of considerable difficulty. This was well illustrated in the early history of the Evangelical Alliance itself, which was initially accused of being a 'do-nothing' organization because it tended to present evangelical unity as a sufficient end in

---

[30] Donald M. Lewis, *Lighten Their Darkness: The Evangelical Mission to Working-Class London 1828-1860* (Greenwood: Westport, Ct., 1986).
[31] James Bentley, *Ritualism and Politics in Victorian Britain* (Oxford: Oxford University Press, 1978), 37.

itself.[32] Moreover the founding international conference in August 1846 became seriously divided over the question of slavery. It is important to emphasize that this was not a simple clash between slaveholders and their militant opponents, positions that were indeed inherently irreconcilable. Rather the issue was one between committed opponents of slavery and the majority of the American delegation who, while generally personally opposed to slavery, believed that excluding slaveholders from membership as others wanted would inevitably limit the potential of the Alliance to recruit in the United States. They also felt that such an exclusion would lead to the EA being seen as another anti-slavery society rather than as a focus for united Christian action on a wider range of fronts.[33]

If this controversy seems remote from present-day concerns it may be useful, if uncomfortable, to suggest an analogy with current tensions over homosexuality. There is similarly no common ground between an active and self-consciously gay lifestyle, and those Evangelicals who hold that homosexuality is unambiguously condemned in Scripture and that any compromise with it is a betrayal of the gospel. However, many contemporary Evangelicals would hold to a middle position, analogous to the stance on slavery of the American delegation in 1847. While believing homosexual practice to be sinful they would still urge that rigid exclusion of practising gay people from any organized Christianity is an abnegation of pastoral responsibility and opportunity, and gives a distorted emphasis to one kind of sin over others. Moreover they see it as generating a popular perception of Christian social and moral engagement as being synonymous with homophobia, thus obscuring issues that they see as more important and more constructive.

The wider implication of this analogy is that a united evangelical front across a diverse range of issues is likely to be difficult to achieve. This is not so much because of fundamental divergence of principle, but because of difference of tactics and because some individuals hold a multi-issue vision, while others are focused on one issue which they then come to see as primary among all others. This tendency was very apparent in nineteenth-century single-issue societies which tended to end up appearing to say, for example, that drink - or even the Roman Catholic Church - was the root of all evil, or that all social and spiritual problems would be resolved if only rigorous Sunday observance were enforced.

---

[32] John Wolffe, 'The Evangelical Alliance in the 1840s: An Attempt to Institutionalise Christian Unity', in W.J. Sheils and Diana Wood (eds.), *Voluntary Religion: Studies in Church History 25* (Oxford: Blackwell/Ecclesiastical History Society, 1986).

[33] *Evangelical Alliance. Report of the Proceedings of the Conference held at Freemasons' Hall, London* (London, 1847), especially 292-3, 401-7; Robert Baird, *The Progress and Prospects of Christianity in the United States of America* (London, 1851), 40-9.

The early history of the Evangelical Alliance, though, also offers a more positive model of how differences could be managed. For example, at the time of its foundation, confrontation between the state churches and Nonconformity was entrenched and extensive, and the Disruption of the Church of Scotland in 1843 had given rise to hopes and fears that state-supported religious establishments were about to break down everywhere. Diametrically opposed views were apparent in the British evangelical constituency, from those who held state churches to be a vital support of the gospel, to those who believed that only with their complete destruction would true Christianity be able to flourish. The EA's response to that situation was to affirm that true unity lay in respecting rather than repressing diversity.[34] In particular it sought to prevent any divisive discussion of relations between church and state occurring at its meetings. This was not sufficient to win over entrenched opinion on either side, but it did provide a basis for effective co-operation between moderates on other issues, and did secure the Alliance a viable long-term future. Clearly, agreements to differ cannot be applied to all controversial issues, otherwise complete inertia would ensue, but they may well be a useful mechanism for dealing with issues of particularly acute divergence which both parties regard as a distraction from other equally pressing concerns.

A further inherent difficulty for pan-evangelical agencies is that they develop an institutional momentum and survival instinct, so that energies and funds become largely expended in maintaining the machinery, rather than in serving the end for which it was originally created. Also for longstanding organizations that survived well into the twentieth century, the need to retain identity by adherence to perceived institutional tradition could easily become a check on effective innovation and engagement with contemporary culture. It would be invidious to name particular bodies here, other than to cite the history of the Evangelical Alliance itself - with its prolonged relative inertia in the early and mid-twentieth century and its subsequent re-invention of itself - as an example of both the pitfalls and the opportunities.[35] It is significant, though, that the transformation of the EA has come in part through better understanding of its institutional history rather than through turning its back on the past.

4. Conclusions

The object of this paper has been to indicate some of the strengths and weaknesses of different evangelical approaches to social transformation, as they have been demonstrated by actual historical experience. This investigation

---

[34] John Wolffe, 'Unity in Diversity? North Atlantic Evangelical Thought in the Mid-Nineteenth Century' in R. N. Swanson (ed.), *Unity and Diversity in the Church: Studies in Church History 32* (Oxford: Blackwell/Ecclesiastical History Society, 1996), 363-75.
[35] For detail see Randall and Hilborn, *One Body in Christ.*

does not lead to a clear-cut preference for any particular approach. All of them have achieved much in the past, and all are subject to significant drawbacks. The broad conclusion would be that the evangelical impact was strongest when all three were working together, as in the early to mid-nineteenth century. This may seem a bland and obvious point, but it is still important to ponder. The EA needs to be careful to resist any natural institutional bias towards a pan-evangelical agency approach. It is therefore encouraging to see much in its *Uniting for Change* manifesto about stimulating local church initiative, but there is a relative lack of measures for raising up, stimulating, and above all sustaining high profile individual leadership of the kind that can really make a difference. [36] Rather than the defeatist assumption that Wilberforces and Shaftesburys will not emerge in our own time, it is better for Evangelicals to ask themselves where such leadership potential can be identified, and also how they can best relate to it when, rather than if, it emerges. Given the vacuum of effective social and political leadership of any kind there are great opportunities and needs here. There is a danger, though, that potential Wilberforces would find the contemporary evangelical subculture restrictive rather than supporting.

In some ways the challenges facing churches at the grassroots are more daunting than they were in the past, because declining active participation has made them much more marginal to the social and cultural life of their localities. Nevertheless the figures given above for Methodist expansion in the early nineteenth century are a reminder of the potential for a seemingly negligible minority to become a substantial and influential minority. Expectations, however, have to be realistic: the main period of Methodist growth extended over half a century, and saw many intermediate fluctuations. Churches need to be encouraged to look to the long term rather than expect instant results and give up when they do not materialize. The extent of the decline in organized Christianity in Britain in the twentieth century can be attributed as much to an internal failure of nerve - to a sense in the churches themselves that they are no longer 'relevant' to the wider community - as to external secularizing forces. [37] A strategy of encouraging churches to strengthen their practical ties with the local community is the best means of restoring a sense of the church as central rather than marginal to the daily life of non-churchgoers. However it is important also to keep on recalling that early Evangelicalism grew in the first instance not by building and organizing community centres, but by preaching Christ as the answer to individual and collective spiritual need. Social transformation must be seen as part and parcel of evangelism, not as an alternative to it. Historical experience suggests, however, that such integration

---

[36] Evangelical Alliance, *Uniting for Change* (London: Evangelical Alliance, 2001).

[37] Jeffrey Cox, *The English Churches in a Secular Society* (New York: Oxford University Press, 1982), 271-4. Significantly, Cox characterizes this crisis of morale as a 'particularly British transformation', not a global one.

is easier to assert in principle than to maintain in practice. In holding to such an integrating vision churches in Britain have much to learn not only from our own past history, but from contemporary church growth in Latin America, Africa and Asia.

There also needs to be serious reflection on the best ways of 'uniting for change' rather than being hamstrung by divisive internal argument. Disagreement and fragmentation have been besetting problems for Evangelicals throughout their history. It can hardly be otherwise to the extent that they are the flip side of strong personal conviction and commitment. Nor is an agreement on essential points, and an 'agreement to differ' on secondary issues always a successful strategy, because some will insist on treating as essential points what others regard as secondary, whether slavery in 1846 or matters of sexual morality in our own times. History tends to offer more by way of cautionary tales than of solutions here, but it does offer the challenge that a truly united Evangelicalism in the twenty-first century would be something historically novel, and hence capable of presenting hitherto unrealized potential for social and spiritual impact. If the EA's Movement for Change is to be catalyst for that unity, however, it will need to avoid succumbing to the temptation of articulating too clear and specific an agenda, which would inevitably alienate some natural supporters. It may therefore be that some questions are better not asked. Rather, the emphasis should be on cultivating states of mind among Evangelicals in which as far as possible painful differences can be accommodated within a spirit of underlying unity. Past thinking by nineteenth-century supporters of the EA may well be worth revisiting here.[38]

Historical models, then, have much to teach us, not as precise blueprints for present action, but as sources of inspiration and encouragement which serve to broaden a sense of the strategies available. Contemporary Evangelicals can have their vision limited either by a lack of historical sense which prevents them seeing how things could ever have been or become different, or by a narrow view of history that over-emphasizes adherence to particular traditions and ways of doing things. Part of a movement for change needs to be an informed understanding of our own past - as individuals, churches, communities, and an overall movement - as a dynamic and creative resource for the future.

---

[38] See Wolffe, 'Unity in Diversity?' for specific examples.

3. Social Transformation in the Missions of Jesus and Paul: Priority or Bonus?

Keith Warrington

Introduction

Social transformation is the conversion of society. It is not clear, however, that this was a priority for the early believers. They do not seem to have attempted to change their communities, but instead concentrated on enlarging the Christian community and improving it. This is not to suggest that society did not need improvement. Nor is it to suggest that Jesus and Paul did not present transformed lives to others, or that they did not expect the same from their followers. It simply recognizes that their priorities lay more with the development of the Christian community than with any wider social programme. Furthermore, it is not necessary to assume that the experience of the early church is a paradigm for today's church. The Spirit who set the first century agenda operates as he wishes, and different contexts may result in different agendas being followed.

There is a great deal in the New Testament about evangelism, its motives and principles.[1] There is also much evidence of transformed lives. People from all strata of society and many cultures are identified as coming to faith in Jesus. They represent different levels of intelligence, wealth and age, while their journey to salvation is varied. However, the one thing they have in common is that they are transformed by the gospel. Thereafter, the practical teaching of the leaders of the early Christian communities almost exclusively relates to the lifestyles and behaviour of these believers. Similarly, the ethical teaching of the New Testament is specifically for those within the church. There is no suggestion that this teaching is to be imposed on those outside. Though some elements of it are transferable and much is admirable, it is particularly a Christian ethic for Christian disciples.[2]

No doubt, as several of the other papers in this collection demonstrate, since the New Testament era Christianity has significantly re-ordered many of the societies in which it has existed. However, little such re-ordering is identifiable from the New Testament itself. More particularly, little explicit indication is given there that the early believers thought the church would or even should

---

[1] Michael Green, *Evangelism in the Early Church* (London: Hodder and Stoughton, 1970), 194-273.

[2] Frank J. Matera, *New Testament Ethics. The Legacy of Jesus and Paul* (Louisville: Westminster John Knox Press, 1996), 10.

transform the wider world.[3] It appears that the early church saw its chief role as being to model an alternative society, which others would be attracted to join. Any change in social norms and practices over and above this is assumed to be coincidental, or a bonus. Indeed, it may have been that for many in the first Christian communities, time was thought too limited before Jesus' return to warrant energy being spent on radicalizing society.

Did the early church transform its society?

Not only is it difficult to locate a New Testament *agenda* for change in society as a whole; it is also difficult to find concrete *evidence* of any wide-scale social change having been effected by the earliest Christians - despite the provocative claim of the mob that they had 'turned the world upside down' (Acts 17:6). Given the nature of the 'motley crew' who made this assessment (17:5), and given their subsequent lies about the preaching of the apostles (17:7), it would be wise to treat this claim with caution.

Furthermore, and by way of example: according to the evidence of the New Testament the legitimacy of slavery was not addressed (though elements of its practice were, albeit in the Christian community (1 Pet. 2:18-21)); political debate was not stimulated (other than to encourage the believers to submit to the government of the day and maintain the status quo (Rom. 13:1-7; 1 Pet. 2:13-17), and detailed strategies were not developed by believers for the transformation of their secular communities. This is not to suggest, however, that the early believers did not positively *affect* those communities. Indeed, there are indications that they did. For instance, the instruction by James (1:27) to support widows and orphans does not appear to apply purely to those in the Christian community. Nevertheless, the limited scope of social reform spurred by the church in its first fifty years or so may seem curious given its subsequent record of bringing radical socio-political change to many regions of the world. There may, though, have been a number of reasons for this slow start:

- The evidence of the New Testament is limited and not intended to be comprehensive. It is possible that the time span covered by the relevant texts was simply too short to have allowed for the development of a coherent programme of social transformation. It appears that the early believers had enough to do with the internal development of their own church communities to formulate clear strategies for the broader

---

[3] E.A. Judge, 'The Impact of Paul's gospel on ancient society', in Peter Bolt & Mark Thompson (Eds.) *The Gospel to the Nations* (Leicester: Apollos, 2000), 297-308; contrast John Howard Yoder, *The Politics of Jesus* (Grand Rapids: Eerdmans, 1972), 136f.

improvement of society. Certainly, amidst the many practical instructions offered by the writers of the New Testament, it is noticeable that little guidance is given on effecting mass structural change within the wider secular world.

- The lack of evidence for an agenda to change society may indicate the limited importance of this to the early church. Instead of transforming the world as such, the earliest Christians sought to change the hearts of their unbelieving neighbours. They may, perhaps, have linked this with an *ulterior* intent to change society at large, but this is not made explicit.

- It is possible that the early believers did not see it as their responsibility to transform the world in which they lived, and it may also be assumed, in the absence of advice to the contrary, that the apostles felt the same. Moreover, the Spirit who set the early church's mission agenda does not appear to have led in this direction as much as he led in the direction of evangelism (Acts 1:8). And if the Spirit was not compelling them to do so, they may have thought that there was little reason to initiate root-and-branch social change.

- It is possible that seeking to turn society around like this might have been premature,[4] and thus counter-productive, in an era when opposition was viewed with grave suspicion and even fear by the authorities, often attracting harsh resistance and punishment. Advocating such wide-scale change so early on might have compromised the first Christians' evangelistic drive. Indeed, evangelism itself was sometimes construed as subversive - let alone more overt 'political' activity. In Philippi, for example, where Paul cast out a demon from a girl (and thus ended her exploitation by her owners), his evangelism was swiftly concluded by imprisonment (Acts 16:16-24) and departure from the city after only a short time (16:40).

- It is possible that the thought of substantively changing their society never occurred to the New Testament believers. They did not live in a democracy and did not enjoy the same opportunities as modern-day westerners to voice their opinions and change the direction of the secular world in which they lived. It is not necessarily that they lacked the desire to bring about change, but simply that they thought attempting to do so was impractical. Those who did make efforts in this direction were best represented by Zealots, who sought to advance their cause by violent means - partly because they perceived that there was no other way. Such an approach did

---

[4] Herman N. Ridderbos, *Paul. An Outline of his Theology* (Grand Rapids: Eerdmans, 1975), 316.

not, however, appear to have been deemed appropriate by followers of the Prince of Peace.

At the same time, the level of corruption and inequality in the fractured society of the Roman Empire should not be overlooked. The lack of a history or framework for social change among the church communities of the New Testament, the small number of believers who comprised them, and the sheer enormity of the task - all these factors ensured that a mass campaign of social transformation would have to have been explicitly commissioned by Jesus or the Spirit before the church would have moved to implement it.

- It is possible that the New Testament believers anticipated the world's ceasing to exist in the near future. Certainly, Paul foresees a serious upheaval in society when he writes to the Corinthians concerning marriage (1 Cor. 7:25-31). The fact that Jesus had said he would return may well have been taken to indicate that this end would occur imminently (Mt. 24:29-35). If so, there would have been limited reason for believers to change the structures of their society. Why expend energy transforming the world if that world was about to cease? Rather, their focus was on developing an alternative ecclesial community - a community which would be fully realized only when the current social pattern was removed for good at the close of the age.

- Finally, the absence of a thoroughgoing scheme of social transformation in the New Testament may be a matter of priorities. The earliest Christian communities described there concentrated on preaching the gospel, and thus, on extending the influence of the church as an alternative society. As such, they sought to embody in their own life and witness what Jesus had so frequently called the 'kingdom of God'. They were not trying so much to change their culture as to model a Christian counter-culture. No doubt both Jesus and Paul expected this latter approach to prove so attractive that significant numbers of people would wish to move from one context to the other. This did not, however, equate to a wholesale replacement of the existing society by a new 'Christian society' - not, at least, before the return of Christ.

Did first century society need transforming?

Life in Israel

Life in the Roman Empire varied a great deal depending on where one lived and on one's social status. The Jews in the first century came under the domination of the Roman Empire, which ruled them either through client kings like the Herods or directly through procurators such as Pilate. The vast majority of people in Israel during the New Testament era were very poor, the wealthy few being the Jewish, often religious, aristocracy, and others who benefited from some close association with Rome. As much as 90% of the people lived with very little surplus income above that which they needed to exist. On top of the financial burden of tithes to the Temple and taxes to the empire - exacerbated as it was by a tax/toll system often administered by Jewish tax collectors - there was the danger of living in a frontier region that bordered the Eastern enemies of Rome. Furthermore, fear dominated the lives of those living in the countryside because of a paucity of law and order outside the major cities. The cities themselves, from Caesarea to Jerusalem, housed often rapacious, oppressive Roman soldiers as well as militias serving the local leaders. Potentially, there was much to be rectified here - much that could have been done to improve the harsh social conditions endured by most Jews in the region. Yet there is no record of Jesus voicing explicit opposition to any of the above - even if his parables and more general teachings do sometimes draw attention to such conditions. Even in the case of Jesus' prophetic forerunner, John the Baptist, the call to radical transformation is focused on those wishing to be baptized, rather than on society as a whole (Lk. 3:12-14).

The political leaders of New Testament times were often insensitive to the culture and practices of those they ruled. Herod the Great terrorized the city of Jerusalem whilst plotting the deaths of his wife, mother-in-law, three sons, nephew, grandfather-in-law and two brothers-in-law, plus countless citizens of the Jewish aristocracy. His surviving sons were little better, one of them being deposed by Rome because of his excessively harsh rule. In his place, procurators were installed who showed little sympathy for the lifestyles, hopes and dreams of Jewish people. Again, there was much that could have been transformed here. But there is no record of Jesus supporting the Jews in any rebellion. On the contrary, when asked where his allegiance lay, he stated that as a member of the Roman Empire one had obligations to Caesar (Mt. 22:21). Later, as David Hilborn shows in his paper for this volume, Paul would offer more detailed teaching on the need to respect and submit to governing authorities (Rom. 13:1-7).

The religious leaders of Israel offered little clear hope for the hard-pressed Jews, and even less cause for joy. They were divided and often hostile to one other: the Pharisees and Sadducees were at odds and the Essenes despised them both, rejecting the temple and all it stood for. Political intrigue, nepotism, corruption and hypocrisy were often too closely linked with religion, and centres created for the worship of God became mere ornaments of ritual. In this context, a case could have been made for Jesus to encourage fundamental social change. His speeches about the Pharisees identify areas where transformation is needed (Mt. 23:2-36), but still they relate to personal spirituality and practice. He chooses neither to associate with nor encourage any popular move towards revolutionizing the religious structures of his day. Even when he cleanses the temple, it is more to assert his spiritual messianic authority over his Father's house than to initiate a transformation of temple regulations and practices. Where he is hailed as the people's king, he prefers to follow a different route, not shaking secular systems but changing human attitudes.

Life in the Empire

Living conditions for the majority of people in the empire were often very harsh. Huge numbers had been forcibly re-located as a result of conquest and slavery, and had endured the hardship and sense of despair which so often attended such displacement. In a strongly patriarchal society the burdens placed on women were often intolerable, while ordinary people routinely looked for some sort of supernatural deliverance from their plight, rather than for a thoroughgoing political solution. Indeed, issues of wealth and poverty, gender and freedom were rarely explored with a view to delivering fundamental change.

Neither is there much evidence that Paul or other leaders in the early church initiated discussions that might lead to such change. Paul was concerned first and foremost to develop Christians in society, not to Christianize society itself - though it may be assumed that he envisaged some broader and longer-term Christianization resulting from this emphasis. Thus, instead of encouraging slaves to demand their freedom or slave owners to release their slaves, Paul guides them in their lifestyles (Eph. 6:5-9; Col. 4:1). His letter to Philemon on behalf of Philemon's escaped and converted slave Onesimus, asking that he be freed by his master (1:16), is a rare example of Paul seeking to change a system or practice associated with his culture. Even while he allows the freedom of women to be developed in contrast to established Jewish and Gentile traditions, and even while he might see this as bearing witness to those traditions, he does not press his reforming vision beyond the confines of the Christian community.[5] Indeed, though some of the church's own agenda might be applicable to non-Christian society, it is not clear from Paul's writings that the church itself was expected to apply it in that wider sphere.

Did Jesus and Paul exhibit socially transforming lifestyles?

Jesus, the transformer of damaged lives

Although evidence for their changing their social order may be limited, Jesus' and Paul's own lifestyles were undoubtedly radical, and both were models of

---

[5] Robert Banks, *Paul's Idea of Community* (Peabody: Hendrickson, 1994) 155-158.

good behaviour for their followers (1 Cor. 10:33, 34; 1 Thess. 1:6). They implicitly challenged the customs and accepted traditions of the dominant culture. This is reflected in the way the gospel writers present the life of Jesus. Thus, shepherds, despised by the majority of law-abiding Jews, are presented with the good news of the birth of Jesus before anyone else, and women, who were treated as inferiors and inadequate witnesses, are presented first with the good news of his resurrection.

Both Jesus and Paul implied that if their lifestyles were emulated by others, a better society would eventually follow. Thus, both advocated the principle of love, the most powerful social transformer of all (Jn. 13:34f; 1 Cor. 13). Thus, both practised a lifestyle of subordination to others marked by a willingness to serve and suffer.[6] Thus, too, Jesus spent time with the apparently least deserving of Jews, such as tax collectors and prostitutes (Mk. 2:15-17, Lk. 18:13, cf. Mt. 21:31-2).

To demonstrate further the reality of this commitment to transforming people's lives, Jesus healed those who, on the basis of Jewish belief, had been punished for their sins by God with sickness or disability. In general, Jewish people held that suffering was part of their lot as human beings. On the whole, however, they did not see it as arbitrarily distributed. Rather, they believed that it resulted from occasions of testing (M. Aboth 5:3; Gen. R. 55:1f; Numbers R. 15:12), or from sinful behaviour (Gen. 32:32; Ex. 15:26; Lev. 26:14ff; Deut. 7:12ff; 2 Sam. 6:7-10; 1 Kgs. 14:10-14). Due to the latter cause especially, they deemed sick people to be impure (Lev. 13f), and attached a stigma to sickness (Ps. 38:11f; Jn. 9:2).

A major element in Jesus' mission and example to future followers was his offer of hope to the marginalized. Although most Jews of the time felt marginalized by Roman rule in any case, those who were ill had particular claim to such a feeling, since their illness was widely taken to be evidence that God was punishing them. Hence by healing them, Jesus offered much more than physical cure; he also enabled them to be accepted again by their communities, and to realize God's desire to bless rather than curse them (Mt. 8:2-4; 9:20-22; 15:21-28; Lk. 7:11-17).

Matthew records the substantial part of Jesus' healing ministry being directed to people at the perimeter of society (8:1-13; 9:1-7, 27-30; 14:14; 15:22; 20:30-34). A similar dedication to the marginalized is also found in Mark's presentation of his healing work, including that conducted among non-Jews (5:1-20; 7:31-37), and the ritually impure (1:40-45; 5:25-34). Luke introduces Jesus' mission to the marginalized sectors of Jewish society (4:16-

---

[6] Yoder, *The Politics of Jesus,* 173-182.

30) by recording a synagogue sermon at Nazareth in which Jesus quotes from Isaiah 61:1f, 58:6, and makes that text's concern for the poor, the oppressed and the blind his own manifesto. These priorities thereafter permeate Luke's gospel (8:48ff; 17:11-19; see also 5:27-32; 7:36-50; 12:32; 14:13f, 21; 19:1-10). Luke records Jesus' ministry as being directed also to Gentiles (7:1-10; 17:11-19), and to those excluded from mainstream society (5:12-16; 8:26-39; 19:1-10). Jesus sought to dissolve the social barriers that separated diseased and infirm people from others,[7] his motivation being 'to restore the *social* wholeness denied to the sick/impure'.[8]

Rudolph Schnackenburg[9] describes Jesus as the one who 'liberates people from their ostracism among the people and their guilt and redeems them from their misery...Jesus is the Savior in a comprehensive sense'. Thus, the gospel miracles are to be understood as 'a record of Christ reaching out to the marginalized, dispossessed, cast out and cursed in society and from faith communities'.[10] Jesus is presented as taking interest in the implications of illness for the sufferer in terms of his/her socially/religiously devalued state. It is the consequential issues of illness - including isolation, rejection and an inability to function in a corporate context - that are of more importance to him. His desire is to restore the sick person to a normal role in society.[11] Percy argues that to view the healings and exorcisms only as demonstrative acts of power is to miss 'the original context and target of Jesus' healings which had radical potential, social and political dynamics'. [12]

Thus, the gospel miracles are to be understood as records of Jesus meeting the marginalized and dispossessed, providing hope for the hopeless and help for the helpless. Through the miracles, he suggests an implicit transformation of Jewish society - socially re-integrating people who because of their illness were once excluded. In doing this, he implicitly critiques the established framework whereby those who were not ill were accepted, while others were rejected. Through his healings, Jesus offers freedom to those bound by illness or demonic influence, and by attendant societal or religious restrictions. As a

---

[7] Joel B. Green, *The Theology of the Gospel of Luke* (Cambridge: Cambridge University Press, 1995), 90.

[8] Ched Myers, *Binding the Strong Man: A Political Reading of Mark's Story of Jesus* (Maryknoll: Orbis Books, 1988), 146 (author's emphasis).

[9] Rudolph Schnackenburg, *Jesus in the Gospels*, Transl. O.C. Dean, (Louisville: Westminster, 1995), 313.

[10] Martyn Percy, 'Christ the Healer: Modern Healing Movements and the Imperative for the Poor', *Studies in World Christianity*, 1.2 (1995) 118, 120f..

[11] Hector Avalos, *Health Care and the Rise of Christianity* (Peabody: Hendrickson, 1999), 68-79. Avalos notes how Graeco-Roman society 'sought to rid society of the chronically ill'.

[12]Percy, 'Christ the Healer' , 122.

result, he makes it possible for them to be reintegrated with society in general, and with their faith community in particular, whilst also enabling them to be productive again. Although not all benefited fully from this potential to actualize their freedom, Jesus' healing plainly encapsulated an integrative mission to weaker humanity. Indeed, although he did not directly address inequality amongst the Jews, he did implicitly challenge it in the very scope and inclusiveness of his healing ministry - a challenge repeated in the healing ministries of the twelve and the seventy (two). The eventual transformation of society is thus embedded in this facet of Jesus' mission, even if not explicitly demanded of the secular community.

Paul, the transformer of damaged communities

In his many instructions to his readers, the apostle Paul advocates a lifestyle that might positively impact the world. In his first letter to the Corinthians, he concentrates on remedying the fractured nature of the Christian community, but implies that a similar process could be applied to the benefit of wider society, affected as it is by significant disharmony. Apart from certain mystery religions, Christianity was distinctive in that it offered the possibility of a close knit, egalitarian society. Although notionally one Empire, the people-groups ruled by Rome were often fragmented one from the other. Not only were there politically and geographically based rivalries between provinces and leaders; there was much else that suggested a society in danger of falling apart. Huge variations in lifestyle were present, and contrasts in status ran deep. Slaves existed in close proximity to wealthy folk, while racial tensions flared between Jews and Gentiles, Jews and Samaritans, Egyptians and Romans, indigenous peoples and immigrants.

Paul presents a gospel that supersedes such divisions, and underlines this in terms that define the nature of the church as a mutually supportive, interdependent community. Foundationally, he describes it as a body and a temple in whom the Spirit of God dwells (1 Cor. 3:16f, 6:18f; Eph. 2:21f). In the Old Testament, God dwelt in the temple; now, the Spirit is described as inhabiting the community of believers, the church (1 Cor. 3:16f). Because the English language does not easily distinguish between singular and plural forms of the word "you", it is helpful to establish the force of Paul's message here by glossing it as follows:

Do you (plural) not know that you (plural) are God's (singular) temple and that God's Spirit dwells in you (plural)? If anyone destroys God's (singular) temple, God will destroy him. For God's temple is holy, and that (singular) temple you (plural) are.

Paul is not stating at this juncture that the Spirit indwells every believer - though he does affirm it elsewhere (1 Cor. 6:18f). The main point is to inform the readers that together, they form a dwelling place of God. As a community, they are the temple in which the Spirit resides. This means that they cannot exist as if other believers do not matter, or as if their actions do not concern the Christian community as a whole. Each believer has an important part to play in this corporate community, and the life of the Spirit is best expressed when they live in harmony. This communal ethos is crucial to Paul's understanding of the church's identity. If it exists in disunity, it loses a major part of its raison d'être.

Thus, in their lives and ministries, Jesus and Paul provide principles of behaviour that, if adopted by others, would benefit them. However, their central message is that these principles can be fully appropriated only in the Christian community.

What were the priorities of Jesus and Paul?

The evidence of the New Testament is that the church grew as a result of evangelism. Although, as we have seen, there is little to suggest that the first Christian believers were encouraged to transform the wider communities of those to whom they witnessed, the considerable, cumulative impact of Christian mission on the Graeco-Roman world through the next three centuries suggests that the seeds of such transformation must have taken root quite early on in this first evangelistic wave.[13] Again, however, it is hard at this stage to identify any deliberate *policy* to effect societal change. Rather, the New Testament churches seem to have functioned much more as conversion-groups, attracting and inducting unbelievers to their new way of life.

Similarly, rather than insisting that their ethics be adopted by society in general, the believers concentrated on making disciples who would adopt the Christian ethic. This does not mean that a wholesale 'monastic' withdrawal from society was deemed appropriate - there is no endorsement in the New Testament of 'Essene'-style ascetic separation. Even so, the New Testament documents seem to suggest that the best mechanism for delivering social transformation would be the Christian community living as Jesus intended - formed by the gospel, responding to the Spirit, and manifesting the radical and life-changing qualities which attracted so many to Jesus himself when he walked the earth.

---

[13] For a readable account of the growing impact of the church on society during this period, see Henry Chadwick, *The Early Church: The Story of Emergent Christianity from the Apostolic Age to the Foundation of the Church of Rome,* Harmondsworth: Penguin, 1967. Especially chapters 3, 7 and 8.

The priorities of Jesus and Paul with regard to their communities may be identified as follows:

- They preached the kingdom of God
- They chose leaders for the community
- They described lifestyle characteristics expected of community members
- They emphasized the importance of the Spirit to the community

It will be helpful to consider each of these priorities in turn, remembering that although they are associated with the Christian community, they provide conduits of change into the secular society.

They preached the kingdom of God

The ministry of Jesus is epitomized by the fact that he preached about the kingdom of God (Mt. 4:23). Although the individual lifestyles of the members of this kingdom were important, the fundamental issue for Jesus was that the kingdom represented a new order in the world. This new kingdom order would not necessarily replace existing social structures - at least not straight away - but it would provide a prophetic alternative to them.

Although the concept of the kingdom is infrequently used in the Pauline literature (Rom. 14:17; Gal. 5:21; 1 Cor. 4:20; 6:9f; 15:50; 1 Thess. 2:12 and see also references to the kingdom in his preaching (Acts 20:25; 28:31)), the life of the kingdom is presented by Paul as life in the Spirit. Thus, the central message is retained, but Paul introduces the Spirit as the one who makes it possible to live according to kingdom principles. Similarly, the ethics of the kingdom, as presented by Jesus, are later linked by Paul more specifically to the influence and enabling power of the Spirit.

'Kingdom life' and 'life in the Spirit' are significant inasmuch as they describe a new community. Having taken seriously the commission of Jesus to make disciples (Mt. 28:19f), Paul stresses the vital importance of how those disciples live together. Indeed, he views their own group transformation as both prior to, and fundamental for, any transformation of the secular world. This is not to suggest that evangelism could be neglected until the church achieved a certain level of spiritual maturity. It does, however, suggest that the priority for the early church's leaders was the protection and purification of the Christian community. As John Howard Yoder puts it when reflecting on this Pauline approach: 'The church must be a sample of the kind of humanity within which, for example, economic and racial differences are surmounted. Only then will it have anything to say to the society that surrounds it about how those differences must be dealt with.'[14]

They chose leaders for the community

Both Jesus and Paul identified leaders to direct their communities. Jesus chose the disciples (Mt. 4:18) and instructed them to make more (Mt. 28:19); Paul chose elders (Acts 20:17) and partnered other believers in his evangelistic activities (Acts 15:22; 16:3; 17:10). One of the roles of such leaders was to identify where the community was failing to fulfil its commission or achieve its purpose. This was often defined as a failure to remain distinct from the surrounding culture (Mt. 6: 2-8; 1 Cor. 6:9-11). As David Bosch suggests, 'Evangelism is only possible when the community that the church evangelizes is a radiant manifestation of the Christian faith and exhibits an attractive lifestyle.'[15] That conclusion does not negate the importance of establishing evangelism as a fundamental element of the activity of the church, but it does emphasize the role of the church in presenting itself as an authentic channel for that evangelism.

They described lifestyle characteristics expected of community members

As with most embryonic organizations, the activity of the New Testament church was concentrated on internal development. Before it looked to change its environment, it spent time changing itself. Rather than looking to transform its setting, it spent time shaping its own life and character. As it did so, it could draw on principles inculcated by Jesus and oriented to growth. For Paul, the experience of the Spirit became a learning platform for the development of the communities that he led. The early years were dynamic and time was invested in adapting and developing.

Specific teaching provided by Jesus in his sermons (Mt. 5-8) relates to the life of the believing community. Paul, throughout his writings, provides continuity by identifying lifestyle characteristics to be adopted (2 Cor. 6:6; Gal. 5:22f; Phil. 4:8; Col. 3:12) and those to be avoided (Rom. 1:29-31; 2 Cor. 12:20; Gal. 5:19-21; Col. 3:5, 8). Both Jesus and Paul anticipate that believers will exist in transformed communities, different from the society in which they

---

[14] Yoder, *The Politics of Jesus*, 150f
[15] David J. Bosch, *Transforming Mission: Paradigm Shifts in the Theology of Mission* (New York: Orbis, 1991), 414.

live and prepared to suffer for their faith, as indeed as they did.[16]

Jesus emphasizes love as the central feature of the life of his followers (Mt. 5:43-48; Mk. 12:30f; John 13:34f; 15:12). This is demonstrated in his teachings, his miraculous activities and his death. Paul also identifies the central role of love, best expressed in 1 Corinthians 13, but also throughout his writings, where he stresses this as a foundational feature of the Spirit (Gal. 5:22), to be worked out through the life of the believer (Rom. 5:5).[17]

The unity of believers was also central to both Jesus (John 17:22f) and Paul (1 Cor. 6:1-8; 12:12-27; Phil 2:1-11), identified graphically in the acceptance of both Jews and Gentiles into the church (Eph. 2:15-22). Accordingly, both offered means whereby this unity could be maintained and developed, establishing activities to be undertaken in a corporate setting. The Eucharist was initiated by Jesus and retained by Paul, a major element of which was that it reminded the believers of their importance to each other (1 Cor. 11:27-34) and the importance of Christ to them all.[18]

Paul draws further attention to unity by using terms like 'body' (1 Cor. 12:12-27) and 'temple' (1 Cor. 3:16f), so highlighting the corporate nature of church. Other words such as *ekklēsia* (church, Mt. 16:18; 1 Cor. 1:2) and *koinōnia* (fellowship, 1 Cor. 10:16) achieve the same purpose, the former identifying a community determined by present conduct and future vision, and the latter emphasizing the core imperative of interdependency.

They spoke of the importance of the Spirit to the community

Jesus identified the Spirit as the one who would continue the work he had begun (Jn. 7:39; 14:17; 20:22) and guaranteed that the Spirit would inspire and empower his followers, not only speaking to them but also through them (Mt. 10:20//Mark 13:11//Lk. 12:12). The same Spirit, who operated in association with Jesus, will now be made available to them (Jn 3:34).

Paul's letters present the Spirit as a personal, immediate, dynamic and perfect guide (Eph. 1:17; 3:4f; Col. 1:9). He speaks and so must be listened to. He is described as being committed to setting believers apart (Rom 15:16; 2 Cor. 6:6; 2 Thess. 2:13), pro-actively transforming them ethically and

---

[16] Hafemann, S., 'Because of weakness' (Galatians 4:13): the role of suffering in the mission of Paul', in Bolt & Thompson, *The Gospel to the Nations*, 131-146.

[17] James D. G. Dunn, *The Theology of Paul the Apostle* (Edinburgh: T. & T. Clark, 1998), 654-661.

[18] N. T. Wright, *The New Testament and the People of God* (London: SPCK, 1992), 448.

spiritually (2 Cor. 3:16-18; 2 Thess. 2:13), inspiring and empowering them to follow his guidance (Rom. 14:17; 1 Cor. 2:4; Eph. 3:16; 1 Tim. 1:18; 4:14). The Spirit expects transformation in the believer, who needs to learn the daily experience of being controlled by him (Eph. 5:18f). This will cause the believers' lifestyle increasingly to reflect the Spirit's own character. Furthermore, the Spirit is committed to relationship with believers and to ensure that that relationship is inclusive of the Father and the Son. Together, they inhabit believers, both individually and corporately.

Summary of Jesus' and Paul's priorities

The basic commission of the church was to make disciples, following the mandate of Jesus. A major role of believers in the New Testament church was to concentrate on their own development, individually and corporately. The leaders concentrated on enabling the believers to live harmoniously in community. The Spirit functioned as the guiding influence and the one who empowered believers to function in community.

Lessons for the contemporary church

Learn from the emphases of Jesus and Paul

Jesus and Paul alike preached the kingdom of God, chose leaders for the community, identified rules and lifestyle expectations for its members, and stressed the importance of the Spirit for its development. The central issue for them was the development of the community of believers. Although there is little by way of an explicit programme to change contemporary society, there is an implicit expectation that it could be changed as a result of the transferable elements of the Christian lifestyle and ethic. The parables identifying the transforming nature of the kingdom presented by Jesus, and the lifestyle changes expected by Paul, are based on the assumption that others will see the distinctive and attractive lifestyles of Jesus' followers, and desire to participate in their unique community.

Incarnational mission: service

Incarnational mission may be defined as living the life of Christ who came to serve (Jn 13:1-17). It flows from a community which recognizes the importance of integration and interdependency. The nature of this incarnational mission is well summed up in the word 'service'. When Jesus spoke about the community of his followers, he challenged them to take responsibility for one other and for their own actions (Mt. 16:8f; 18:15-35). Similarly, Paul explores the need for believers to recognize their responsibility for the welfare of other believers (Rom. 15:1-7), with love as their guiding influence (1 Cor. 8:9-13).

These principles can fit uncomfortably with a society which has grown used to individualism and democracy, where personal rights have come to dominate. Indeed, our present western context only serves to point up the counter-culturalism of the New Testament message, throwing into sharp relief the church's vocation to be a 'peculiar people' whose lifestyle is determined not by an assertion of entitlements, so much as by consideration of other's needs.

Incarnational Christianity, then, is living the life that Christ would live. Such a life may be identified as the life of Christ in the lifestyle of the believer or, in the words of Paul, 'For me to live is Christ' (Phil. 1:21). If a Christian community does not recognize the importance of fellowship and interdependency, it is not functioning as it was intended to. If it realizes that it is a partnership-based community, a *koinōnia,* shaped by a manifesto originating in love, it will portray a righteousness, justice, liberty and wholeness that cannot help but be noticed by the wider community. Even if members of that wider community decline to join it, its memory and influence is unlikely to be forgotten.

Crucifixional mission: suffering

This key motif confirms that if it wishes to transform society in accordance with the gospel, the church must be prepared to suffer in the process. Tellingly, the gospel writers focus on the final few days of the life of Jesus, omitting the majority of his life in favour of what is central – namely, the salvation he wrought for men and women by his passion, his suffering and his death on the cross. The Evangelists also underline the fact that Jesus' followers must be ready to take up their own cross as they follow his path (Mt. 16:24f; Lk. 14:27-33). As Bosch puts it, 'When the risen Christ commissioned his disciples…it was the scars of his passion that revealed to them who he was (Jn. 20:20).'[19] The connection between self-sacrifice and mission is clear.

Paul sees suffering in the life of the believer as an important element of mission (2 Cor. 4:10; Phil. 3:10f). This understanding, too, is grounded in a recognition that the Christian is crucified with Christ (Gal. 2:20). Not only is such suffering seen as normative for the Christian (Phil. 1:29; 2 Tim. 3:12); it is also regarded as instructive for others, suffering being a means by which the life of Jesus is manifested to society at large (2 Cor. 4:7-12).

---

[19] Bosch, *Transforming Mission,* 513.

As Jesus suffered in serving others, so the identification of the church as a community of people who desire to serve others, despite the suffering which might result, becomes a powerful statement to a sceptical world.

Pneumatological mission: Spirit

The New Testament does not set a pattern of mission or social transformation that must be replicated in every setting or age. Different contexts and cultures often demand different responses. Although the basic behavioural characteristics portrayed by Jesus are to be properly emulated, the context in which one lives needs to be considered. The mission of the church in one society, age or setting may be very different to that in another. Seeking to find a New Testament paradigm for social transformation is not particularly helpful, since that was not the main focus of the early church's leaders: they were looking to establish an alternative society, not to change society as such. This is not to suggest that they advocated an especially pietistic approach to life, in the sense of a life cut off from socio-political realities. On the contrary, Jesus speaks of disciples functioning as salt and light within their society (Mt. 5:13-16), and he presents the normative Christian life in the Beatitudes as one which impacts wider society through peacemaking and acts of mercy (Mt. 5:7, 9). Similarly, Paul accounts seriously for social relationships formed with unbelievers (1 Cor. 5:9-12; 10:27).

What seems plain, however, is that neither Jesus nor Paul mapped out any detailed plan for delivering societal transformation, other than through the witness of the believing community. Even the vivid parable of the sheep and the goats in Matthew 25:35-46, which encourages charitable care for people in need of sustenance, housing or visitation, is presented by Jesus as a contrast between authentic and inauthentic commitment to him, rather than to the needy alone.

John records the teaching of Jesus on the role of the Spirit in guiding the believer. The onus is not on the believer to glean guidance and support from the Spirit, though that is appropriate. Rather, the Spirit is described as providing the necessary support for the believer. This emphasis contrasts markedly with much first century religious activity, be it Jewish or Gentile. In most cases, to benefit from a supernatural source it was assumed that a correct ritual had to be observed. John, however, advocates no such ritual; instead, he offers a relationship - a relationship with the Spirit. Even though the apostles would die, the church would not be leaderless, nor would there ever come a time when it would not be in receipt of divine wisdom. In situations not experienced before, and not covered by previous apostolic teaching, the Spirit would be on hand to provide the necessary instruction and wisdom.

The book of Acts illustrates the role of the Spirit in guiding believers, especially in respect of their mission (8:29; 10:19; 11:12; 13:2, 4; 15:28; 16:6, 7; 20:22f). A further example of the wisdom imparted by the Spirit is contained in 1 Corinthians 7:40, where Paul suggests that widows should not remarry - a conclusion that he believes has been prompted by the Spirit. As with many other such pastoral issues, there was no specific instruction on this in the Old Testament. The Spirit's involvement in a believer's life is in this sense unique. In situations where divine guidance is not located in the text, Paul anticipates that the Spirit can still offer direction.

The concept of living in the Spirit is particularly significant in prompting social transformation which is contextualized and appropriate. In seeking to apply the gospel to the world, the church has three main sources to which it can turn: first, the Bible, and then also the wisdom of the members themselves as they interpret and apply it. But this process of interpretation and application is in turn empowered and validated by the Spirit. Thus, Jesus promises the Spirit as the one who will guide the fledgling church (Jn. 14:26; 16:7, 13). Similarly, Paul, who offers specific advice concerning behaviour (Gal. 5:13-15; Eph. 4:25-6:9), also encourages the believers to see the Spirit as their Teacher (Gal. 5:16, 25).

The Spirit not only introduces the believers to God's wisdom in the form of the gospel; he also serves as the inexhaustible source of wisdom for all areas of life. The implications of this are momentous. The Spirit's boundless wisdom is present in the life of the believer to provide direction and facilitate growth. Furthermore, because it is boundless, such wisdom extends to politics and social policy, to civic institutions and business, to the media and the arts. As such, it can inform the church's interaction with these spheres of wider society, and help it formulate a contextually relevant witness among them. The church is called to listen obediently to this dynamic Spirit, who not only energized mission in the early church era, but sets the agenda for Christian mission today.

Conclusion

In exploring the mission of the church through the writings of Jesus and Paul, no thoroughgoing strategy emerges that would indicate society's being transformed other than through evangelism and the enlargement of the Christian community. It is through converging towards the church that the renewal of the wider community is best anticipated. However, although this is a useful first conclusion, it does not provide the full picture, because the New Testament most immediately reflects a first-century context which is in many ways very different from our own.

Not all the guidance needed for mission in today's world can be assumed to reside explicitly in the pages of the New Testament. Vital principles may be identified there, but more specific application of those principles may require the use of models (e.g. from management theory or local custom) which are not so obviously 'biblical'. It is partially for this purpose that the Spirit was given to the church - to inspire, fuel and accomplish mission that will transform the context in which the church exists, whilst at the same time prompting the Christian community to listen for God within that context. As mission is renewed and re-contextualized in this way, the Spirit will lead the process, as indeed he did in the lives of Jesus and his disciples.

The primary missional task of the church is thus to walk with the Spirit as he manifests the life of Christ among believers, purifying and empowering them to bear the gospel to 'the ends of the earth'. As Yoder sums it up, 'God is working in the world and it is the task of the church to know how he is working.'[20] Part of this knowledge will undoubtedly come through the development of wider social initiatives, but such initiatives will be truly Christian only inasmuch as they can be said to share 'the good news of God's love, incarnated in the witness of a community, for the sake of the world' - with, I might add, the empowering presence of the Spirit.[21]

---

[20] Yoder, *The Politics of Jesus*, 155.
[21] Bosch, *Transforming Mission*, 519.

4. God, Self and Society: Variations on a Trinitarian Theme

Graham McFarlane

Introduction

A strange irony lies at the heart of any attempt to locate a specifically *evangelical* theology. On the one hand, as D. H. Williams points out, 'Defining twentieth-century Evangelicalism is notoriously difficult because of its doctrinal and historical diversity...There is no one identifying confession, and many evangelical groups which share the Free Church legacy renounce the very idea of confessionalism.'[1] Thus, with no common consensus to which the movement as a whole can appeal, it has never arrived at one mind on its key beliefs in any articulated and consensual manner. Nor is there any one spokesperson or group who may speak with singular authority on behalf of Evangelicals as a whole. Given its undoubted influence within and beyond the church, one might assume that Evangelicalism seeks to address issues from an established canonical position. However, at closer inspection, such a position becomes hard to define in detail. Rather, evangelical identity and belief has comprised something more akin to a constellation of core values. John Stackhouse identifies five criteria that sum up well what this constellation entails: the gospel of salvation centring on Jesus Christ; the authority of the Bible; the need for conversion; the call to mission, and the combination of all four which Stackhouse identifies as transdenominationalism.[2]

The reason for this almost bi-polar nature of evangelical theology, it may be suggested, lies in the fact that both evangelical theology and identity emerge from two distinct and quite different sources. On the one hand, there is the obvious historical and theological context, namely, Evangelicalism's biblical Reformed, Puritan and Pietistic inheritance. These historical influences have very much conditioned twentieth-century Evangelicalism. On the other, however, is the wider cultural influence of Modernity - that worldview, and the theologies it facilitated, which collectively have been perceived as detrimental to true biblical and evangelical faith. As such, one of the major influences upon the movement has been its evolving relationship with the wider culture within which it has existed, since this has given Evangelicals something against which

---

[1] D. H. Williams, *Retrieving the Tradition & Renewing Evangelicalism* (Grand Rapids: Eerdmans, 1999), 3.

[2] John G. Stackhouse Jr. (ed.), *Evangelical Futures: A Conversation on Theological Method* (Leicester: Apollos, 2000), 41-42.

to identify themselves. This is a pertinent point, for, as John Thornhill reminds us, the ideology we describe as Modernity 'is a five-centuries-long movement within our western tradition of such complexity that it would seem to defy the making of an overall interpretation. However a great deal of light is shed upon the nature of this movement...when it is recognized that the central concern of its originating moment was emancipation from late medievalism's heavy reliance upon the authority of tradition. Modernity would replace this authority with the accountability of a shared intellectual inquiry.'[3]

Thus, evangelical faith has traditionally sought to express itself within a wider culture conditioned by the Enlightenment quest for certainty and epistemological foundations. In so doing, evangelical faith has assumed a somewhat dialectical identity. On the one hand, it took its bearing from specifically rational and foundationalist tendencies, evidenced in its quest for absolute truth. Yet, on the other, it, too, had its own reactions to such rational faith and thus developed its own theological versions of Enlightenment Romanticism, whether 19th century pietism or 20th century charismaticism. Either way, it can be seen that each expression reflects not only internal aspects of the movement drawn from its biblical identity, but also external aspects drawn from the wider surrounding culture. This latter part is particularly relevant to the subject matter of the present chapter: the different aspects of evangelical theology are to be understood in relation to their cultural and historical locations. Perhaps Webber puts it most simply, proposing as he does three cycles of Evangelicals in the twentieth century, where the first represents a time when they were known more for what they did *not* believe than for what they did, i.e., a time of anti-intellectualism. However, after the Second World War a further cycle was defined by the emergence of a 'new kind' of Evangelical, one open to the challenge of articulating a specifically evangelical faith and working out its social implications. This, in turn, was to lay the foundations for the third cycle, which Webber represents as a diversification of evangelical concerns, both intellectually and socially.[4]

The moot point is this: much evangelical theology is the product of core beliefs *and* surrounding cultural concerns, both negative and positive.[5] Like Judaism, Evangelicalism is very skilled at adapting to the wider culture. On the one hand, it has adopted an overtly *rational* emphasis in the expression of its faith. As such, Evangelicalism, on the whole, has batted more from a

---

[3] John Thornhill, *Modernity: Christianity's Estranged Child Reconstructed* (Grand Rapids: Eerdmans, 2000), 5.

[4] Robert E. Webber, *The Younger Evangelicals: Facing the Challenge of the New World* (Grand Rapids: Baker, 2002), 25-40.

[5] For a concise example of this phenomenon see: Derek J. Tidball, *Who Are the Evangelicals?* (London: Marshall Pickering, 1994), 63-66.

foundationalist epistemological wicket than from anything distinctly social. In doing so, the predominantly Cartesian nature of western culture finds its Christian counterpart in Evangelicalism's typically robust theologies and apologetics. On the other hand, and at the same time, Evangelicalism has cloaked its concern for social transformation in predominantly missionary guises, so that most of its interests in social action and wider social polity have been absorbed or overshadowed by missionary concerns. The gospel imperative has thus mandated a counter-approach to the wider social ills facing society. Consequently, Evangelicalism has reflected its own internal concerns, tending to reify conversion over social activism.

Admittedly, this is to simplify the issues. As John Stott reminds us, 'It is exceedingly strange that any followers of Jesus Christ should ever need to ask whether social involvement was their concern, and that controversy should have blown up over the relationship between evangelism and social responsibility. For it is evident that in his public ministry Jesus both "went about...teaching...and preaching" (Matt 4:2; 9:35) and "went about doing good and healing" (Acts 10:38). In consequence Evangelism and social concern have been intimately related to one another throughout the history of the church...Christian people have often engaged in both activities quite unselfconsciously, without feeling the need to define what they were doing or why.'[6]

However, despite protestations to the contrary, the general silence among evangelical theologians on social issues stands in stark contrast to both the wider theological agenda and to contemporary trends within western theological circles. For if anything defines the church's agenda during the latter part of the twentieth century and the beginning of the twenty first, it is a twofold concern over both the social identity of God - what we might loosely call *social trinitarianism* - and the social needs facing the human race. It is not surprising, then, that as the shift in emphasis has moved from the epistemic to the social, significant theological contributions have emerged. Whilst few can realistically be called 'evangelical', their impact on emerging twenty-first century evangelical theology is not to be underestimated. Indeed, I shall argue that this move from a modalistic trinity to a more social expression of God's life and purpose is not an example of theology projecting its cultural needs upon the Divine, but rather, an example of how our understanding of divine identity impacts our own human modes of relating.

---

[6]John R.W. Stott, *Issues Facing Christians Today* (London: Marshall Morgan and Scott, 1984), 3.

One, Three, Many

Historically, western theology has been dominated by a model of God established by Augustine.[7] This *psychological* model of God, so described because of Augustine's analogies for divine identity drawn from the human mind or consciousness, became the *leitmotif* for subsequent expressions of divine identity. This model prioritized the One, talking of 'God' as though divine identity was singular and easily reducible to a single category. In turn, if divine identity is 'one' then so must be its human image: the individual substance with a rational nature.[8] Descartes only expanded the logic of this modalistic expression of personal identity when he located certainty about knowledge in the human mind with his *cogito*. Despite the centuries separating them, Descartes' *cogito* and Margaret Thatcher's 1980s dictum 'no such thing as society' make good bedfellows. However, like all good things, this fellowship has come to an end with the demise of the Enlightenment project.

Admittedly, like any long-standing tradition the legacy of the psychological model will remain part of western theology's history. Yet it is not without rival. Modernity simply drowned out any rivals in its quest for total homogeneity, for the One. However, with its demise, we are better placed to consider the alternatives. Perhaps the most important of all is that which comes to us with an equally aristocratic background, namely the *social* model of the Trinity developed by the Cappadocian Fathers of the Eastern Church.[9] Historically, Basil the Great, Gregory of Nazianzus and Gregory of Nyssa developed a more communitarian model of divine identity where the one God is identified in terms of Father, Son and Spirit. What distinguishes this model from Augustine's is that the different personal relations are identified in terms of their relations to one another. Thus, it is the relation of being Unbegotten that personally distinguishes the Father, the relation of being Begotten that personally distinguishes the Son, and the relation of Proceeding that personally distinguishes the Spirit. In turn, each relation cannot be understood autonomously of the other two, as though it stands independently of them. Rather, they are understood *perichoretically*, that is, in terms of mutual interdependence and interpenetration.[10] Thus, the foundations for a social

---

[7] See Catherine M. La Cugna, *God For Us* (New York: Harper Collins, 1991), 81ff.

[8] See Ralph Del Colle, 'The Triune God', in Colin E. Gunton (ed.), *The Cambridge Companion to Christian Doctrine* (Cambridge: Cambridge University Press, 1997), 132-133.

[9] R.P.C. Hanson, *The Search for the Christian Doctrine of God* (Edinburgh: T&T Clark, 1988), 676-790.

[10] What the Latin West understands as *circumincessio*.

vision of the Trinity and of the *imago dei* are established.[11] What is of interest, however, is the influence this alternative model has had on contemporary theological debate - an influence which can be sub-divided into three main categories: the doctrinal, the ethical and the social. As Stanely Grenz lucidly points out, 'feminist and liberation theologians close ranks with each other and with evangelical, philosophical and process colleagues in suggesting that God is best viewed as the social Trinity.'[12]

The theological

Standing behind every trinitarian theologian of the late twentieth and early twenty-first century is the figure of Karl Barth. It was Barth who decisively broke away from the purely speculative trinitarianism of modern theology. However, since we are concerned here with contemporary theologians, we shall simply acknowledge his formative influence on modern western trinitarianism and move on to his successors, the most influential of whom is Jürgen Moltmann. Whilst the impact of Barth can be detected in Moltmann, he is no Barthian. He is equally influenced theologically by the Romanian scholar, Dumitriu Staniloae[13] and politically by Ernst Bloch's Marxism.[14] This broad range of influence, in turn, is developed in what the late Colin Gunton described as a more journalistic interpretation of the Trinity. Thus, his systematic theology follows a trinitarian pattern of focusing on the Father,[15] moving onto the Son,[16] and then to the Spirit.[17]

---

[11] Admittedly, this Eastern understanding of the immanent Trinity is to be understood differently from what contemporary western social trinitarians argue: as Sarah Coakley rightly points out, what Gregory of Nyssa argues stands in stark contrast to that being suggested by Alvin Plantinga and other social trinitarians. Sarah Coakley, '"Persons" in the 'social' Doctrine of the Trinity: A Critique of Current Analytic Discussion', in S.T. Davis, D. Kendall & G. O'Collins (eds.) *The Trinity* (Oxford: Oxford University Press, 1999), 123-144.

[12] Stanley J. Grenz, *The Social God and the Relational Self: A Trinitarian Theology of the Imago Dei* (Louisville: Westminster John Knox Press, 2001), 5.

[13] See Dumitriu Staniloae, *Theology and the Church* (Crestwood, NY: St Vladimir's Seminary Press), 1980

[14] See Wayne Hudson, *The Marxist Philosophy of Ernst Bloch* (London; Macmillan, 1982).

[15] Jürgen Moltmann, *The Crucified God* (London: SCM Press, 1974). Note that for Moltmann a monarchical Father leads to a monarchical government: a social Trinity can lead to proper social strata that facilitate freedom.

[16] Jürgen Moltmann, *The Way of Jesus Christ* (London: SCM Press, 1990); *The Trinity and the Kingdom of God* (London: SCM Press, 1981).

[17] Jürgen Moltmann, *The Life Of the Spirit,* London: SCM Press Ltd, 1992

It is with the latter that Moltmann completes his specific understanding of a trinitarian history of God in such a way that historical time becomes part of the inner reality of God.[18] In doing so, Moltmann unpacks his argument that social belief and expressions of such belief are themselves expressions of deeper beliefs about God or the gods. As such, the Christian doctrine of the Trinity establishes a direct point of contact with human reality: as the Father embraces history through the Son's passion on the cross, so the Spirit is now released upon the world, uniting history with the very being of God himself. In this, the mandate for both human social intercourse and human freedom are established. Herein lies the mandate for social transformation: the social trinitarianism of Moltmann suggests political socialism, since the freedom won on the cross and expressed through the kingdom of God has to be worked out in concrete terms in winning freedom for all men and women. Set free from any hierarchical framework that legitimates only those in power, the trinitarian theology of Moltmann mandates a social politic that impacts every level of society in terms of the freedom he perceives to lie at the heart of the gospel. Admittedly, such an understanding sails very close to the universalist wind, both in terms of universal salvation and panentheism. Such criticisms, however, cannot be levelled against two of Moltmann's most significant successors, Miroslav Volf and Stanley Grenz. Of significance here is the fact not only that Volf and Grenz develop Moltmann in their own way, but that each has significant links to the evangelical constituency.

Volf extends Moltmann's political application of theology within a very specific context, namely, the conflict zone of his native Croatia. Whilst his output is limited, his significance is growing disproportionately, a reflection of the quality and contemporaneity of his two volumes, *Exclusion and Embrace* [19] and *After Our Likeness*.[20] In the first, Volf unpacks his political theology within the context of human suffering. Here resonances with Moltmann's seminal study *The Crucified God* emerge with profound imaginative force: on the cross, God embraces the full implications of our sin by readjusting himself to our situation and making space for us, in a manner similar to our embracing of

---

[18] Such a vision began with Moltmann's 'Theology of Hope', in which the notion of 'future' constitutes divine identity and a future deeply embedded in the future of creation: Jürgen Moltmann, *Theology of Hope* (London: SCM Press, 1967, Trans. J.W. Leitch). This, however, is not to say that Creator and Time are interdependent, but rather expresses God's self-transcendence to identify with created history: Jürgen Moltmann, *The Coming of God: Christian Eschatology* (London: SCM Press, 1996), 330-332.

[19] Miroslav Volf, Exclusion & Embrace: a Theological Exploration of Identity, Otherness, and Reconciliation
(Nashville: Abingdon Press, 1996).

[20] Miroslav Volf, *After Our Likeness: The Church as the Image of the Trinity* (Grand Rapids: Eerdmans, 1998).

others.[21] Again, within the contours of political reality, the notion of judgement is outworked in terms of exclusion: where boundaries are crossed and consequences are realized. If there is a weakness in his theology here, it is in the area of the church, where Volf does not sufficiently expound what it means to be a community of the embraced and embracing. However, this aspect is picked up in *After our Likeness*, as Volf seeks to develop the notion of an *ecclesial self* or *catholic personality*, where person and community exist in terms of co-habitation and co-indwelling.[22] Here, he unpacks what the doctrine of the Trinity implies for the formal relations between person and community - firstly for church, and latterly for wider social intercourse. However, any understanding of human community that is modelled on the Trinity will be conditioned by two criteria: firstly, that it will be analogous rather than univocal, and secondly, that it will be shaped by historical contingencies.[23] Thus, the doctrines of creation and sin guide our understanding of how the Trinity relates to human identity.[24]

If Volf seeks to earth his social trinitarianism within cultural and ecclesial contexts, Stanley Grenz, a PhD student of Moltmann's, looks to develop an explicitly trinitarian ideology. For Grenz, it is towards the *imago Dei* that human existence is eschatologically oriented. This is the creation imperative that comes into view only in the act of recreation. Thus, Grenz writes, "the creation of humankind in the divine image...can mean nothing less than that humans express the relational dynamic of the God whose representation we are called to be".[25] This communitarian vision, in turn, is extended to all human social groups.[26] In a recent ambitious beginning to a six-volume systematic theology, Grenz seeks to synthesize the insights from contemporary trinitarianism to the field of theological anthropology. In the first volume,[27] interestingly, Grenz shares the same vision as Volf, namely the construction of an *ecclesial self*.[28] Here, the relational self, as one created in the image of the Triune God, finds true identity narratively in a social rather than individual sense. Such a narratival identity operates on two levels: firstly in the sense that each person discovers true identity in relation to the Christian narrative - the true self is disclosed in the wider textuality of the Christian story. However,

---

[21] Volf, *Exclusion & Embrace*, 29.

[22] Volf, *After Our Likeness*, 3.

[23] Miroslav Volf, 'The Trinity is our Social Program', *Modern Theology* 14:3 (July 1998), 405, (401-423).

[24] Volf, 'The Trinity is our Social Program', 406; also, Miroslav Volf, 'The Final Reconciliation', *Modern Theology* 16:1 (January 2000), 100 (91-113).

[25] Stanley J. Grenz & John R. Franke, *Beyond Foundationalism: Shaping Theology in a Postmodern Context*, (Louisville: Westminster John Knox Press, 2001), 201.

[26] Grenz & Franke, *Beyond Foundationalism*, 229.

[27] Grenz, *The Social God and the Relational Self*.

[28] Grenz, *The Social God and the Relational Self*, 305, 312ff.

Grenz proffers a second understanding of a narrative identity: here the individual is *read*, as being someone *in Christ*, whose own story is to be understood in relation to another, namely Jesus Christ and the church of Jesus Christ.[29] Once again, human being is interpreted within the wider context of social trinitarianism: that is, the author's understanding of divine identity impacts his understanding of human identity in such a way as to subvert the modern view of the person as an individual free from external contingencies.

The ethical

If Grenz and Volf offer a theological (and to some extent, abstracted) notion of trinitarian anthropology, the same cannot be said for two representatives of what we may describe as ethical expressions of Christian faith within the wider marketplace. It is significant, too, that both examples are theologians who do not fit easily in the status quo of theological inquiry. Whilst neither can be described as 'evangelical', their impact upon emerging evangelical theologians is significant. They are Stanley Hauerwas, professor of Theological Ethics at Duke Divinity School, and Walter Wink, professor of Biblical Interpretation at Auburn Theological Seminary. What links these two scholars most significantly is their trenchant critique of contemporary culture in the light of the gospel and person of Jesus Christ.

Wink is most famous for his trilogy, *Naming the Powers,*[30] *Unmasking the Powers,*[31] and *Engaging the Powers.*[32] Here we are presented with a systematic identification and critique of the domination system (the powers) that operates within the world today. In it, Wink presents an ethical challenge concerning the forces that wreak havoc on the lives of those who inhabit planet earth at the turn of the millennium. Certainly, Wink presents what might be described as a robust metaphysic - that is, an interpretation of reality which stands in stark contrast to the way the surrounding culture understands itself. Wink proposes that a powerful 'domination system' possesses both societies in general, and the churches which belong to those societies in particular. The call of the gospel, he asserts, is to break such systems of domination. Thus, the language of power, traditionally expressed in terms of Satan, demons, angels, gods and elements of the universe, is reinterpreted to show that these forces manifest today as

---

[29]Grenz, *The Social God and the Relational Self,* 329.

[30] Walter Wink, *Naming the Powers: The Language of Power in the New Testament* (Minneapolis: Fortress Press, 1984).

[31] Walter Wink, *Unmasking the Powers: the Invisible Forces that Determine Human Existence* (Minneapolis: Fortress Press, 1986).

[32] Walter Wink, *Engaging the Powers: Discernment and Resistance in a World of Domination* (Minneapolis: Fortress Press, 1992).

patriarchy, economic inequality and other structures of oppression which
disable the many for the benefit of the few. Consequently, one of the major
challenges facing the church is to recognize or 'name' such powers, to
disempower or 'unmask' them, and to take them on or 'engage' them in the
authority of an alternative counter-power.

Wink's critique of these modern-day powers highlights the fact that they
operate through a system of violence: those at the top of the pyramid exist
solely at the expense of those at the bottom. What constitutes a radical
alternative, according to Wink, is to offer a response of *non-violence*. This
Wink develops from Jesus' teaching and exemplification of non-resistance - of
turning the other cheek (forcing the opponent to treat you as an equal rather
than as someone beneath you); of giving up your cloak (and your underclothes
and thus exposing your opponent as being shameless), and of going the extra
mile (and thus turning your opponent into the transgressor of the Roman law).
Hence for Wink, the *social* dimension of the gospel expresses itself in ethical
and personal demonstrations of an alternative use of power, the power of non-
violence.

This avowal of non-violence is also a hall-mark of Hauerwas' ethics. A
pacifist rooted in an alternative churchmanship, Hauerwas' writings constitute a
major attempt at recovering the significance of the virtues for our
understanding of the nature of the Christian life. What makes Hauerwas so
interesting is that he is conversant with a broad range of disciplines, drawing
from systematic theology, through ethical theory (and applying it to a wide
range of contemporary ethical issues), to political discourse and philosophy.
And yet, what stands at his centre is a similar perspective to that found in Wink
- namely, that the gospel and the God we meet in Jesus Christ call human
beings to a counter-culture.[33] Here, we may identify two key dimensions of his
thought that touch on our present concerns. On the one hand, Hauerwas insists
on the development of Christian virtues that are transformative.[34] The ethical
imperative is traced back to the teaching of Jesus in such a way that Hauerwas
will not allow the gospel to be reduced to a set of doctrines or principles. Why
not? Because neither actually change people's characters! Indeed, if the
Christian faith is to be reduced to such principles, then it is these, and not Jesus
himself, that we should worship. There is, however, no ethical transformatory
power in them alone. It is only in relation to Jesus Christ that we are

---

[33] Stanley Hauerwas, *In Good Company: The Church as Polis (Revised Edition)* (Notre
Dame: University of Notre Dame Press, 1995).

[34] Hauerwas outlines what this might mean in concrete terms in a series of articles in *A
Better Hope: Resources for a Church Confronting Capitalism, Democracy, and
Postmodernity* (Grand Rapids: Brazos Press, 2001).

transformed, thus becoming *resident aliens* whose very existence reveals that there is indeed an alternative on offer.[35]

On the other hand, Hauerwas argues for an understanding of Christian life that is both informed and constituted by the narrative of church, for it is only church that can rightly tell the stories of transformation.   His is a radical critique of enlightenment individualism, and it is best articulated in his study *Community of Character: Toward a Constructive Christian Social Ethic.*[36] The significance of this text cannot be underestimated: it was justly selected as one of the 100 most important books on religion in the 20th century. Within it, the call to an understanding of Christianity that is ethical in its impact upon wider society is made with force. Here, the myth of the autonomous self, the unaccountable Christian, is debunked. While Volf argues for a more catholic *self*, Hauerwas' calls further for a more catholic *polis* - that is, for a Christian counter-culture which is expressed both politically and economically as the church lives out the teaching of Jesus not in work but in character, not just doctrinally, but ethically, too.

The social

If Wink and Hauerwas engage wider society from an ethical, and admittedly privileged, position, the same cannot be said for the laicized Franciscan priest, Leonardo Boff.   Professor at the Faculdade de Filosofia e Teologia dos Fransciscanos in Petropolis, Rio de Janiero, Boff, along with his brother Clodovis, represents an increasingly sophisticated form of liberation theology. In the process, Boff has paid the high price of being forced out of his mother church.   Given the nature of contemporary globalization, the significance of this particular theologian cannot be underestimated. For Boff, the context of the poor and disenfranchised of Latin America has demanded new ways of doing theology. This *new theology* he identifies by five criteria, in which he gives priority to: the human over the church; the ideal over the fact; the critical over the dogmatic; the social over the individual, and praxis over doctrine.[37] Thus, he argues that 'God abides in the realities of justice, love and freedom. He is not automatically present in pious words. If we do not include the realities of freedom, justice, and love when we speak of God, then we are speaking of some ideal and not of the living God'.[38] It is clear that for Boff, the social and

[35] Stanley Hauerwas (with William Willimon), *Where Resident Aliens Live: Exercises for Christian Practice* (Nashville: Abingdon Press, 1996).

[36] Stanley Hauerwas, *A Community of Character: Toward a Constructive Christian Social Ethic* (Notre Dame: University of Notre Dame Press, 1981).

[37] Leonardo Boff, *Jesus Christ: Liberator* (Maryknoll: Orbis, 1980), 44-47.

[38] Leonardo Boff, *Church: Charism and Power* (London: SCM Press, 1985), 24.

the religious have an almost symbiotic relationship: the two realities come together as one, wherein the religious sheds light on the oppression so offensive to God, and the social embodies what God genuinely desires.

With Boff we confront a full-blown social expression of the gospel which mandates Christians to identify with the cause of the poor and work out the gospel in terms of liberation. Here we detect resonances of the similar theological anthropologies of Volf and Grenz as well as the ethical insights of Wink and Hauerwas put into action. The emergence of liberation theology, for Boff, enables the church to identify with the poor and the oppressed. This is social trinitarianism in action. As such, what is needed is not reform: such a process works within already existing structures, and for Boff (as for Wink) the whole point of the gospel is that the structures *themselves* are corrupt and oppressive. Rather, such social trinitarianism demands liberation, in which the poor actively break out of their oppression by means of strategic social change. The impetus for such change comes from what Boff describes as a dynamic communion with the Trinity. This, indeed, becomes for him the basis for integral and social liberation.[39] Just as the Trinity represents the fruitful communion of three divine persons, so for Boff it offers a source and model of fruitful human society - a society in which political, economic and social justice thrive. Yet this social trinitarianism is not abstracted: Boff has not lost his cutting-edge. In the face of growing globalization, the challenges that first precipitated the *comunidades de base* ('base communities') of South America 20 years ago are now faced by communities world wide - that is, wherever fundamental issues such as work, health, food, shelter are to the fore.

Conclusion

There can be no doubt that profound challenges face the contemporary, western church. As the Enlightenment paradigm continues to recede, we are left wondering about its successor. At the same time, the degree to which Evangelicalism is married to this retreating worldview is beginning to be tested. The individualism that stands as the hallmark of modernity is being challenged at both theoretical and practical levels. At the same time, contemporary theologians have been empowered to rise to this new state of affairs as they have engaged with and embraced different aspects of what we have called the *social* Trinity.

---

[39] Leonardo Boff, *Trinity and Society* (Tunbridge Wells: Burns & Oates, 1988), VII, 123-154.

There is much to be applauded in such an approach: the vacuum left by individualism[40] is all-too easily filled by postmodern versions of consumerism, and by drawing instead on social trinitarianism, western theologians find resources for addressing the issues they face daily. From Volf and Grenz, as well as others, new foundations are laid that facilitate more dynamic means of perceiving the self in relation to others. As Evangelicals, we need fresh and vibrant ways of addressing the ills we face both internally in respect of church and externally in respect of culture. In addition, from Wink and Hauerwas, we are emboldened to see that sin, as a relational dysfunction, impacts not only the *I-Thou* relationship, but also the millions of *I-Them* relationships about which we have become increasingly aware in our global village. Sin is not merely personal: it is corporate, and it is only from within the Christian story that we are able to identify it as such. The 'powers' are real. Whilst the story of redemption drives home the fact that they have been dislodged, they have not, as yet, been removed. Lastly, from Boff, we catch glimpses of the End breaking into the Present through creative and powerful counter-communities modelled on the Trinity. Here we confront not only faith seeking understanding, but also its application.

It should be acknowledged, then, that contemporary evangelical theologians owe much to the serious theological engagements made by a range of non-evangelical counterparts. The task facing evangelical theology as it engages with these new neighbours - whether in relation to the more immediate challenges of postmodernism or the complex processes of globalization - is not without its difficulties. However, it is the role of the theologian both to identify the problems facing the contemporary church and to offer solutions and alternatives - ways of perception that resonate with a baptized imagination. Whilst the social strategies named above may never quite sit comfortably within a purely evangelical context, they can nevertheless serve a prophetic function, stirring us up to meet the wider and deeper challenges which face us in the world today.

The significance of this cultural and theological state of affairs is immense. From the emergence of Tudor England and the religion it spawned, through the various denominational responses to this Anglicanism, and the Reformation background against which those responses were made, the British evangelical church has matured within a modern, Enlightenment culture. The gravity of the challenge to this dying culture, and therefore to the evangelical expression of Christian faith in the western church itself, is considerable. If, as we have argued, Evangelicalism has been substantially conditioned by modernity, then unless procedures for transition can be developed, and implemented with some

---

[40] Colin Gunton holds that much of the malaise can be traced back to Augustine: Colin E. Gunton, *The Promise of Trinitarian Theology* (Edinburgh: T&T Clark, 1991), 94.

degree of unity, the future looks very bleak. In essence, no amount of evangelical spin or faddism[41] will support the necessary crossover. Rather, what is needed is, in the words of Morris Berman, a 'monastic option'.[42] This is no call to withdrawal into a religious community: quite the reverse, for Berman is no Christian theologian. Rather, it is to grasp that as a culture dies, it requires pockets of resistance - pools of antibodies that offer at best correctives to what is taking place in the wider social fabric, and at worst, safe-houses for the protection of all that is good in the unravelling culture. Interestingly, such communities operated both at the fall of the Roman Empire and in the Dark Ages. And whilst they may not fully have understood what they were doing, they nevertheless acted as conveyors of the good in culture. As such, they facilitated change between what was collapsing and what was emerging.

Nearer to home and more importantly, the present cultural transition offers evangelical theologians an opportunity to refocus, so that as Jim Packer suggests, we might maintain our trajectories.[43] Evangelicals have sustained a biblical theology that is strangely both at odds with its surrounding culture, yet also too much identified with that culture. We readily commend the Pauline imperative - 'Do not be conformed to this world, but be transformed by the renewal of your mind, that you may prove what is the will of God, what is good and acceptable and perfect' (Rom.12:2). Likewise its Johannine equivalent: 'Do not love the world or the things in the world. If any one loves the world, love for the Father is not in him. For all that is in the world...is not of the Father, but is of the world. The world passes away, and the lust of it; but he who does the will of the Father abides for ever' (1 John 2:15-17). Yet both ironically serve as pertinent warnings to our own models and methods. For an evangelical churchmanship long proven at adapting itself the world it intends to convert, there is indeed an urgent need for renewed 'monastic' counterparts. As we have seen, one such viable and dynamic possibility is rooted in the social trinitarian theologies produced by Moltmann, Grenz, Volf, Hauerwas, Wink and Boff. In these theologies lie creative possibilities for transition from what is dying to what will emerge. It remains to be seen whether evangelical theologians will assimilate these theologies and engage this transition while yet maintaining their appointed trajectories - that is, while upholding orthodox doctrine,

---

[41] For a penetrating analysis of the degree of faddism that has taken over the serious and weighty business of theological reflection, see I.R. Stackhouse, *Revivalism, Faddism and the Practices of the Church: a Theological Trajectory for Charismatic Renewal in the United Kingdom*, (Unpublished Ph.D., Brunel University, 2003).

[42] Morris Berman, *The Twilight of American Culture* (New York: W. W. Norton & Co., 2000), esp.ch.2.

[43] J.I. Packer, 'Maintaining Evangelical Theology', in John G. Stackhouse Jr. (ed.), *Evangelical Futures* (Grand Rapids: Baker Books, 2000), 186.

searching the Scriptures faithfully, and enhancing the church's mission to this rapidly changing world.[44]

---

[44] Packer, 'Maintaining Evangelical Theology', 186-188.

5. Ethical Models for the Twilight Zone of Church and Culture

Anna Robbins

When you spell things out you're accused of politics. If you don't spell them out, you're accused of being an interesting social philosopher. David Warlock

Without a common and focal Gospel we fall easy victims to limitation of a more serious kind - to the idiosyncrasies of an individual, the fashion of an age, or the egoism of Humanity. P. T. Forsyth

I

The American social gospel champion, Walter Rauschenbusch, once delivered a paper detailing his enthusiasm for the ideals of the kingdom of God to be realized in society. Although lauded for his deep passion and breadth of vision, he was criticized for not being more specific in terms of how he expected his ideas to have real, practical application. Speaking on a further occasion, Rauschenbusch responded to the criticism:

> Several of you criticised the lack of programme, the absence of suggestions how our social conditions could be made better. It was not within the scope of that paper to develop a plan of action, and yet the complaint was just. Discussions of social questions usually drag us out of the City of the Present with its crooked but definite streets and alleys, and leave us facing the fields of the Future, where only a net-work of calf-paths invites our hesitating feet. It is so much easier to criticize the present than to construct the future. The one requires merely an open ear and eye for the evils thick about us, and sympathy enough to hate wrong. The other requires a very rare faculty, a constructive imagination.[1]

It is rare to find a passionate social gospel advocate who wrestles seriously with this perennial difficulty of social ethics. 'If some one, like myself, is young and good-natured enough to respond to the demand and attempts to construct a positive programme,' Rauschenbusch wrote, 'he sails between Scylla and Charybdis. If he goes into tangible details that appeal to the imagination, his critics bid him go back to his home in Utopia. If he confines himself to large guiding principles, they want to know if we are to risk the future of our civilization on such glittering generalities. So the most experienced social thinkers are slow to take their seat on the Delphic tripod.'[2]

---

[1] Walter Rauschenbusch, 'How can the Aims of the Social Movement be Realized?' Unpublished paper, American Baptist Historical Archives, Rauschenbusch Family Papers, Record Group 1003, Box 19,2.

[2] Rauschenbusch, 'social Movement', Box 19,2.

One hundred years on, the difficulty of bridging the gap between theory and practice remains. Yet, as someone who is young by relative standards, generally good-natured, and given to pursuits of the imagination, I cannot resist the call to launch out in my craft and attempt to sail thus. I do this without aspiring to the Delphic tripod, if indeed such a tripod is still standing upon its battered foundation. Indeed, the treachery of the sea journey itself is compounded in the present intellectual and social climate, where contemporary social thinkers define the Scylla of foundationalism and the Charybdis of difference.[3] Is this forced dichotomy appropriate? Must we really choose between the six-headed monster of particularity, foundationalism, and moralism, and the disorienting whirlpool of generality, ambiguity, and difference? Is the gospel able, even across differences of philosophy, theology, geography, and experience, to help the evangelical churches chart a common course of confident social ethics in this stormy sea? I do not think it is naive to answer 'yes' to this question, though it will be a 'yes' served with many qualifications and limitations. After all, if Odysseus could elicit a safe sailing route from Circe, who was responsible for setting the original dilemma, might we not also express hope in the possibility that our Creating and Redeeming God will give clues for navigating similarly treacherous waters? While we remain constantly mindful of our limitations in grasping his instructions, and build such recognition into our ethical methods, it is now, as much as at any time in history, that the confident voice of the church needs to be expressed and heard, and its empowered body released for service. Though the question of *how* is an infinitely difficult one, an attempt to answer it is imperative. Otherwise, 'between the great thing we cannot do, and the little thing we will not do, life passes. And nothing will be done.'[4]

But as we set out to make some suggestions about *how* to do Christian ethics in today's complex world, should we really see evangelical ethics as *either* moralism *or* moral theology, where moral theology indicates a careful and ongoing thoughtful process of ethical matters, and moralism suggests rigid dogmatism? It is true that moralism has adopted negative connotations over recent years. This is especially so in light of American evangelical calls to take up the weapons of the culture war. The lack of depth of ethical reflection of both a theological and philosophical sort have prevented the culture warriors from taking adequate account of competing interpretations of Scripture, the facts of a pluralistic political economy, and the damaging witness which results from personal hurt overlooked in attacks on 'issues'. It is my perception that on

---

[3] John Milbank, *Theology and Social Theory: Beyond Secular Reason* (Cambridge: Basil Blackwell, 1990), 327-8.
[4] William H. MacGuffey, cited in Walter Rauschenbusch, *Dare We Be Christians?* (1914, reprint Cleveland: Pilgrim, 1993).

the whole, British Evangelicals appreciate the complexities involved in relating faith to contemporary culture, and have no illusions about any attempts to 'Christianize' the culture in which we live. The fact that postmodern thought and social existence have been readily engaged by many Evangelicals here suggests that, despite the continuing existence of an established church, there is wide acceptance of the end of Constantinian Christianity, and at least a hesitant willingness to explore new ways of engaging culture with all of the resources of the Christian community. To say that this task demands moral theology and *not* moralism seems obvious. And yet to say it *feels* as though we are giving something up as Evangelicals: the right to suggest that there are moral imperatives and ethical truths which indicate right and wrong behaviour. While I would be among the first to say that Christian ethics should never be pursued without theological and philosophical reflection - the more the better - I would not wish to prohibit those prophetically-minded from *ever* issuing a warning of judgement, or a suggestion of transgressed boundaries. Steering between these extremes means holding a number of factors in balance.

The challenges of doing ethics in today's world are unique. We must be careful not to fall into the danger of correcting one extreme view by presenting an exclusively opposite view. Thus for contemporary ethics, it is not a matter of choosing authority *or* freedom, but both; not foundations *or* coherence, but both; not act *or* essence, but both. Drawing these elements together means making a number of affirmations about the nature and character of evangelical ethics.

I proceed, then, amidst much fear and trembling, to offer a constructive proposal for evangelical ethics in Britain today. I begin by making some affirmations about the nature of evangelical ethics. I will then test several methods of ethics against these affirmations, with respect to their potential for balancing the factors of authority and freedom, foundations and coherence, act and essence, in order to make a recommendation for which method might be most appropriate for Evangelicals to pursue.[5]

II

Characteristics of evangelical ethics

A. Evangelical ethics are ecumenical ethics

The fact that Evangelicals recognize their need to belong together, and to wrestle with what that means in the light of revealed truth, despite all their

---

[5] These categories are not unpacked in explicit detail here, though they lie beneath the concerns which are explored.

disagreements and diversity, testifies to the need for our ethics to be ecumenical. In other words, Evangelicals understand, interpret and live out the faith in many different ways. And yet we recognize at the heart of our faith something we share in common, across denominational, national, cultural and theological boundaries. It is the truth that lies at the heart of, and which we seek to manifest in, Christian life which brings us to unity despite our differences, and which makes us an ecumenical community.

As a community of faith which desires unity, we do not gloss over our diversity, but acknowledge our doctrinal differences. In acknowledging them and discussing them - without any illusions about universal agreement - we display the unity that is ours in Christ. If we believe that our ethics are to be theological, then we have to be willing to discuss our differences without fragmenting into sectarian camps when we happen to disagree. For that reason, our ethics, as ecumenical ethics, will be *both* doctrinal and dialogical.

DOCTRINAL

The role of doctrine in ethical method has been fought over in the past, and debate continues in the present. In the year of my own birth, and a at time when it was fashionable to do so, Paul Ramsey indicated his reluctance to step from the pages of Scripture directly to debates in the public realm.[6] There was a significant doctrinal task which needed to take place in the space between the two. More recently, referring to Ramsey's reluctance, Keith Clements accuses him of compartmentalizing the public voice of the church, arguing that public concern is far more tied into the entire life of the church than Ramsey allowed.[7] Clements instead points to work by Mark Ellingsen to argue that ecumenical dialogue involves more than theological agreement. Yet Ellingsen's research actually demonstrates a lack of scriptural or doctrinal warrant displayed in many, if not most, ecumenical ethical statements.[8] His own view - and that of Clements - is that theological disagreement need not preclude the possibility of agreement on common action. Yet, this was the guiding myth of the first ecumenical ethical consultations in Stockholm in 1925 - 'doctrine divides, but service unites' - and the ensuing years demonstrated its vacuity. Doctrine and service may equally divide or unite. A common pronouncement on some ethical matter which means nothing because its words can be interpreted as

---

[6] Paul Ramsey, *Who Speaks for the Church?* (Nashville and New York: Abingdon, 1967).
[7] Keith Clements, *Learning to Speak: The Church's Voice in Public Affairs* (Edinburgh: T&T Clark, 1995), 21.
[8] Mark Ellingsen, *The Cutting Edge: How Churches Speak on Social Issues* (Grand Rapids: Eerdmans and Geneva: WCC, 1993).

meaning anything should not be the goal of Christian ethics. Our statements, like our actions, will reflect our deepest philosophical commitments. For evangelical Christians, our ethical statements and actions ought to reflect our deepest theological commitments.

Doctrine forms the heart of ethical method. Oliver O'Donovan suggests that 'Christian ethics must arise from the gospel of Jesus Christ. Otherwise it could not be Christian ethics.'[9] Esther Reed similarly affirms their theological nature, indicating, 'The work of Christian ethics and moral theology has to do with discernment of the truth and the gospel itself. It is about both the 'what' and the 'so what' of God's revelation in human form and the calling of the church today.'[10] Alister McGrath reminds us that 'Christian doctrine is what sets Christian ethics apart from the ethics of the world around us. It defines what is distinctive, what is Christian about Christian ethics. To lose sight of the importance of doctrine is to lose the backbone of faith and to open the way to a spineless ethic.'[11] McGrath recalls Dorothy Sayers' reaction against those who suggest that our commitment to other people matters more than doctrine. She responded:

> The one thing I am here to say to you is this: that it is worse than useless for Christians to talk about the importance of Christian morality, unless they are prepared to take their stand upon the fundamentals of Christian theology. It is a lie to say that dogma does not matter; it matters enormously. It is fatal to let people suppose that Christianity is only a mode of feeling; it is virtually necessary to insist that it is first and foremost a rational explanation of the universe. It is hopeless to offer Christianity as a vaguely idealistic aspiration of a simple and consoling kind; it is, on the contrary, a hard, tough, exacting and complex doctrine, steeped in drastic and uncompromising realism.[12]

Her strong statement has been confirmed by my own forays into ecumenical ethics: where ethical issues have proved most divisive for churches, it is usually differences in doctrinal understanding, or lack of doctrinal understanding, which lead to schism. Where there has been little or no doctrinal commitment, or weak doctrinal underpinning, ethical commitments have tended to reflect secular philosophical values instead, and have proven ineffective for the church in the long run.

---

[9] Oliver O'Donovan, *Resurrection and Moral Order: An Outline for Evangelical Ethics*, 2nd Ed. (Leicester: Apollos, 1994), 11.

[10] Esther Reed, *The Genesis of Ethics* (London: DLT, 2000), xx.

[11] Alister McGrath, 'Doctrine and Ethics,' *JETS* , 34/2 (June 1991), 145.

[12] Dorothy L. Sayers, *Creed or Chaos* (London: Methuen, 1947), 28, cited in McGrath, 'Doctrine and Ethics', 146-147.

P. T. Forsyth lamented the result for the Christian faith when social aims replace theology and cause the church to lose an appreciation of historic dogma. For those who place ideology before theology, the truth 'is not found in a great and final liberating Word for the moral Soul.' To such as these, dogma rooted in historical truth is abhorrent 'because a historic redemption is so, or a final revelation, or an absolute gospel. The growth of such freedom is only the growth of human nature turned religious.' God 'is a Liberator rather than a Redeemer. It is natural freedom rarefied and refined. It is not regeneration.' On this matter, as indeed on many others, Forsyth was irrepressible:

> The essential thing about dogma is not is length, breadth nor thickness but its finality. And the fundamental difference between a dogmatic and an undogmatic Christianity is that for the former Christ has done the final thing for the human soul while for the latter He has but won the highest height. The one prizes Christ for His grace, the other for His excellency. The one calls Him Saviour in the new creative sense (and nothing is so final as creation); the other calls Him hero - the soul's hero no doubt but still its *beau ideal* and not its Redeemer.[13]

It matters for our ethics what we think about God, about creation, redemption and the nature of Christ and the work of his spirit.

This may sound like an argument *for* evangelical moralism. But we should not see it as a kind of moralism which is narrow and exclusive of all but a carefully selected 'bouquet of believers' who see the world exactly the same as 'I' do. Appreciating the crucial role of doctrine in moral theology need not render our ethic sectarian, or philosophically weak. To the contrary, 'An obedient response to truth is a mark of intellectual integrity.'[14]

We are saved from narrow and constraining moralism when we recognize the limits, as well as the value, of doctrine for our ethics. While 'theology is not a creative act but only a praise of the Creator,'[15] we do not, as Ramsey rightly reminded us, step directly from the pages of Scripture to a contemporary ethical issue. For that reason, our doctrinal underpinnings are always under construction, and reflect a tentative, rather than final understanding of what God's will desires for each situation. As Evangelicals seek to balance personal piety and social engagement, they are invited to 'recognize that for each of us the school of thought where we feel most at home is not the only theology

---

[13] Peter Taylor Forsyth, *Theology in Church and State* (London: Hodder & Stoughton, 1915), 114.

[14] Forsyth, *Theology in Church and State*, 150.

[15] Karl Barth, *Evangelical Theology*, trans. Grover Foley (Grand Rapids, Eerdmans, 1963), 17.

which is enlightening.'[16] J. S. Mill reminds us that 'He who knows only his own side of the case knows little of that.'[17] Accordingly, evangelical ethics which are doctrinal must also be dialogical.

DIALOGICAL[18]

Dialogue occupies a critical place in ecumenical method, as it must be present at various levels of engagement.[19] It is perhaps best thought of in this context as an attitude rather than a simple discussion. Dialogue reminds us of the open and ongoing discussion which must take place between us regarding our doctrinal commitments and our understanding of their relationship to our ethics. Dialogue means that we come to discussions with a certain degree of openness that God, by his Spirit, and his grace, may direct us to a new understanding of each other, and of him. It means that we take each other, and our unity, seriously. Dialogue takes place between us as members of an ecumenical community seeking to formulate ethical positions. It focuses on doctrine, but also on hermeneutics as we extend the dialogue to include the Bible and culture. It means discussing the different ways we use the Bible, and apply our various understandings of its teaching to our lives as individual Christians, and as a community. In the light of ecumenical failures at ethical dialogue, Evangelicals are well-poised to learn from the mistakes, and to offer a fresh perspective which is confident in truth, but open to wide participation by theological, philosophical and practical experts in the various disciplines their ethics seek to address.[20] The level of agreement attained in dialogue will in turn

---

[16] Albert van den Heuvel, 'The Honest to God Debate in Ecumenical Perspective,' *The Ecumenical Review* XVI (3 April 1964), 289. For more on this theme, see Anna Robbins, 'After Honesty: The Honest to God Debate Revisited,' in *Full of the Holy Spirit and Faith* (Wolfville: Gaspereau Press, 1997), 23-39.

[17] J. S. Mill, cited in Ramsey, *Who Speaks for the Church?*, 25.

[18] Esther Reed has recently sought to ground principles of dialogue ontologically in the authority of God. Her theological affirmations give further support to these more practical principles which were reached independently of her conclusions. Her work nevertheless has encouraged me to pursue this concept further as a method for practical ethical deliberation. See Reed, *The Genesis of Ethics*, 58-118.

[19] Although many perceive a postmodern philosophical ethos to preclude the possibility of dialogue, Alasdair MacIntyre (unlike many who have fed upon his thought) offers suggestions of how dialogue might continue to be engaged even across varying traditions. See Alasdair MacIntyre, *Whose Justice? Which Rationality?* (London: Duckworth, 1988), chapter 19.

[20] This is especially so in light of recent failures in ecumenical ethics, and subsequent critiques which seek to retrieve the best of earlier study methods from the ecumenical tradition. See Ronald Preston, *Confusions in Christian Social Ethics* (London: SCM,

dictate the extent of action which may take place without compromising unity. Yet, even here we should not grow complacent, but rather always be seeking opportunities to engage issues beyond the point where we feel we have reached even unanimous resolutions. Dialogue further prevents us from pretending to agree when we really do not, and from building walls when we reach that point of recognizing our differences. It keeps us talking through the tough times, and leads us always to clarify our philosophical presuppositions.

But if dialogue is built around our doctrine, what is that place of culture in all of this? Does doctrine dictate the agenda for dialogue, or does our context? These questions lead us to the next point of affirmation - that evangelical ethics are realist ethics.

B. Evangelical ethics are realist ethics

Ethical realism has as many descriptions as advocates.[21] My use of the term must therefore be clarified. First, I use it negatively to distinguish evangelical ethics from any form of ethical idealism. Idealism suggests that God's spirit is immanent and therefore ethics are in some sense determined or universal. Such a view obscures the Creator-creature distinction, and fails to adequately balance God's presence in the world with his transcendence as judge over it. Second, I use the term positively to indicate that evangelical ethics are concerned to apply real truth to real situations. This usually means that we accept our ethics as being less than perfect, as the world, ourselves, and our relationships are vulnerable to sin. If the love of Christ is the supreme ideal for Christian ethics, realism recognizes that the objective of social ethics will always be incomplete. We may uphold the reality of a moral ideal, and believe equally in the real limitations of human achievement. This sort of realism is not 'a formal doctrine or even a set of positions on issues' but rather 'a dynamic orientation to the world, a cultivation of tension in one's apprehension of it.... The living of Christian realism promote[s] changes of opinion as the Christian constantly renegotiate[s] the balance between taking the world as it [i]s and demanding

---

1994); and also unpublished reports and correspondence of the Berlin Group which met occasionally through the 1990s.

[21] Rufus Black has recently described moral realism as the contextual natural law ethic of Grisez, whereas Robin Lovin relates realism to the work of neo-orthodox theologians such as Reinhold Niebuhr. See, for example, Robin Lovin, *Reinhold Niebuhr and Christian Realism* (Cambridge, CUP, 1995); Rufus Black, *Christian Moral Realism: Natural Law, Narrative, Virtue, and the Gospel* (Oxford: OUP, 2000). One author goes so far as to suggest that all Christian ethics are realist! See Michael Beaty, Carlton Fisher and Mark Nelson (eds.), *Christian Theism and Moral Philosophy* (Macon: Mercer University Press, 1998).

that it embody higher standards of justice.'[22] Realism then, in this sense, seeks to take seriously *both* the ethical principles which are derived from Scripture and Christian doctrine *and* the context they seek to address.

PRINCIPLED

Discussion of ethical principles and a commitment to their development reminds us of the limits of lifting precepts directly from Scripture. It also precludes any notion of an exemplar Christ.[23] The facts of their Christian nature means that they have something distinct about their content, though that does not exclude them from relevance to other people on some common rational ground.[24] Ethical principles derived from Scripture will have a doctrinal basis, and an appeal to truth. That does not mean that they are the final word on any matter, but rather that they reflect the best that is possible at the moment.

Not everyone is enamoured with the notion of ethical principles. Duncan Forrester writes that 'Dogmas, principles and ethical systems are time-bound endeavours to give an account of the significance of the story in terms of a particular culture and age.' It is the story, rather than principles, which give guidance.[25] As Lesslie Newbigin states, principles can too easily become demonic, or once the principles are distilled from the story, the story itself is

---

[22] Richard Fox, 'Reinhold Niebuhr - The Living of Christian Realism,' in Richard Harries (ed.) *Reinhold Niebuhr and the Issues of Our Time* (London and Oxford: Mowbray, 1986), 10.

[23] This is not a potential pitfall only for liberal theologians to avoid. Much of contemporary evangelical theology brings to mind the similarly broad landscape which characterised evangelicalism at the time of the social gospel. Cf. Gary Dorrien, *Imagining Progressive Religion: The Making of American Liberal Theology 1805-1900* (Louisville and London: WJKP, 2001). See also Brian Stanley, 'Evangelical Social and Political Ethics: An Historical Perspective,' *EQ* 62:1 (1990), 19-36.

[24] Oliver Barclay and Chris Sugden write that we commend ethics 'ultimately on the basis of God's revelation. But given the fragmentary awareness that humanity has of that revelation, we can also commend on a non-revelational basis without using that fragmentary awareness as a primary framework ourselves.' See Barclay and Sugden, 'Biblical Social Ethics in a Mixed Society,' *EQ* LXII (January 1990): 13. Cf. N. H. G. Robinson, *The Groundwork of Christian Ethics* (London: Collins, 1971). Alan Sell has compared the bases for an ethic driven by reason, and by experience *viz.* philosophical idealism. While he has found neither to provide sufficient grounds for a Christian ethic, this does not preclude either from being considered as *part* of a Christian ethic. See Alan P. F. Sell, *Confessing and Commending the Faith: Historic Witness and Apologetic Method* (Cardiff: UWP, 2002); cf. *Philosophical Idealism and Christian Belief* (Cardiff: UWP, 1993), and *John Locke and the Eighteenth-Century Divines* (Cardiff: UWP, 1997).

[25] Duncan Forrester, *Beliefs, Values and Policies* (Oxford: Clarendon, 1989), 28-29.

too easily jettisoned.[26] However, it may be quickly added that the story *need not* be jettisoned when the ethical principles are derived from it, especially if those principles are held as a tentative rather than final word. In this regard, Ramsey argued that ethical principles 'cannot say what should or must be done but only what may be done.'[27] In contrast to the older 'middle axiom' approach, Ramsey's concept of intermediate principles would serve the dual purpose of *informing* 'the ethos and conscience' of nations and political leaders, and *affirming* that Christian opinion will not abandon magistrates if particular actions are taken.[28]

Perhaps not surprisingly, Forrester believes that such an approach does not go far enough. He suggests that 'it also requires to be recognized that a lot of men and women do not find statements of such generality as speaking for them, or addressing their condition. They look for some word that is more specific and concrete.' Moreover, 'there are still multitudes of problems about how to relate the measured theological statements that are intended to give guidance in a variety of situations and the responses to particular crises and problems which take full account of the experiences, emotions, and sufferings involved.'[29] His concern that principles meet the real context of people's experiences is an important one to be heard.

Yet, there is nothing to prevent the contextualization of overarching ethical principles on the local level, by the people directly concerned. This would seem to represent true contextualization while avoiding the danger of confusing principle and precept.[30] Forrester seems to caricature Ramsey's method by suggesting that he *never* permits a specific word.[31] But Ramsey does not preclude the possibility of issuing a specific word; rather, he insists that it should be clarified when and why a specific word should be given, and that in most instances, specificity is more properly addressed at the local level than at the inter-denominational level of ethical dialogue.

---

[26] Lesslie Newbigin, cited in Forrester, *Beliefs, Values and Policies*.

[27] Ramsey, *Who Speaks for the Church?*, 152.

[28] Ramsey, *Who Speaks for the Church?* 154, 120. Ramsey builds this idea on the affirmation made by the Archbishop of Canterbury on the situation in Rhodesia. Cf. Ronald Preston, 'Middle Axioms in Christian Social Ethics,' in *Church and Society in the Late Twentieth Century: The Economic and Political Task* (London: SCM, 1983), 141-156.

[29] Forrester, *Beliefs, Values and Policies*, 57-58.

[30] The distinction between principle and precept in ethics is highlighted by P. T. Forsyth in *Socialism, the Church and the Poor* (London: Hodder & Stoughton, 1908), 59.

[31] Forrester, *Beliefs, Values and Policies*, 58.

CONTEXTUAL

Nevertheless, it is obvious that the idea of ethical principles must be held in balance with an appreciation of the context to which they may be applied. The very identification of issues which precipitates dialogue for the development of ethical principles will be a contextual exercise. It will be important to understand what questions the Christian community and wider society are asking; to appreciate the character of contemporary culture; to anticipate changes and issues for the future and not only for the present. Christian ethics will always have a contextual element. But the matter of context carries with it certain dangers too.

In the present philosophical climate, which is working itself out in practical life, contextualisation brings with it two particular dangers: the danger of social fragmentation; and the danger of doctrinal sectarianism. Douglas John Hall, in responding to the World Council of Churches process for Justice, Peace, and the Integrity of Creation, explains how the current refusal to move beyond context in doing theology and ethics threatens those very things which give us our identity as Christians. 'To say it in a sentence,' he writes, 'the real danger of contextualism is that it will devolve into the kind of regionalism or localism that threatens both the unity of the church and the unity of truth. With the reduction or demise of earnest attempts at global theology, we might see the emergence of a theological tower of Babel where, in contrast to Pentecost, the various provinces of "Christendom" could no longer communicate with one another.'[32] Hall suggests that it is 'precisely because we have begun to think contextually' that 'we are in all the more need' of a 'dialogue that can be a forum for testimony and interchange among many differing contexts.' This means 'we shall have to learn not only how to be forthright about our own contexts and their quite explicit demands upon the faith; we shall have also to learn how to listen intelligently to the testimonies of those who speak out of socio-historical contexts very different from our own.'[33]

Taking ideology rather than theology as an ethical starting-point leads to the kind of contextualism that inhibits dialogue and real effectiveness in ethics.[34]

---

[32] Douglas John Hall, 'The State of the Ark: Lessons from Seoul,' in D. Preman Niles (Compiler), *Between the Flood and the Rainbow: Interpreting the Conciliar Process of Mutual Commitment (Covenant) to Justice, Peace, and the Integrity of Creation* (Geneva: WCC, 1992), 37.

[33] Hall, 'The State of the Ark', 37-38.

[34] This is evidenced in the fragmented Marxism which characterised much of liberation ethics. Charles West points out that, 'If one takes its doctrine of ideology with final seriousness, the result is complete relativism both moral and metaphysical.' Charles West, 'Faith, Ideology, and Power: Toward an Ecumenical, Post-Marxist Method in Christian Ethics,' in Shin Chiba, George Hunsberger and Lester Ruiz (eds.), *Christian*

John Bennett describes it this way:

> In the writing of some contextualists two conceptions take the place of principles: the discernment of what God is doing to humanize man in a situation, and the idea of the *koinonia*. The first raises questions as to how we know what God is doing in the very ambiguous situations which we continually confront unless we have in our minds some criteria - drawn, it may be, from the very idea of humanization. Such criteria would be necessary protection against aberration, such as in the case of many churchmen who saw God at work positively in Hitler. The *koinonia* also raises questions that point beyond itself. If the *koinonia* is a kind of cell group of Christians working together in a revolutionary crisis...it may be necessary to choose between such groups. This would involve some criteria. If the koinonia is the larger church, it is in continual need of reformation in the light of some criteria.[35]

In other words, ethics demands more of the church than simply identifying what we think God is doing in the world and getting on board with it. It demands more than simply deciding what action to take based on the needs and perspective of our local fellowship. Although Bennett's example is dated in the sense that it relates specifically to the situation presented by Marxist liberation ethics, his critique resonates anew when we consider the contemporary tendency for some Evangelicals to define our ethical needs on the one hand by what God is doing in the world today, and on the other, by what we perceive our needs are in very narrowly-defined homogeneous Christian communities.

On the other hand, when they do not slide into sectarianism, contextual aspects of theology may enrich and positively challenge our ethics.[36] They give ethics their vitality and relevance to life. They challenge us to think outside of the narrow bands of our particular communities and to think of the whole life of the church, along with its blessings and challenges to people who may see things quite differently from ourselves. At very least, we must acknowledge that our context, in part, determines the way we see God and the world.[37] That

---

Ethics in Ecumenical Context: Theology, Culture and Politics in Dialogue (Grand Rapids: Eerdmans, 1995), 45.

[35] John Bennett, *Christian Ethics in a Changing World* (New York and London: SCM, 1966), 376-377.

[36] Cf. Alan P. F. Sell, *Commemorations: Studies in Christian Thought and History* (Calgary: University of Calgary Press and Cardiff: University of Wales Press, 1993), 51-55.

[37] I say 'in part' very specifically to counterbalance those aspects of Stanley Hauerwas's thought which suggest that the contextual formation of character is very nearly the whole of ethics. See Hauerwas, *Character and the Christian Life* (San Antonio: Trinity University Press), 1975; cf. Gene Outka's critique of this point, 'Character, Vision and

is a vision that is always reforming and transforming, as we encounter others and learn more about what it means to be disciples of Christ in this time and place.

All of this raises a further important question: what is it in our contexts which ethics must address, or of what does it form a part? Is it our individual lives, our life as a community, or structures which we seek to transform? Considering these questions leads us into our third affirmation of evangelical ethics.

C. Evangelical ethics are responsible ethics

Differences in ethical approaches often centre on who, or what, is perceived to be the agent, and who or what is perceived to be the object of Christian ethics. Very rarely are these differences even recognized, let alone acknowledged and discussed. Yet at their heart is a matter crucial for ethics of any kind - the matter responsibility with respect to action and essence. Evangelical ethics must be clear about who is acting: society, the church, or individuals. They must equally be clear about the object of transformation, as it has significant implications for how ethics function and what outcome is not only expected, but possible. In the words of T. S. Eliot, 'A good deal of confusion could be avoided, if we refrained from setting before the group, what can be the aim only of the individual; and before society as a whole, what can be the aim only of a group.'[38] Are evangelical ethics a matter of people or structures - or both? To such considerations we now turn.

INDIVIDUAL AGENCY

We recognize the responsibility of each individual person before God. An evangelical doctrine of sin reminds us of its universality in the human race, and its permeation of all aspects of human life, including structures of society. It is widely acknowledged that structures themselves seem to take on a life of their own and act back on individuals,[39] and that they thus have 'an effect on the sin

---

Narrative,' *RSR* 6 (1980), 110-118; and also Black's discussion in *Christian Moral Realism: Natural Law, Narrative, Virtue, and the Gospel* (Oxford: OUP, 2000), 247ff.

[38] I have since misplaced the exact source of this quote, but similar sentiments may be found in T. S. Eliot, *The Idea of a Christian Society* (London: Faber & Faber, 1939).

[39] Karl Marx, interpreting Feuerbach, believed that 'It is not the consciousness of men that determines their being, but on the contrary their social being that determines their consciousness.' Preface to *A Contribution to the Critique of Political Economy* (Chicago: Charles H. Kerr, 1904), cited in Charles C. West, 'Faith, Ideology, and Power', 40. Alistair Kee indicates that despite disagreement with Feuerbach, 'Marx quite correctly observed that Feuerbach was actually presenting a very fruitful model for

of people' - though only a few of the more discerning will acknowledge that structures are actually 'impersonal and cannot themselves sin, though the people responsible can do so.' Despite evidence which implicates them in the very thing they argue against, Chris Sugden and Oliver Barclay helpfully clarify the nature of structural sin, rightly redefining it as structural evil:

> ...we are very reluctant to call this social evil structural sin. First, the phrase 'structural sin' confuses societal and personal categories. Second, the terminology of structural sin suggests that we have only to repent of it and we could put it right, and arrive at utopia. In fact when we recognize evil in the structures of society we may repent ourselves, but we cannot necessarily put them right and we can never put them perfectly right. No one knows for sure what a perfectly righteous structure would look like in today's world. We can guess, but we have to accept less than the ideal and strive for the improvement of the situation. Third, to speak of structural sin also often has the consequence of shifting the guilt on to others or even on to impersonal forces as if all the evil lies outside ourselves. We can be angry about structural evil and work hard to reduce it. To repent of it can be idle and ineffective.[40]

While we may not be eager to jettison the term 'structural sin', the caveat to be clear about what we mean by it is well taken. Reinhold Niebuhr argued similarly, suggesting that whereas sin is rooted in the will of the individual, only individuals are able to access forgiveness by grace, effecting a true repentance. For that reason, though he believed in the possibility of collective sin, he believed only in an individual repentance which could approximate love. On the level of society, love may not be applied directly, but only relatively. Love applied to society is justice, which is divisible, meaning higher and lower forms are possible, but always falling short of the ideal of perfect love revealed in Christ. In this approach, he maintained the responsibility of the individual, but sometimes displayed a rather cynical view of collective humanity.[41] This meant his method was vulnerable to the accusation of individualism, and lost any sense of the distinctive, collective identity of the church in ethics. [42]

---

the understanding of the development of human consciousness and indeed societal life. It is a theory of a dialectical movement of externalization, objectification and internalization. Man has the capacity to conceive of ideals and to project them away from himself. They then take on objective form in the external world, in the form of institutions. Finally these institutions come to have an independent reality over against the individual. They act back and control man's life.' Alistair Kee, *Domination or Liberation? The Place of Religion in Social Conflict* (London: SCM Press, 1986), 63.

[40] Barclay and Sugden, 'Biblical Social Ethics in a Mixed Society', 6-7.

[41] See Reinhold Niebuhr, *The Nature and Destiny of Man* (New York: Scribner's, 1941).

[42] Under the influence of Niebuhr and others, 'Christians can lose any sense that the way they think about the world is different than how others may think about the world'. So

COLLECTIVE AGENCY

While we need to acknowledge both individual and collective agency, and
clarify our ethical statements and actions in this regard, the matter is
compounded when we consider the collective action of the church.   In his
response to the World Council of Churches *Ecclesiology and Ethics* study,
participant and co-moderator Duncan Forrester issued an important caveat by
suggesting that 'it is of greatest importance that Christians are not trapped in
the individualism characteristic of post-enlightenment ethics.'[43] Stating that,
'one cannot be a Christian in isolation, only in relationship,' Forrester follows
Stanley Hauerwas's lead in equating Christian ethics and church ethics, though
he stops short of endorsing the type of ethical witness advocated by Hauerwas.

Understanding ethics as a matter of character development - as individuals
but more importantly as a community - Hauerwas compromises the idea of
agency by suggesting that people do not make actual ethical decisions through
reason. Rather, they act in accordance with their virtuous nature, which for
Christians is formed by the narrative of the community. While this may be true
in part, Hauerwas draws criticism for making it form the whole of his Christian
ethic. He drowns the individual under the collective agent of the church, and
thus compromises the sense of moral responsibility which is required of an
ethic which reflects an external authority.

Oliver O'Donovan has noted the methodological significance of Hauerwas's
starting point in contrast to his own: '...where I turn to the Christ-event and to
the apostolic witness, he turns first to the practices of the church.'[44] He explains
that Hauerwas has 'strong reservations about ...a theology not determined by
tradition, a theology that can transcend particularistic communities.'[45] As *the*
political community, Hauerwas defines the church in terms of collective moral
agency, through an ethic of moral formation - one which is less than satisfying
on a number of fronts.[46] It neither takes consideration of the self who accrues
the character of experience, nor does it account for any discernment of the
negative or morally bad features of character which might emerge. It fails to do
justice to the competing allegiances and webs of relationships which
characterize human life, and ends up drowning the responsibility of the
individual beneath the collective of the church.

---

says Stanley Hauerwas, *In Good Company: The Church as Polis* (Notre Dame: UNDP),
157.

[43] Duncan Forrester, 'Living in Truth and Unity', in Thomas Best and Martin Robra
(eds.), *Ecclesiology and Ethics: Ecumenical Ethical Engagement, Moral Formation and
the Nature of the Church* (Geneva.: WCC, 1997), 97.

[44] O'Donovan, *Resurrection and Moral Order*, xv.

[45] Cf. Stanley Hauerwas, *After Christendom?* (Nashville: Abingdon, 1991), 89.

[46] See especially Rufus Black, *Christian Moral Realism*, 258ff.

However, insights about the collective agency of Christian community may be best appreciated when balanced with a dynamic of individuality. Bonhoeffer challenged that we recognize only as we are within the fellowship that we can be alone 'and only he that is alone can live in fellowship. Only in the fellowship do we learn to be rightly alone, and only in aloneness do we learn to live rightly in the fellowship. It is not as though the one preceded the other; both begin at the same time, namely, with the call of Jesus Christ.'[47] Finding a balance between individual and collective aspects of moral agency is crucial to resolving the contemporary impasse, remembering that Christ, and not the church, is the centre and source of our salvation. 'The Christian Church on earth was designed and fitted to be the home where Christian might meet with Christian, and hold fellowship together; it was neither designed nor fitted to be a substitute for the union and fellowship of the sinner with his Saviour'.[48] And yet Hauerwas and John Howard Yoder serve to remind us that we must be wary of those who seek to turn the church into a political messianic community, whose sole interest is the 'Christianizing' of society and culture through means of conflict and power.[49] But to see Christian ethics as solely a matter of individual *or* collective conscience and responsibility is to neglect a full appreciation of these two aspects of moral agency.

Thus far we have made some rather bold assertions about the form of evangelical ethics. We have suggested that they are ecumenical, realist and responsible, and must learn to balance doctrine and dialogue, principles and contexts, individuals and communities. It will remain to be seen whether a particular method of ethics best accommodates or reflects these concerns as suggestions are made about preferable methods of ethics for Evangelicals to pursue.

III

Ethical models in the contemporary world

How, then, are we to view the contemporary setting? As far as ethics is concerned, it is a matter of particular urgency. The issues raised by philosophy and the changing culture have left confidence in truth, reality and our apprehension of them shaken, if not shattered. Amongst others, Evangelicals find themselves wrestling over whether it is right to say that our beliefs in

---

[47] Dietrich Bonhoeffer, *Life Together*, Trans. John W. Doberstein (London: SCM Press, 1954), 57-58.
[48] James Bannerman, cited in Alan P. F. Sell, *The Spirit of Our Life* (Shippensburg, PA: Ragged Edge Press), 55.
[49] Cf. John Howard Yoder, *The Politics of Jesus* (Carlisle: Paternoster, 1994).

things represent anything more than cultural or personal preferences, and in such a climate, we may end up saying and doing little. There is a sense that western culture is moving into a twilight zone between what is often described with the all-encompassing term 'modernity', and the equally ambiguous period to follow, 'postmodernity.' As the sun sets on one epoch of western civilisation, we are uncertain as to whether the sun will rise again for a new day (as in the land of the midnight sun), or if the setting sun suggests an impending period of darkness. We are unsure whether the destiny of the church is bound up with that of culture, and how closely we should tie our fortunes together. For Christian ethics, this is the twilight of uncertainty.

Yet, in the twilight, there is a challenge for Evangelicals to regain our ethical confidence. We do not need to feel that we must hide behind the privatizing shade which has been pulled down in front of religious life; though we should be realistic about the extent of our witness that is possible and desirable. Nor should we rejoice *too* loudly in the relativizing freedom such privacy affords, thinking that a turn towards nebulous spirituality will feed, rather than feed on, the church. Still less should we retreat into ghettoized existence, or seek to be the moral guardians for the whole of western society. It is important that we take stock of the contrast between ethical methods whose qualities are yet discernible in the muted shades of the twilight in order to identify which approach might best facilitate our moral witness to our culture.

I would identify four possibilities for Evangelicals in the present climate. They are the culture war; action-reflection; moral formation; and study-dialogue. Evangelicals will most likely be found amongst the advocates of all of these positions, for reasons of pragmatic or emotional predisposition, if not out of theological and philosophical commitment. It seems important, therefore, to discover whether they are compatible, or if one is preferable for Evangelicals to follow in an era of new cultural challenges, new diversities, and renewed commitment to social engagement.

The previous section indicated the nature of contemporary Christian ethics as a) doctrinal and dialogical, b) principled and contextual, and c) individual and collective. This highlights three important challenges: the need to maintain unity-in-diversity; the significant hermeneutical task in ethics, and the need for expert participation from theological and relevant topical sectors.[50] How do

---

[50] These three aspects are elaborated further by a group of leading ecumenists who are critical of the ethical direction of the WCC in recent decades. Organising secretary for the group was Paul Abrecht, and a body of unpublished reports and correspondence points to these concerns, e.g. 'Report on the Meeting with the World Council of Churches on the Future of Ecumenical Social Thought, at the Ecumenical Institute, Bossey, Switzerland, February 18-19', 1994, 4. Cf. Roger Shinn, 'Friendly Dialogue,'

these three ethical methods fare when tested against these three characteristics and requirements?

A. The culture war

In the United States in the early 1990's, James Davison Hunter identified the struggle over the moral direction of the nation as a 'war'.[51] He identified two streams in American culture which appealed to two opposing sources of moral authority. One stream appealed to biblical foundations for their position, and the other to foundations of autonomous human reason. They both posed a threat to democracy, he suggested, in that many Christians sought to accomplish too much through politics, and the libertarians sought to shut the Christian voice out of their agenda. These positions became embedded in mutually exclusive stances which are expressed in a struggle to control the morality of the nation through political means.

The term 'culture war' does not describe a phenomenon which is new. In fact, it has been a constant theme in the development of American society, as one which was founded on *both* principles of freedom *and* Godly authority. For the founding fathers, these concepts were complementary; in postmodern culture they are often seen as diametrical opposites. For some Evangelicals, to surrender the 'war' for Christian values to rule the political agenda is to abandon the faith.

Obviously, the situation in Britain has been quite different. The fact of established religion has offered more correlation between faith and culture than is the case where there is no state church. On the one hand, this has meant there has been little antagonism of the political kind which has sometimes characterized the Christian voice in American politics. On the other hand, it means the church has often been too comfortable in its cultural skin and not always lived up to its prophetic responsibilities. In the present day, Evangelicals must be prepared for the political disestablishment of the church, even as they acknowledge that moral disestablishment has already taken place.

Does this mean that we will be forced to engage an American-style culture war, as what is left of the Christian foundations of society slips away? It may well be that for the church to offer a challenge on some issues is desirable or necessary, but it is crucial to think carefully whether negative, antagonistic confrontation is the most effective method of moral witness in our present cultural climate.

One World (April 1994), 13; Ronald Preston, 'Middle Axioms'. See also Anna Robbins, *Methods in the Madness* (Carlisle: Paternoster Press, forthcoming 2004).

[51] James Davison Hunter, *The Culture War* (New York: Oxford University Press, 1993).

It is unlikely that the church's mission will proceed thus, even if it were decided to be the preferable option. It is not the case in Britain that there are two opposing streams of thought. Rather, there are *many* streams of authority and none, and the pluralism of our political culture reflects this reality. This may be seen as a welcome challenge for the church: in a pluralistic democracy, evangelical Christians may have every expectation that their voices may be heard and their actions seen in the public forum. Indeed, their voices may be welcomed even by non-Christians who seek the guidance of those who have somewhere firm to put their feet in the shifting sands of relativistic culture. If the church is to meet this opportunity effectively, it needs methods which allow for creative engagement with culture.

An emphasis on doctrine over dialogue, principles against context, and disrespecting the individual-collective tension in ethics means that this method does not yield the desired balance for evangelical ethics in today's world. Because of this, unity-in-diversity is not attained, hermeneutics are easily brushed over, and expert advice avoided. The totalizing vision of the culture war does not leave much room for gentle persuasion or inclusion of differing views, and fails to be sufficiently self-critical. By its very nature it highlights the negative rather than positive aspects of Christian ethics. In the present situation, it would seem that engaging the methods of a 'culture war' are inappropriate to the developing vision of the Evangelical Alliance.

B. Action-reflection

The term action-reflection I use to describe those methods which emphasise ethical practice over theological truth. This is not to say that advocates of such a method are *un*concerned about truth, but rather that they take their cues from what is actually happening 'on the ground.' They want to find out 'what God is doing in the world' and get 'on board' with it, rather than studiously contemplate the right hermeneutical method or deepest theological concern. Action-reflection ethics begin by considering how to be involved in actively transforming the structures of society. The intention is to be committed to praxis first, after which the experience may be reflected upon theologically. This may sometimes create a closed hermeneutical circle, where experience takes precedence over theology, and the Bible is allowed to speak only contextually.

Advocates of this method believe that the scriptural affirmations about love and justice are directly applicable to society, and do not require translation and adaptation, or have any measure of ambiguity about them. It should be clear to all who are Christians what love requires in a given situation, and it may be expressed in either evolutionary or revolutionary terms. In the past, the action-reflection approach has been embodied in the social gospel and in liberation movements.

Action-reflection methods tend to reflect an idealist philosophy which considers God's immanence in priority over his transcendence. They will focus on incarnation, justice and peace, and how to achieve a full humanity. Targets for reform tend to be structures rather than individuals or groups. Like the 'culture war' approach, it may be totalizing in its vision.

Because this approach rests on a philosophically tenuous basis, and its theology may often be compromised to the demands of action, it is difficult to recommend it as appropriately relevant for Evangelicals or for the contemporary culture. Its universality offers no means for mediating disputes, or moderating different points of view, and it tends to focus on collective agency to the exclusion of individual agency. As a method, its stress on action often ignores the importance of the role of hermeneutics in devising ethical strategies. It tends to translate the gospel in light of experience rather than seeking to understand experience in light of the gospel. Its one-sidedness binds it to culture and renders it evangelistically untenable in the long run. Like the social gospel and the ethics of revolution, when the cultural context shifts, it may find itself left behind.

C. Moral formation

Moral formation is that approach which is most fashionable in many theological circles today. It takes seriously the challenges of postmodern society, and favours a narrative approach to ethics. It begins with accepting Alasdair MacIntyre's suggestion that we are in a new Dark Ages for community and morality in the world today, and concludes that developing a community ethic of virtue is the way to respond to the current crisis.

Influenced supremely, though certainly not exclusively, by the work of Stanley Hauerwas, the moral formation approach has broad appeal for a number of reasons. First, it acknowledges the fragmentation of contemporary culture, and welcomes the demise of Constantinian Christianity. It suggests that the true role of the church is one of witness, through the development of a community of character which resists 'Christianizing' society through means of conflict and power. Moral formation accepts that culture has rejected totalizing metanarratives while embracing the notion that its life and ethic are formed by its own narrative. It does not accept a plurality of narratives since its creation arises from the only narrative it comprehends and embodies. To wrestle ethically in the public realm is to acknowledge a plurality in which the church does not participate; to discuss ethics as a matter of policy or decision-making is to accept rational autonomy rather than recognising that we always end up making decisions in harmony with our virtuous character. The role of the church in ethics, then, is to build up virtuous faith communities which will live a common   life of integrity and witness. More than that, the community becomes the very continuation of the incarnation of Christ in the world.

It should not be surprising if this approach has immediate appeal for many Evangelicals.[52] As a method, it recaptures the centrality of theology for ethics, and supports a view of discipleship which resonates with those who are committed believers. It takes its cues for ethical content from the church rather than the world, and seeks to be a radical witness by displaying a life which does not participate in moral conflict and power struggles. Moreover, it accepts the cultural rejection of foundationalism as recognition that there was never any epistemological foundation apart from Christ.

As much as we might value these aspects of a moral formation method, there are concerns to be raised. First, by rejecting any form of decision-making ethics, the method fails to acknowledge that despite the formative role of community discipleship, Christians as individuals are often faced with moral decisions where they truly do not know what to do, and seek guidance for those decisions. Moral formation offers them no such help. Second, the method fails to recognize that individuals embody several communities at one time, which may well make competing moral claims upon them. The method offers no means of resolving the conflicts which may arise for individuals, within communities, or across differing traditions of the wider church community. Third, its acceptance of a narrative epistemological approach precludes any common ground for ethical agreement with groups outside of the moral community. As Christians, that means overlooking the *imago dei* aspect of creation which suggests there is at least *something* which the church has in common with the wider community.

In a surrender of foundations for coherence, an unwillingness to wrestle with the boundaries between church and world, and an exclusive focus on essence over action, the moral formation model is unable to hold together the practical strands of ethical method. Diversities are glossed over, and hermeneutics are reduced to story-telling. Theological expertise is recovered, but there is no acknowledgement of the role of experts in the fields of activity which Christian ethics might seek to address.

---

[52] Hauerwas is not surprised to find much in common with James McClendon, of whom he says that the epistemological shattering of foundations could not shake a Baptist who, in any case, could conceive of no other foundation than Jesus Christ.

D. Study-dialogue

Study-dialogue is a term I will use to describe the style of ethics pursued in ecumenical circles in the early days of the movement. It held sway primarily from the 1930s into the 1950s but a lack of sufficiently wide commitment to its principles allowed it to demise, though some still argue for its resurrection to a place of pre-eminence today.

The method acknowledges that Christian ethics is more complicated than simply applying the ideals of love to society. It recognizes that deriving scriptural principles for ethics requires disciplined hermeneutics; that our appropriation of that kind of knowledge will always fall short of God's ideal because of our sin; that applying biblical principles to real situations requires an expert knowledge and understanding of the situation itself; and that a certain degree of diversity will always be present when Christians gather together to deliberate these complicated issues.

In ecumenical circles, the method faded into the background as revolutionary approaches moved to the fore. A certain frustration with a lack of visible results from study-dialogue led many to abandon it for a method which they believed would yield tangible action. Yet, there is significant reason to believe that the retrieval and application of a modified study-dialogue method may be desirable and appropriate for Evangelicals in the contemporary world.

The study-dialogue method approaches ethics with a certain humility, Recognising that its attempts at realizing justice will be limited when measured against God's perfect justice. Yet it does not surrender to complete relativism, because it suggests that there is at least some correspondence between our apprehension of moral truth and its reality in God. It is a dialectical method in that it approaches situations from both a biblical perspective and a cultural one, seeking to bring the two together in transforming ways. For that reason, it wrestles continuously with hermeneutics, and seeks the input of experts in whatever field of ethics it seeks to address. This forms the study aspect of the method.

The dialogue aspect of the method is also a continuous activity. It is comprised of dialogue across evangelical denominations; dialogue with Scripture, and with experts in the field. In this broad conversation, issues are raised, studied, prayed over and addressed. This dialogue preserves unity in diversity, because it allows many voices to be heard, and encourages as much action as the level of agreement permits. If an issue has universal agreement, then a great deal of focused action may take place. If an issue has less agreement, then a more limited degree of action may be taken. However, the dialogue continues even when parties disagree, and potential action is negligible. This maintains the unity of the evangelical church, as participants recognize that their common commitment to Christ even though they may differ, sometimes significantly, over ethical issues. This is crucial in an age of relativism when fragmentation may too easily split the voice and action of the church, rendering it less effective, and hampering its witness.

This discussion may be taken further. Agreement on statements and actions could progress as far as consensus allows. When consensus breaks down, it would be the task of participants to continue study and dialogue, and to elaborate their reasons for their differences. At least in this activity, dialogue could continue, even though participants may find they encounter strong disagreement. Various groups could then outline the options they believe may be taken by Christians, along with the reasons why they support these positions. It would be left to the Churches and individuals within them to discuss them further and apply them in their respective contexts. In the other direction, if an issue arises from a particular context and is brought to the table for debate, it ought to be pursued towards as much agreement as possible. This approach not only prevents wider bodies such as the EA from being too outspoken on issues which enjoy only a small measure of agreement, but balances the development of gospel principles with the necessities of context. In such situations, consensus is recognized as the goal and ideal, but is usually considered a rare possibility. Most times, debate, discussion and dialogue about possible alternatives, and their accompanying theological and philosophical arguments, will be expected. Thus the integrity of individual contexts and the collective body will be maintained.

A Study-dialogue method is focused more on speaking *to* the church than *for* the church. That does not preclude the possibility of *ever* issuing a public statement, rather it will need to be abundantly clear to all involved when that occasion arises. This not only prevents the church from 'leapfrogging' from issue to issue, but it preserves the balance between those potentially contradictory aspects which characterize evangelical ethics, and it meets the rigorous cultural demands of the day by balancing authority and freedom, foundation and coherence, act and essence. This method seeks to reflect equally upon the truth of Christian doctrine, and the reality of the situation in which such doctrine (or story) is lived out, and it dissuades the church from claiming for itself more expertise than it possesses on a given issue.

In this respect, Paul Ramsey believed that rather than a single policy line, alternatives need to be elaborated, especially when attempts are made to speak for the church. In a day of increased diversity, it may be said that this is appropriate when transdenominational bodies such as the EA are speaking *to* the church, and speaking or acting *as* the church. While the church goes on continually with the business of moral formation, informing the ethos of church and society as it lives out its mission in the world, there are times when a public word is needed. In such cases, it may be more appropriate to affirm that Christian opinion will not abandon magistrates if particular actions are taken, than to suggest which actions *ought* to be taken.[53] If the church is engaging this sort of activity with diligence, it will inevitably make its witness clear in an engaging and realistic way, without compromising authority and freedom, foundations and coherence, action and essence.

IV

Whether contemporary ethicists like it or not, ethical decision-making will always be a part of the Christian life. Neither history, nor philosophy, nor theology nor Scripture is able to affirm the contention that Christians will always 'do the right thing' in accordance with their virtuous nature, especially when they are considered together in all of their diversity as the body of Christ.[54] Neither will mere structuralism suffice, just as a simplified individualism which pays scant attention to the dynamics of society is inadequate. This is particularly acute in an age which is torn ideologically between disturbing visions of violent individualism and totalizing collectivism.[55] The church has particular resources to bring to bear on these subjects, if it will resist the trend to retreat into its own cosseted narrative, or fragment into homogeneous units, to the neglect of a whole humanity inhabiting a shared space.

Now, more than ever, Christians live in a world full of complexities and contradictions which forces decisions upon them if they lack the courage or conviction to make decisions for themselves. Equipping the saints for the ministry of the church as individuals, working together for the good of the whole community, speaking and acting with conviction when required, and remaining silent when there is nothing helpful to be said requires diligence and discipline. Yet this hard work is necessary if the church is to continue to offer a foundation for belief, and a means of speaking and acting prophetically and authoritatively in the midst of particular situations.[56] Ethical integrity will mean

---

[53] This follows Ramsey's recommendations.

[54] For a clear and concise criticism of Hauerwas on these points, see Black, *Christian Moral Realism.*

[55] The one represents views following Lyotard, Bauman, etc.; the other follows from those who suggest we are being swallowed by a globalizing consumer culture.

[56] Cf. John de Gruchy, *Liberating Reformed Theology* (Grand Rapids: Eerdmans, 1991). The integrity of this task depends on a commitment to the whole gospel. This will yield not only 'a commitment to the evangelical doctrines as affirmed in early catholic traditions and retrieved by the Reformation but also a commitment to the biblical

that 'Christian ethical reflection will be theological reflection; and Christian praxis will be devotional praxis - it will flow from gratitude to God. In Christian ethical theory, gift and demand will be held together as an indissoluble whole; in Christian praxis there will be a constant concern - a striving - to ensure that the actions performed are consistent with the gospel proclaimed.'[57] Through rigorous study and patient dialogue, may the church receive the wisdom and grace to sail on and thrive in the twilight, for the good of God's world, and the glory of Christ.

---

prophetic witness to God's purposes of justice and equity within society.' Thus, 'while a tradition can wither and die - or worse, become an albatross around our necks - it can also be retrieved as a source of empowerment in the present, providing the symbols not only for its own revitalisation and renewal, but for society at large', 39-40.
[57] Alan P. F. Sell, *Aspects of Christian Integrity* (Louisville: WJKP, 1990), 61.

6. The State and Social Transformation: Evangelicals and Politics

John Coffey

The resurgence of religion in politics

The last three decades have witnessed a dramatic resurgence of religion in global politics. In the 1960s, sociologists and radical theologians lined up to announce the inevitability of secularization. By the close of the twentieth century, such predictions looked seriously misleading. In the era between the Iranian Revolution of 1979 and the attack on the World Trade Center on 11 September 2001, Islamic 'fundamentalism' and various forms of religious nationalism emerged as a major force in contemporary politics.[1] During the same period, Christian churches threw their weight behind democracy movements and human rights campaigns, and played an important role in the collapse of Communism in Eastern Europe and the ending of apartheid in South Africa.[2] Sociologists of religion began to talk about 'the revenge of God' and 'the return of the sacred'. Peter Berger, perhaps the most influential of the 1960s secularization theorists, announced that he had been 'essentially mistaken'. In *The Desecularization of the World: Resurgent Religion and World Politics* (1999), Berger wrote that 'the assumption that we live in a secularized world is false. The world today, with some exceptions…is as furiously religious as it ever was, and in some places more so than ever'.[3]

To an extent that is only now becoming clear, Evangelicalism was heavily involved in this desecularization of politics. The politicization of Evangelicalism has been most evident in the United States, where Jerry Falwell's Moral Majority became a major political player in the 1980s, and Pat Robertson's Christian Coalition took up a similar role in the 1990s. Evangelical activists protested against abortion, pornography, the teaching of evolution, and gay rights, and campaigned for the Republican party, helping to secure the election of Ronald Reagan, George Bush Snr., and George Bush Jnr. If the

---

[1] See Martin Marty and Scott Appleby (eds.) *Fundamentalisms and the State* (Chicago: University of Chicago Press, 1993); David Westerlund, *Questioning the Secular State: The Worldwide Resurgence of Religion in Politics* (London: Hurst and Co, 1996).

[2] See John De Gruchy, *Christianity and Democracy* (Cambridge: CUP, 1995); D. Martin, *Forbidden Revolutions: Pentecostalism in Latin America, Catholicism in Eastern Europe* (London: SPCK, 1996).

[3] Peter Berger, *The Desecularization of the World: Resurgent Religion and World Politics* (Grand Rapids: Eerdmans, 1999), 2. See also John Coffey, 'Secularisation: is it inevitable?' *Cambridge Papers*, 10:1 (2001).

Christian Right garnered most press attention, there was also a smaller Evangelical Left, led by influential activists like Jim Wallis and Tony Campolo.[4]

In the Third World, mass Evangelicalism was also becoming a major political force, as Paul Freston has demonstrated in his pioneering study, *Evangelicals and Politics in Asia, Africa and Latin America* (CUP, 2001). There have been evangelical presidents in Guatemala, South Korea, the Philippines, Kenya, Zambia and Nigeria, and evangelical political parties have become a significant force in several Latin American countries. But as in the United States, the character of evangelical politics is very diverse. Some Evangelicals are human rights and democracy activists, whilst others have supported authoritarian regimes. In Kenya, for instance, Evangelicalism was 'both bulwark of the Moi regime and one of its most important opponents'. Third World Evangelicals are also divided over whether the state should be non-confessional or explicitly Christian; some only seek political equality with other religions, whilst others display a triumphalist zeal for the rule of the godly. Because the shape of evangelical politics is affected by a wide range of local factors (its numerical size, its competitors, its social and denominational composition, its political context etc), Freston warns against easy generalizations. But the growing importance of Evangelicals as political actors is unmistakable.

To turn from the United States, Africa and Latin America to the UK is to enter a different world. Western Europe is the one region where secularization theory still seems to make sense. Unlike the United States and many Third World countries, Britain does not have a mass evangelical movement that can exercise substantial electoral clout. Whereas around 40% of the US population are regular churchgoers, in Britain the figure is around 7%. Moreover, like other Western Europeans, the British tend to feel uncomfortable when politicians invoke God. Tony Blair, though not an Evangelical himself, is satirized for his 'evangelical' style, with *Private Eye* famously depicting him as the trendy but vacuous guitar-strumming 'Vicar of Albion'. But in reality, Blair avoids parading his piety or pushing an overtly Christian agenda. And there is nothing in Britain to compare to the powerful Christian Right in the US. Few British Evangelicals promote the same distinctive blend of capitalism, patriotism and moralism. Even if they did, they could not draw on the support of a massive churchgoing constituency.

---

[4] For a useful (if somewhat dated) overview of American evangelical politics, see James Skillen, *The Scattered Voice: Christians at Odds in the Public Square* (Grand Rapids: Zondervan, 1990).

Yet even in secular Britain, the political influence of religion should not be underestimated. The reality of secularization needs to be set alongside the development of a multi-faith society, in which Islam is an increasingly prominent presence. The political pronouncements of senior religious figures such as the Archbishop of Canterbury and the Chief Rabbi continue to attract extensive media coverage. The Westminster Parliament has a substantial number of Christian politicians. The Christian Socialist Movement has 36 member MPs (including the Prime Minister), whilst the Conservative Christian Fellowship and the Liberal Democrat Christian Forum are also well supported both within Parliament and beyond.[5] Outside the main parties, the Movement for Christian Democracy brings together a broad coalition of Christians interested in politics, and provides a variety of helpful resources.[6] Evangelicals are a significant presence within these various movements, and have become politically engaged in other ways too.[7] The Keep Sunday Special Campaign inspired by the Jubilee Centre was the only pressure group to inflict a parliamentary defeat on Margaret Thatcher's government in the 1980s (though this was later overturned). Evangelicals were also actively involved in establishing the high profile Jubilee 2000 Campaign for Third World debt relief. Its success prompted the commentator Will Hutton to write that 'it is no longer Morris, Keynes and Beveridge who inspire and change the world - it's Leviticus'.[8]

There has also been a welcome revival of Christian political thought. Oliver O'Donovan's book, *The Desire of the Nations*, is the most important work of evangelical political theology to be published in many years. Alongside the work of Tom Wright, it reminds us of how political themes are woven into the very fabric of the New Testament.[9] It has also inspired a groundbreaking dialogue with other Christian scholars about the political use of the Bible.[10] Moreover, in *From Irenaeus to Grotius: A Sourcebook in Christian Political Thought, 100-1625* (Eerdmans, 1999), Oliver and Joan O'Donovan have

---

[5] For further details on this see the useful gateway website of Christians in Politics: <http://www.christiansinpolitics.org.uk>

[6] See the MCD website: <http://www.mcdpolitics.org>

[7] For evangelical reengagement with politics and society from the 1960s onwards, see Timothy Chester, *Awakening to a World of Need: The Recovery of Evangelical Social Concern* (Leicester: IVP, 1993). See also the autobiographies of two leading evangelical politicians: Sir Fred Catherwood, *On the Cutting Edge* (London: Hodder & Stoughton, 1995); and Brian Mawhinney, *In the Firing Line* (London: HarperCollins, 1999).

[8] Will Hutton, 'The Jubilee line that works', *The Observer*, 3 October 1999.

[9] Oliver O'Donovan, *The Desire of the Nations: Rediscovering the Roots of Political Theology* (Cambridge: CUP, 1996); N. T. Wright, *Jesus and the Victory of God* (London: SPCK, 1996).

[10] Craig Bartholomew et al (eds.) *A Royal Priesthood? The Use of the Bible Ethically and Politically* (Carlisle: Paternoster, 2003).

assembled a remarkable anthology of texts designed to help Christians reengage with a rich intellectual tradition. O'Donovan's work is the most outstanding example of a growing body of political reflection by evangelical theologians, biblical scholars, philosophers, political theorists, lawyers, historians and activists.[11]

This essay adds to the discussion by offering an historical perspective on a key issue - the role of the state in social and spiritual transformation. As we will see, Evangelicals have differed amongst themselves over what they should expect from the state. For some it is the key to transforming society, whilst for others it is at best an irrelevance. Surveying a variety of evangelical political attitudes will not yield straightforward answers to our questions about the role of the state. But it should give us a better grasp of the issues, the options, the potentials and the pitfalls of Christian involvement. It should also give us a greater sense of historical perspective on our own tradition. Evangelical Protestants have often been deeply engaged with politics over the past five centuries. Their successes and failures can usefully inform contemporary evangelical political thinking. [12]

The irrelevant State

For some Evangelicals, of course, the state is essentially *irrelevant* to the

---

[11] See for example the following works published during the past twenty years: Richard Mouw, *When the Kings Come Marching In: Isaiah and the New Jerusalem* (Grand Rapids: Eerdmans, 1983); Nicholas Wolterstorff, *When Justice and Peace Embrace* (Grand Rapids: Eerdmans, 1983); Charles Colson, *Kingdoms in Conflict* (London: Hodder & Stoughton, 1988); Richard Bauckham, *The Bible in Politics* (London: SPCK, 1989); N. T. Wright, 'The New Testament and the "state"', *Themelios*, 16 (1990), 11-17; Richard Mouw et al, *Pluralisms and Horizons: An Essay in Christian Public Philosophy* (Grand Rapids: Eerdmans, 1993); Os Guinness, *The American Hour* (New York: Macmillan, 1993); James Skillen, *Recharging the American Experiment: Principled Pluralism for Genuine Civic Community* (Grand Rapids: Baker, 1994); Jim Wallis, *The Soul of Politics* (Grand Rapids: Zondervan, 1995); Mark Noll, *Adding Cross to Crown: The Political Significance of Christ's Passion* (Grand Rapids: Eerdmans, 1996); Miroslav Volf, *Exclusion and Embrace* (Nashville, TN: Abingdon Press, 1996); Robert Song, *Christianity and Liberal Society* (Oxford: Clarendon Press, 1997); Paul Beaumont (ed.), *Christian Perspectives on Law and Relationism* (Carlisle: Paternoster, 2000); Nigel Wright, *Disavowing Constantine* (Carlisle: Paternoster, 2000); Jonathan Chaplin, 'Prospects for an Evangelical Political Philosophy', *Evangelical Review of Theology*, 24 (2000), 354-73; Paul Beaumont (ed.), *Christian Perspectives on the Limits of Law* (Carlisle: Paternoster, 2002).

[12] In this chapter, I will draw my examples from the broad evangelical Protestant tradition that began with Luther and was renewed by successive waves of revival and awakening in subsequent centuries.

Christian. Whilst they acknowledge that the state is ordained by God to restrain evildoers, its task is minimal and quite unimportant. Although one should pay one's taxes and obey the law of the land, it would be a mistake to invest time, energy and expectations in the political process. After all, Christ's kingdom is 'not of this world' (Jn. 18:36), and believers are 'aliens and strangers' in this world (1 Pet. 2:11). In Glenn Jordan's excellent book, *Not of this World? Evangelical Protestants in Northern Ireland* (2001), the apolitical stance is clearly articulated by someone called Chris: 'When you go away on holiday and people you meet just want to talk about the Troubles in Belfast, all I want to talk about is Jesus, and how he can bring changes to the lives of individuals. I don't want to talk about Protestants or Catholics, I want to talk about Jesus the life changer. I want to be known as a guy who is in love with Jesus and who doesn't want to be fussed about anything else'.[13]

On one level, this apolitical quietism embodies a certain wisdom. In Northern Ireland, the politicization of Protestantism and Catholicism has fostered bitter communal division, and one can understand Chris's distaste for Ulster politics. Political issues can also become a source of division within churches, which is why John Wesley forbade political debates within the Methodist movement.[14] Moreover, Christians sometimes become more excited about the state than about the church, and so politically engaged that they lose their focus on the need for Christian conversion. When this happens they need to heed the advice of Stanley Hauerwas: 'the primary social task of the church is to be itself'.[15] Christian political involvement is important, but we must appreciate the limitations of politics and the potential of the local church. As Bill Hybels explains:

> For eight years during the decade of the nineties I went to Washington, D. C., every month to meet in the foremost centres of power with some of the highest elected officials in our country. What I discovered was not how powerful these people are, but how limited their power really is. All they can actually do is rearrange the yard markers on the playing field. They can't change a human heart. They can't heal a wounded soul. They can't turn hatred into love. They can't bring about repentance, forgiveness, reconciliation, peace…in a very real way the future of the world rests in the hands of local congregations like yours and mine.[16]

---

[13] Glenn Jordan, *Not of this World? Evangelical Protestants in Northern Ireland* (Belfast: Blackstaff, 2001), 125.

[14] David Bebbington, *Evangelicalism in Modern Britain: A History from the 1730s to the 1980s* (London: Unwin Hyman, 1989), 72. This did not stop Wesley pronouncing on political issues, such as the evil of the American War of Independence against Britain!

[15] Stanley Hauerwas, *The Hauerwas Reader* (Durham, SC: Duke University Press, 2001), 113.

[16] Bill Hybels, *Courageous Leadership* (Grand Rapids: Zondervan, 2002).

But if quietists are right to recognize the limits of what the state can do, they are wrong to see political involvement as intrinsically unspiritual. Tom Wright argues that Christ's statement that his kingdom was 'not of this world' is not a reference to 'an other-worldly, Platonic, non-physical kingdom' in the next life. Instead, it is a declaration that 'the kingdom he is inaugurating is not world*ly* in its methods'.[17] As Paul explained, 'though we live in the world, we do not wage war as the world does. The weapons we fight with are not the weapons of the world' (2 Cor. 10:3-4). Moreover, when Peter tells Christians that they are 'aliens and strangers in the world', he does not go on to advocate withdrawal from public life; instead, he urges believers to abstain from sinful desires, live exemplary lives among the pagans, and submit to political authorities (1 Pet. 2:11-17). Ironically, those who insist on a withdrawal ethic reduce the opportunities for Christian witness in the midst of our society. They also leave a vacuum that will be filled by others. Chris's disengagement from Northern Ireland politics, for example, arguably allows more strident voices to dominate the political scene. And it displays a startling disinterest in a major sphere of human existence. Far from being irrelevant, the state affects our lives in a multitude of ways, far more so than it did in past societies. Since the modern state impacts the economy, education, health care, foreign policy, the environment, and many other spheres of existence, it must surely be a focus of Christian concern. This is not to say that every Christian is called to be a political activist, but it is to say that the Christian community as a whole cannot afford to ignore the state.

Christian involvement is all the more important given the dramatic decline in civic engagement across western societies over the past forty years. As the Harvard sociologist Robert Putnam demonstrates in his powerful study, *Bowling Alone*, the trends have all been downward whether we are talking about political, civic or religious participation, or informal social connections. Putnam notes that evangelical churches constitute one of the most striking exceptions to this decline in 'social capital'. But although evangelical churches have bucked the trend by growing when other institutions are in decline, Putnam suggests that their social capital 'is invested at home more than in the wider community'. They are more likely to create *bonding* (or exclusive) social capital than *bridging* (or inclusive) social capital. Whereas mainline Protestants 'provided a disproportionate share of leadership to the wider civic community', Evangelicals tend to 'put more emphasis on church-centred activities'. [18]

We may wish to challenge Putnam's generalisations, but his argument should give us pause for thought. Clearly there is a danger in the liberal Protestant model, where Christian energies are invested in civic life at the

---

[17] Wright, 'The New Testament and the "state"', 13.

[18] Robert Putnam, *Bowling Alone* (New York: Simon and Schuster, 2000), 77-78.

expense of the church itself. But Evangelicals often tend toward the other extreme, shunning 'the world' and turning the church into a ghetto from which we rarely emerge. If being 'in the world, not of it' is the Christian's goal, then we need to ensure that believers are not only deeply rooted in the church but also actively involved in life of the wider community. We need to rediscover and cultivate an ethic of public service. The Old Testament tells the stories of faithful Hebrews who served in pagan courts, bringing benefit to their own people, but also serving their fellow citizens. If Evangelicals are to be a movement for change, we need more people like Joseph, Esther, and Daniel.

The ungodly state

But what should one do if the state is *unjust* or *ungodly*? Is there a place for *resistance*, and if so what form should it take? The legitimacy of resistance to the state has generated intense debate among Christians. The key text, of course, has been Romans 13, where Paul declares that 'Everyone must submit himself to the governing authorities, for there is no authority except that which God has established. The authorities that exist have been established by God. Consequently, he who rebels against the authority is rebelling against what God has instituted' (Rom. 13:1-2). Many see this as an unambiguous text, which flatly denies the legitimacy of 'rebellion' against any government, however tyrannical and ungodly. For centuries, Romans 13 has been invoked by conservatives against revolutionaries. It was a favourite text of Royalists in the English Civil War, and of Loyalists in the American War of Independence.

Yet there is also a long and vigorous tradition of resistance theory among evangelical Protestants. Although Luther was initially an advocate of passive obedience to the state, he soon changed his mind when the Reformation was threatened by the Catholic powers. Calvin was also reticent about resistance to magistrates, but many of his followers (including Theodore Beza and John Knox) became zealous advocates of resistance to (Catholic) tyrants. The tradition of Calvinist resistance theory was developed by the French Huguenots fighting against the Catholic monarchy in the late 16th century; revived by English Puritans and Scottish Covenanters during the British Civil Wars of the 1640s; and put to use once more by the Patriots in the American War of Independence in the 1770s. Together these groups assembled a formidable body of political thought, one which drew on natural law theory, Roman law and common law, Christian tradition and the Bible.[19]

---

[19] See Quentin Skinner, *The Foundations of Modern Political Thought, Vol. II: The Reformation* (Cambridge: CUP, 1978). For primary texts, see A. S. P. Woodhouse (ed.),

In dealing with the problematic text of Romans 13, resistance theorists argued that one must not stop at verse 2. In verses 3-4, Paul goes on to argue that the state has been instituted as 'God's servant' to do good to the righteous, and to be 'an agent of wrath to bring punishment on the wrongdoer'. The authorities to which Paul refers, suggested these theorists, were not tyrannical authorities that persecuted the righteous and promoted criminals, for such authorities would be the reverse of what Paul had in mind - a terror to their good subjects and not to evildoers. As such, they would no longer conform to the pattern of divinely instituted 'authorities', and Paul's command to 'submit' would no longer apply. Like Old Testament tyrants such as Ahab, they could be resisted and overthrown by force of arms.[20]

The controversies of the early modern era may seem very distant today, but they have profoundly shaped the way we think about the state. Resistance theorists popularized key convictions of modern democratic politics: political authority is rooted in popular consent; governments must be limited by the rule of law; governments are accountable to the people; tyrannical rulers can be resisted by force of arms. Moreover, the question of resistance to the state has been a live one for many Christians in the past century. As David Hilborn's paper for this volume demonstrates, German Christians under Hitler, Russian Baptists under Communism, and South African Evangelicals under apartheid all wrestled with the implications of Romans 13.

In the UK, of course, Christians are not confronted by an authoritarian state. But it would be naïve to suppose that liberal democratic states cannot act in ways that are offensive or even oppressive to the Christian conscience. Indeed, there are signs that some liberals want to exercise a kind of 'homogenizing pressure on ways of life that do not embrace autonomy', by mandating compliance with a liberal sexual ethic or restricting religious 'proselytism'.[21] Fortunately, parliamentary democracy permits peaceful resistance to state policy through public protests and political lobbying. In recent years Christians have actively campaigned against a variety of government policies, including legalized abortion, the arms trade, and Sunday trading. This willingness to critique the state is healthy. As David Hilborn suggests, 'unqualified

---

Puritanism and Liberty (London: Everyman, 1992); Ellis Sandoz, *Political Sermons of the American Revolution* (Indianapolis: Liberty Fund, 1991).

[20] For the resistance theory of a prominent Scottish theologian, see John Coffey, *Politics, Religion and the British Revolutions: The Mind of Samuel Rutherford* (Cambridge: CUP, 1997), ch. 6.

[21] For an important analysis and critique of this autonomy-based liberalism and its hostility to religious communities, see William Galston, *Liberal Pluralism* (Cambridge: CUP, 2002). Quotation from p. 23.

acquiescence' is a dubious stance for the Christian, and there is a place for 'biblical dissent'.

The Christian state

For some, the best solution to the problem of the unjust or ungodly state lies in the establishment of a *Christian* state. The magisterial Reformers, including Luther and Calvin, firmly believed that the state had a crucial role to play in the promotion of Christianity. Magistrates were 'nursing fathers' of the church, and they had a solemn duty to uphold and enforce both tables of the Decalogue, including man's duties towards God as well as towards other men. Christian magistrates were in the same position as the godly kings of Israel, and they should reform the church of its corruption, suppress idolatry and heresy, and promote true religion among the population.[22]

This magisterial Reformation vision of a confessional state was the mainstream Protestant view, but there was an alternative tradition articulated by a small minority of radical Dissenters. Contintental Anabaptists, for example, tended to disassociate themselves from political power. The true believer, they argued, could not hold public office as a magistrate since he would then be implicated in the state's use of 'the sword' against criminals and other States.[23] Radical English Puritans disagreed with this, but they maintained that the purposes of the state were 'merely civil', not religious. Roger Williams, the founder of the colony of Rhode Island in New England, argued at length against the magisterial Reformation vision of a Christian state in his book, *The Bloody Tenent of Persecution* (1644). Williams suggested that Christians had taken a wrong turn in the fourth century, when under the Emperor Constantine Christianity had started the journey towards becoming the established religion of the Roman Empire. By creating 'Christian nations' modelled on Old Testament Israel, Christians had departed from the example of the New Testament church and tried to promote the faith with worldly weapons. Christianity had become a civil religion and a persecutor of its rivals. Williams believed that Christianity must return to its New Testament roots. The church must be reconstituted as a *voluntary* community, and the state must be reconceived as an essentially *civil* institution with no competence to judge

---

[22] See John Coffey, *Persecution and Toleration in Protestant England, 1558-1689* (Harlow: Longman, 2000), ch. 2.

[23] For an excellent overview of Anabaptists and other radical Protestants see Meic Pearse, *The Great Restoration: The Religious Radicals of the 16th and 17th Centuries* (Carlisle: Paternoster, 1998).

matters of religion. If this was done, religious freedom would be secure, and the state could govern a peaceful, prosperous and pluralist society.[24]

The dispute between magisterial and radical Reformers constitutes one of the key fault lines within the evangelical Protestant political tradition. Although it is often papered over, it has not gone away. In the nineteenth century, Anglican defenders of the State Church found themselves at odds with Dissenters campaigning for disestablishment. In our own day, the debate rumbles on. A small minority of Theonomists or Christian Reconstructionists long for a return to the full-blooded Protestant state of Calvin's Geneva, or at least of Cromwell's England.[25] For most Evangelicals this is a pipe dream, and an unattractive one at that. But many would follow O'Donovan in favouring a kinder, gentler Christian state that is both confessionally Christian and tolerant of other faiths, and there is still a good deal of support for the Anglican establishment.[26] By contrast, Evangelicals like Nigel Wright argue for disestablishment and a non-confessional state. They believe that we are entering a 'post-Constantinian' era, when the church will need to learn to live without state support.[27]

Each of these positions generates a very different political agenda. Advocates of a theonomist state, a tolerant Christian state, and a non-confessional state may make common cause over a particular issue like abortion, but their ultimate aims are sharply divergent. Evangelicals are divided over the very nature of the state.[28] But there is a good deal of common ground between defenders of a tolerant religious establishment and principled pluralists who support a non-confessional state. Both groups are firmly opposed to a Christian triumphalism or religious nationalism that would undermine the civil rights of non-Christians. Principled pluralists would warmly welcome Lesslie Newbigin's ringing endorsement of 'the principle of religious freedom' and his

---

[24] See Coffey, 'How should Evangelicals think about politics? Roger Williams and the case for principled pluralism', *Evangelical Quarterly*, 69 (1997), 39-62.

[25] See Stephen Perks, *A Defence of the Christian State* (Taunton: The Kuyper Foundation, 1998). I should add that this is a book-length critique of my own article on Roger Williams.

[26] O'Donovan, *Desire of the Nations*, chs. 6-7. See also Lesslie Newbigin et al., *Faith and Power: Christianity and Islam in 'secular' Britain* (London: SPCK, 1998); David Holloway, *Church and State in the New Millennium* (London: HarperCollins, 2000).

[27] Wright, *Disavowing Constantine*. This position is also supported by Evangelicals inspired by Dutch neo-Calvinism, including James Skillen, Richard Mouw and Jonathan Chaplin. See also the influential writings of the American theologian, Stanley Hauerwas, especially two books he has written with William Willimon, *Resident Aliens* (Nashville: Abingdon Press, 1989); and *After Christendom* (Nashville: Abingdon Press, 1991).

[28] See G. S. Smith, ed., *God and Politics: Four Views on the Reformation of Civil Government* (Phillipsburg, NJ: Presbyterian & Reformed, 1989).

rejection of a 'territorial' view of the faith.[29] Moreover, both groups are critical of the modern liberal attempt to entirely secularize public life and public discourse. Advocates of the Christian state would applaud the efforts of principled pluralists to defend the use of religious arguments in political discourse, and the rights of faith-based charities to apply for public funding.[30] Although there is significant disagreement over the idea of a Christian state, there are important shared principles.

The moral state

Historically, the role of the state in promoting or even enforcing *morality* has been less controversial among Christians than its role in promoting true religion. Even radical Dissenters who rejected religious establishments still believed that the state should enforce a basic morality derived from natural law. Early modern Protestants commonly believed that the second table of the Decalogue encapsulated universal moral principles accessible to all rational people. Political authorities were duty bound to punish those who committed theft, murder and adultery (if not those who disobeyed their parents, coveted their neighbour's ox, or told lies). The state could be an agent of moral renewal.

At times, the evangelical Protestant drive for moral transformation through the state has reached epic proportions. In John Calvin's Geneva, the Reformer instigated a far-reaching programme of social transformation that resulted in dramatic changes to the city's mores. A series of laws were passed against gambling, blasphemy, drunkenness and adultery, and there were even laws against the singing of dirty songs and the naming of children after Catholic saints. The results were spectacular; by the 1560s, Geneva had some of the lowest rates of illegitimate births (0.12%) and prenuptial conceptions (1%) ever recorded in Europe.[31] In England, during the Puritan Revolution, an even more ambitious effort was made to create a godly nation. Puritan magistrates targeted a miscellany of evils, including Sabbath-breaking, maypole dancing, adultery, drunkenness, blood sports, and even the 'popish' celebration of Christmas. At one point, Oliver Cromwell went so far as to empower his Major-Generals to suppress vice and promote virtue. But the campaign for moral reformation was

---

[29] Newbigin et al, *Faith and Power*, 141.

[30] See especially Robert Audi and Nicholas Wolterstorff, *Religion in the Public Square* (Lanham, MD: Rowman & Littlefield, 1996); Stephen Monsma, *Positive Neutrality: Letting Religious Freedom Ring* (Grand Rapids: Baker, 1995); Stephen Monsma, *When Sacred and Secular Mix: Religious Nonprofit Organisations and Public Money* (Lanham, MD: Rowman and Littlefield, 1996).

[31] P. Benedict, *Christ's Churches Purely Reformed: A Social History of Calvinism* (New Haven: Yale University Press, 2002), 98-103.

a failure, and after just one year Cromwell was forced to abolish the rule of the Major-Generals. When Charles II was restored to power in 1660, there was rejoicing in the streets because the old festive culture of 'Merrie England' had returned.[32]

The failure of the Puritans did not spell the end of the evangelical Protestant vision of the state as a moralizing force. Campaigns for the reformation of manners received a new lease of life in the 1690s, and continued to attract Evangelicals thereafter. Like their Puritan forbears, eighteenth- and nineteenth-century Evangelicals often urged political authorities to clamp down on sexual immorality, sabbath-breaking and drunkenness.[33] In the United States, many Evangelicals moved from supporting voluntary temperance campaigns to promoting a coercive government policy of prohibition. But in the 1920s, the attempt to enforce morality backfired, and the Prohibition experiment was eventually ended.

Several decades later, in the 1960s, a wave of liberalizing legislation on abortion, divorce, censorship and homosexuality re-ignited evangelical protests, which were orchestrated by the Nationwide Festival of Light. The new permissiveness clashed with the evangelical passion for godliness and moral purity. Here too, vigorous Christian campaigning failed to reverse the tide of government legislation or contemporary mores, though they did give birth to important lobbying organizations like CARE.

Evangelical morality campaigns have tried to tackle real problems in society, such as male alcoholism, violent sports, and pornography. But they have often had unintended consequences. They have produced the stereotype of the evangelical Protestant as a puritanical killjoy - one recalls Lord Macaulay's quip that Puritans were opposed to bear baiting not because it inflicted pain on the animal, but because it gave pleasure to the spectators. Although Evangelicalism is a religion of grace, its morality campaigns have made people think of it as a religion of law. This was not helped by the fact that Evangelicals sometimes lost a sense of moral proportion, becoming obsessed with swearing or drunkenness but remaining indifferent to racism or poverty. Moreover, it is hard to deny that Evangelicals have often expected too much of the state, and too much of their fellow citizens. There has been a utopian strain in evangelical campaigning, a rather odd sense that sin can be conquered with a few good laws. Sometimes Evangelicals need a dose of Augustinian realism.

---

[32] See C. Durston, *Cromwell's Major-Generals: Godly Government during the English Revolution* (Manchester: MUP, 2001).
[33] See Bebbington, *Evangelicalism in Modern Britain*, 134-5.

But Evangelicals would be mistaken if they just gave up on their moral critique of contemporary society. In our pluralistic, postmodern society, where moral discourse has become so fragmented, it is tempting to drop the whole idea of public ethics, and adopt an essentially sectarian posture. But the example of the early church suggests that we should be reluctant to do so. Early Christian apologists also wrote in a pluralistic context, but they still believed that it was possible to engage in moral dialogue with pagans. As Markus Bockmuehl points out, 'Christianity inherited from the Old Testament and Judaism the tradition of an international morality on the basis of which ethical discourse was possible', and the early Christians were convinced that certain basic principles of right and wrong would be 'recognized by cultured peoples everywhere'. These included: (1) respect for God, (2) respect for life, and (3) commitment to sexual morality. These universal ethical principles were drawn from the Noachide Code of Genesis 9, but could also be found in Stoic natural law ethics, and the apologists recommended them to the pagans on the grounds that they fostered a truly humane way of life.[34]

In today's climate, it may be more difficult to get non-Christians to agree on these principles, but Bockmuehl argues that we can learn much from the early Christian apologists:

> We will realize that part of Christian public ethics involves the intelligent criticism of pagan morality, not in a merely judgmental vein but by appealing to the very same principles which the best of pagan moral philosophy itself affirms. The chief emphasis, as for the early Christians, should probably fall on the criticism of three aspects of modern life: idolatry, i.e. all that claims ultimate significance for that which does not have it; illicit sex, which cheapens commitment and thus destroys the very integrity of our essential human relatedness; and "blood offences" of violence and disrespect for human and animal life. Our task is to present these errors in terms which a pagan society can understand and acknowledge. But above all, Christians will embody a living and publicly visible alternative, which carries its own persuasive power. They will not be ghetto dwellers but public witnesses of the liberating and humanizing effect of the gospel in every area of life.[35]

What this means in political terms is open to debate. We need to bear in mind the distinction between the *moral* and the *legal*. Not everything that is morally wrong should be criminalized, and the mixed record of Christian attempts to enforce morality against the popular will suggests the need for caution and discernment. But neither should we buy into the contemporary liberal notion that the state should be morally neutral between alternative

---

[34] M. Bockmuehl, 'Public ethics in a pluralistic world? Lessons from the early church', *Crux*, September 1992, 2-9.

[35] Bockmuehl, 'Public ethics in a pluralistic world?', 9.

versions of the good life. The Catholic natural law theorist Robert George has mounted an impressive critique of contemporary liberalism, and a reasoned defence of morals legislation.[36] Evangelicals may question his optimism about reason or his opposition to contraception, but in many ways his arguments stand in the best tradition of the early Christian apologists. Christians do have a responsibility to bear witness to high moral ideals in a culture that is often allergic to them. We do this primarily in our churches, where we 'embody a living and publicly visible alternative'. But Christian witness on ethical issues will also involve public debate and political campaigning.

The welfare state

The moral agenda of evangelical Protestant politics has often been criticized as hard and punitive. But there was also a tender and compassionate side to Protestant activism. A just state would not only punish the immoral, it would also be concerned for the *welfare* of the poor and the outcast. Here Evangelicals were once again guided by Scripture, which repeatedly taught the Israelite community to provide for the poor and the alien, and condemned those who oppressed the weak. Bono, lead singer of the rock band U2 and campaigner for Third World debt relief, is fond of saying that the Bible contains 2103 verses about the poor.[37] One could argue about the statistic, but the overwhelming biblical emphasis on caring for the poor is impossible to deny.

In the Reformation era, many Protestants believed that caring for the poor was a responsibility of political authorities as well as individual Christians. The town of Dorchester had a good claim to be the most Puritan town in England in the early 17th-century. As David Underdown has shown in his marvellous study, *Fire from Heaven*, Dorchester's Puritan governors combined the tough and the tender, discipline and care. On the one hand, their 'relentless pursuit of drunkards, fornicators, sabbath-breakers and masterless people' reflected their desire for 'a sober, godly and disciplined population'. But on the other hand, 'Dorchester's reformers also showed a striking concern for relieving the deserving poor; for feeding, clothing, and educating their children; for providing shelter for the elderly and fuel for the indigent'. They raised extraordinary sums in order to establish a hospital, a school, and almshouses. Underdown suggests that under the Puritans Dorchester became a mini-welfare state.[38]

---

[36] Robert George, *Making Men Moral* (Oxford: OUP, 1995); *In Defence of Natural Law* (Oxford: OUP, 2001); *The Clash of Orthodoxies* (Wilmington, DE: ISI Books, 2001).
[37] See Cathleen Falsani, 'Bono's American prayer', *Christianity Today*, March 2003, 43.
[38] David Underdown, *Fire from Heaven: Life in an English Town in the Seventeenth Century* (London: HarperCollins, 1992), 108.

The evangelical belief that political authorities could promote human welfare flourished once again in the nineteenth century, when Wilberforce, Shaftesbury and a host of lesser-known figures campaigned against slavery, child labour and other evils. These Evangelicals believed that by lobbying Parliament they could put a stop to particular social evils and create a more humane civilization. In his great speech to Parliament in 1789 on 'reparation to Africa', Wilberforce talked about both the *iniquity* and the *inhumanity* of slavery:

> Let us put an end at once to this inhuman traffic - let us stop this effusion of human blood...Wherever the sun shines, let us go round the world with him [the African], diffusing our beneficence; but let us not traffic...setting millions of our fellow-creatures a-hunting each other for slaves, creating fairs and markets for human flesh, through one whole continent of the world, and, under the name of policy, concealing from ourselves all the baseness and iniquity of such a traffic.[39]

Wilberforce and his allies pioneered a new style of passionate ethical campaigning in politics that is alive and well two centuries later, as the Jubilee 2000 Campaign for global debt relief has demonstrated. Arguably, this model of campaigning - with its crusading zeal and mass lobbying - has been one of the most important legacies of the evangelical movement to secular politics.

But if national campaigns still have their place, local cooperation between government and church-based charities may be just as fruitful in coming decades. The Welfare State established in Britain after 1945 was partly inspired by Christian concern for the poor and the needy, but it also confirmed that the state had replaced the church as the main dispenser of welfare in western societies. However, as the Christian MP Stephen Timms has observed, there are growing signs of a fresh partnership between the state and faith-based charities inspired by a 'new Christian activism'. He cites the work of an employment project in south London (Pecan: Peckham Evangelical Churches Action Network), a homelessness project in Edinburgh (Bethany Trust), and a drug misuse project in north London (Victory Outreach). These projects are rooted in the life of local churches, but they have also forged productive alliances with government that benefit some of the most vulnerable people in our society.[40] They stand in a venerable Christian tradition of social concern, and remind us that the church can prompt the state to provide for human welfare.

---

[39] Brian Macarthur (ed.), *The Penguin Book of Historic Speeches* (London: Penguin, 1996), 135-6.

[40] Stephen Timms' Tawney lecture can be found on the website of the Movement for Christian Democracy: <http://www.mcdpolitics.org>

The liberal democratic state

For all its benevolent achievements, Evangelicalism can still provoke suspicion and even trepidation. Its critics sometimes talk as if it is a monolithic movement bearing down upon the ungodly and endangering *liberal democracy*. The successes of the American Christian Right, for example, appear profoundly threatening to the secular left, and have even inspired a classic dystopian novel by Margaret Atwood. *The Handmaid's Tale* (1985) conjured up a liberal nightmare - a patriarchal, puritanical 'Republic of Gilead' run by biblicist zealots in North America. Academic surveys of the political opinions of ordinary American Evangelicals reveal a far less lurid and more complex reality.[41] Evangelicals in the US are politically diverse. There are major differences, for example, between white Evangelicals (a majority of whom lean towards the Republican party), and black Evangelicals (who remain overwhelmingly Democrat). If George W. Bush is a self-confessed Evangelical, so was Jimmy Carter. And only a minority of right-wing Evangelicals embrace the theocratic agenda associated with the Christian Reconstructionists.

Moreover, historically evangelical Protestants have helped to create liberal democratic polities. We have already noted that Calvinist resistance theory contributed to the foundations of modern political thought. And although the great seventeenth-century debates over religious toleration deeply divided English Puritans, radical Protestant tolerationists did sow the seeds of later liberalism. Baptists and other radical Puritans provided much of the leadership and rank-and-file support of the Levellers, who have some claim to be the first modern liberal democrats.[42] As the historian David Wootton explains:

> The Levellers are the first modern political movement organized around the idea of popular sovereignty. They are the first democrats who think in terms, not of participatory self-government within a city-state, but of representative government within a nation-state. They are the first who want a written constitution in order to protect the rights of the citizen against the State. The first with a modern conception of which rights should be inalienable: the right to silence...and to legal representation; the right to freedom of conscience and freedom of debate; the right to equality before the law and freedom of trade; the right to vote and, when faced with tyranny, to revolution. The Levellers are thus not merely the first modern democrats, but the first to seek to construct a liberal State.[43]

---

[41] See Christian Smith, *Christian America? What Evangelicals Really Want* (Berkeley/London: University of California Press, 2000).

[42] For a good anthology, see Andrew Sharp (ed.), *The English Levellers* (Cambridge: CUP, 1998).

[43] David Wootton, 'The Levellers', in John Dunn (ed.), *Democracy: The Unfinished Journey* (Oxford: OUP, 1992), 71.

Although the Levellers were a political failure in their own day, their goals were largely realized in nineteenth-century Britain, when once again dissenting Protestants and other Christians were actively involved in the promotion of liberal politics.[44]

The Christian roots of 'early modern liberalism' have been highlighted by Oliver O'Donovan. O'Donovan realizes that Christians cannot simply dismiss 'the liberal achievement', not least because it embodies so much Christian wisdom about freedom, merciful judgement, natural right and openness to speech.[45] As he explains:

> The liberal tradition...has right of possession. There is no other model available to us of a political order derived from a millennium of close engagement between State and Church. It ought, therefore, to have the first word in any discussion of what Christians can approve, even if it ought not to have the last word.[46]

However, like many Evangelicals, O'Donovan feels uneasy over 'late modern liberalism', with its radical stress on individual autonomy and its apparent hostility to moral communities.[47] The Chief Rabbi Jonathan Sacks has also lamented the shift from earlier 'liberalism' to contemporary 'libertarianism', and Evangelicals could learn much from his thoughtful diagnosis of our current ills and his prescription for future recovery.[48] As the human costs of permissiveness and individualism become clearer, Evangelicals will need to think hard about realistic and practical policies that can repair the damage and rebuild relationships and communities.[49] And we will have to learn to critique the excesses of contemporary liberalism, whilst holding on to the very real achievements of the liberal tradition.[50]

---

[44] See the work of two evangelical historians: Eugenio Biagini, *Liberty, Retrenchment and Reform: Popular Liberalism in the Age of Gladstone* (Cambridge: CUP, 1992); Timothy Larsen, *Friends of Religious Equality: Nonconformist Politics in Mid-Victorian England* (Woodbridge: Boydell Press, 1999).

[45] O'Donovan, *The Desire of the Nations*, 250-71.

[46] O'Donovan, *The Desire of the Nations*, 77.

[47] O'Donovan, *The Desire of the Nations*, 271-84.

[48] Jonathan Sacks, *The Politics of Hope* (London: Random House, 1997). Robert George, *The Clash of Orthodoxies*, makes a similar distinction between a 'conservative liberalism' and a radical secular liberalism.

[49] Some of the most interesting Christian proposals have emanated from the Jubilee Centre and the Relationships Foundation. See their websites: <http://www.jubilee-centre.org/>; <http://www.relationshipsfoundation.org>

[50] For evangelical engagements with liberalism see: Jonathan Chaplin, 'How much cultural and religious pluralism can liberalism tolerate?' in J. Horton (ed.), *Liberalism, Multiculturalism and Toleration* (London: Macmillan, 1993); Paul Marshall,

Politics and the cross

Finally, we must not forget the cross. In his reflections on evangelical politics, the historian Mark Noll has noted that politically active Evangelicals often focus more on the kingly rule of Christ and the restoration of creation than on the cross. Noll warns that 'A Christian politics that forgets the cross, a Christian politics that neglects the realities of redemption, a Christian politics that assumes a God-like stance toward the world - is a Christian politics that has abandoned Christ'. He suggests that the message of the cross has a number of important implications for Christian politics. Most fundamentally, it reminds us that we are sinners saved by grace. This realization shows up the folly of demonizing our enemies or acting as if we were God himself. A politics centred on the cross, writes Noll, 'will display humility, a willingness to question one's own motives, and the expectation that reform of political vision will always be needed because even Christian politics is carried out by individuals who know they are still sinners, however glad they are to be sinners saved by grace'.[51]

'Liberalism, pluralism and Christianity', *Fides et Historia* (1989), 4-17; Julian Rivers, 'Liberal constitutionalism and Christian political thought', in Beaumont (ed.), *Christian Perspectives on the Limits of Law*; Song, *Christianity and Liberal Society*.
[51] Mark Noll, 'Evangelical Politics: A Better Way', in his *American Evangelical Christianity* (Oxford: Blackwell, 2001), ch. 10.

7. Church, Society and State: Romans 13 in Evangelical Practice

David Hilborn

Evangelicals and the debate about the state

Sooner or later, Christians who are serious about social transformation must work out their relationship to the state. They had to so in the early church, as they lived and worshipped under a pagan Roman Empire. Momentously, they had to so again in the fourth century, as that empire turned from antagonist to sponsor under the patronage of Constantine. Arguments about this Constantinian legacy abound today - not least in the United Kingdom. Not only is there disagreement about how far British society can still be called 'Christian'; opinion is also deeply divided on whether such institutionalization of the gospel was a good thing in the first place. Echoing the critique levelled by D. L. Munby against T. S. Eliot's *Idea of a Christian Society* in the early Sixties,[1] robust disavowal of the Constantinian paradigm has entered the mainstream of British theological discourse thanks, among others, to Alistair Kee, Nigel Wright and Alan Kreider.[2] Conversely, while alive to the problems inherent in the Constantinian tradition, Oliver O'Donovan, Paul Avis and Wesley Carr have offered notably more constructive accounts of the 'Christian State', and of its persistence within the civic structures of the UK.[3]

---

[1] D. L. Munby, *The Idea of a Secular Society and Its Significance for Christians* (London: Oxford University Press, 1963). See also Munby's *God and the Rich Society* (New York: Oxford University Press, 1961). Cf. T.S. Eliot, *The Idea of a Christian Society* (London: Faber & Faber, 1939).

[2] Alistair Kee, *Constantine Versus Christ: The Triumph of Ideology* (London: SCM Press, 1982); Nigel Goring Wright, *The Radical Evangelical* (London: SPCK, 1996), 103-119; *Disavowing Constantine* (Carlisle: Paternoster, 2000); Alan Kreider (ed.), *The Origins of Christendom in the West* (Edinburgh: Continuum International Publishing Group - T & T Clark, 2001). Kreider is American, but taught for a number of years in Britain, and published widely on this topic while resident in the UK. Both Kreider and Wright are, however, particularly indebted to the work of the American anabaptists John Howard Yoder and James McLendon Jr.: John Howard Yoder, *Christian Witness to the State* (Newton, Kansas: Faith and Life Press, 1964); *The Politics of Jesus: Behold the Man! Our Victorious Lamb* (Grand Rapids: Eerdmans, 1972; Second Edition published jointly with Paternoster Press of Carlisle, 1994); James Wm. McLendon Jr., *Systematic Theology: Ethics* (Nashville: Abingdon, 1986).

[3] Paul Avis, *Church, State and Establishment* (London: SPCK, 2001; Oliver O'Donovan, *The Desire of the Nations: Rediscovering the Roots of Political Theology* (Cambridge: CUP, 1996); Wesley Carr, 'Crown and People: Reflections on the Spiritual

No doubt this debate bears significantly on the Evangelical Alliance's resolve to foster a 'movement for change' in present-day Britain. Yet I want to suggest that merely 'taking sides' on Constantine will only get us so far. Whatever traces of Constantinianism abide in British culture, the rise of modern secular democracy, with its *de facto* distinctions between church and state power and its pluralist attitude to religion, demands a somewhat more nuanced approach. We may no longer be able to rely on the state actively to promote, and still less to fund, Christian mission as it did in its high Constantinian phase. Neither, however, do we face the violent, state-sponsored persecution meted out to Christians by Constantine's predecessors. As we shall see, more subtle challenges may well come our way, whose apparent benignity could in fact stifle the spread of the gospel where the blood of the early martyrs once seeded it. Still, to equate ourselves too readily with those martyrs and their context both misconstrues our situation in twenty-first century Britain, and insults those many Christians elsewhere today who *are* actually tortured and executed by their governments for daring to follow Christ.[4] Rather, the more religiously 'neutral' civic sphere with which we are now engaged challenges us to cultivate what Lesslie Newbigin called a 'gospel friendly' society by *gradualist* means - that is, through the development of localized social projects and charitable partnerships. David Bebbington and John Wolffe clearly show in their papers for this book that precedents for such projects and partnerships can be traced some way back into British evangelical history - even if applying them to our current milieu might require significant adaptation and revision. Indeed, one of the most salutary lessons to be gleaned from these precedents concerns the need to balance short-term activism with long-term vision and strategy.

As Kathleen Heasman notes in her detailed study of their missions during the Victorian period, British Evangelicals have often failed to match impressive grass roots relief work with grander, more thoroughgoing social programmes.[5] Likewise, John Wolffe has elsewhere pertinently observed of Evangelicals in modern Britain that our engagement with the world has been most typically 'pervasive' but 'unfocused'.[6] The same, incidentally, does not quite apply to the

---

Dimensions of Establishment', Lecture given at Westminster Abbey, 16 September 2002. Text at < http://www.westminster - abbey.org / event / lecture / archives / 020917_jubilee.htm>.

[4] For a chilling record of such modern-day persecution, see Paul Marshall (with Leila Gilbert), *Their Blood Cries Out: The Worldwide Tragedy of Modern Christians Who Are Dying for Their Faith* (Dallas: Word, 1997).

[5] Kathleen Heasman, *Evangelicals in Action: An Appraisal of their Social Work* (London: Geoffrey Bles, 1962), 293.

[6] John Wolffe, 'Introduction', in John Wolffe (ed.), *Evangelical Faith and Public Zeal: Evangelicals and Society in Britain 1780-1980* (London: SPCK), 7.

United States. America was settled by devout Puritans whose successors developed the Christian social doctrine of their nation's 'Manifest Destiny' - a doctrine whose tenets have resurfaced most recently and most obviously in the worldview of the Moral Majority, in the theology known as Reconstructionism, and in the prominent Christian wing of Neo-Conservatism.[7] Having said this, the US Constutution's explicit separation of church and state has meant that in practice, most civic expressions of the Gospel in America have still tended to come through local churches and communities, as part of what James Davison Hunter calls 'voluntarism'.[8]

For Evangelicals on both sides of the Atlantic, such gradualist and voluntarist approaches have reflected a typically moderate theology of the state - a theology framed in response to the relative 'impartiality' of modern western governments towards the church. Yet as the twenty-first century dawns, it would be unwise to view this relationship complacently. Indeed, it is hardly fanciful to suggest that it might soon turn from impartiality to a something rather less accommodating. In his recent study on the decline of Christian allegiance and public influence in the UK, Callum Brown concludes that 'the culture of Christianity has gone in the Britain of the new millennium', and adds that 'Britain is showing the world how religion as we have known it can die'.[9] While the finer points of Brown's analysis may be open to debate, there can be little doubt that the privileged position enjoyed by the church in British life is significantly diminishing. Granted, what is being put in its place in the present political situation is hardly an atheistic or apostate political tyranny; indeed, it is not even particularly secular*ist* in its ideology. Rather, as Prince Charles famously noticed in 1994, it tends towards a pluralization of faith rather than systematic exclusion of 'the Faith'; a willingness to endorse 'faith-based initiatives' rather than 'churches' as such; a diversification of 'faith schools' rather than an outright, French-style ban on state-sponsored religious education.[10]

On one level, this pluralization can be seen as a natural extension of those basic religious liberties which, until at least the late Nineteenth century, were

---

[7] Clifford Longley, *Chosen People: The Big Idea That Shaped England and America* (London: Hodder & Stoughton, 2003).

[8] James Davison Hunter, *American Evangelicalism: Conservative Religion and the Quandary of Modernity* (New Brunswick, NJ: Rutgers University Press, 1983), 25.

[9] Callum Brown, *The Death of Christian Britain* (London: Routledge, 2001), 198.

[10] In an ITV television interview with Jonathan Dimbleby, broadcast on 29 June 1994 under the title 'Charles: The Private Man, The Public Role', the Prince voiced the idea that it might be more appropriate in modern-day, multicultural Britain that he be called 'Defender of Faith' if and when he ascends to the throne, rather than 'Defender of *the* Faith' - namely the Protestant faith of the established Church of England, as defined in the present Coronation Oath.

denied to many Evangelicals in this country – and specifically to those from Nonconformist traditions.[11] Yet as bodies like the Evangelical Alliance seek to deal with such pluralization and prepare to take their place on a growing government guest list of interest groups and 'community organizations', it is worth considering what might happen should the purported even-handedness of this approach come in time to cloak a more sinister disqualification of Evangelicals from the civic sphere. If this does occur, we will almost certainly be ostracized on the grounds that we ourselves reject the philosophical and moral relativism which is presumed to underpin this pluralizing agenda. To extend the metaphor: in a postmodern context, the more the state-as-host deems such things as street evangelism, broadcast sermons and theologically specific employment policies to be 'intolerant' and even 'illegal', the less we will be able to count on its hospitality, or even its protection of our liberties. David Bebbington alludes to this possible shift at the end of his paper for this book, and suggests that we might have seen portents of it in recent laws passed in France and Belgium, designed to restrict the public witness of certain smaller evangelical groups in the name of a 'tolerant', 'multi-cultural' and 'plural' society. Yet there is evidence that the shift is already taking place in Britain.

Recently, the Evangelical Alliance has found it necessary to critique or oppose UK legislation which prejudices its own basic freedoms, and the freedoms of its members, in at least three significant areas. First, we have sought to modify the adoption into law of the European Equal Treatment Directive, which in draft form denied the right of Christian organizations to employ only those who accord with their own stated doctrinal and moral ethos. In particular, this has meant demonstrating the invidiousness of an evangelical charity's being forced to retain a member of staff who is expected to promote marital fidelity and chastity, but who practices, or even comes to advocate, an adulterous or homosexual lifestyle. Second, we have questioned proposed changes to the civil registration of marriages which would eliminate the requirement to record the sex of the two people involved, on the grounds that this might compromise a minister who could not in conscience officiate at a marriage where one partner or another is transsexual. Closely linked with this, we have challenged plans to allow transsexual people to obtain a new birth certificate which conceals their intrinsic biological identity from clergy - and not least from clergy in the Church of England, who are obliged to marry any legally eligible adult within their parish. Third, we have supported the claim of Premier Radio and other Christian broadcasters to national terrestrial licenses, positively on the grounds of their right to free expression, and negatively in opposition to current legislation which in a discriminatory fashion specifically withholds such licenses from religious broadcasters.

---

[11] For an account of these restrictions, and their gradual repeal during this period, see D. W. Bebbington, *The Nonconformist Conscience: Chapel and Politics, 1870-1914* (London: Harper Collins, 1982).

The irony of such cases is that they demonstrate just how illiberal and intolerant certain liberal versions 'tolerance' of can become - most especially when defined according to secular pluralist precepts and legally enforced as such on religious bodies who do not themselves share that definition. The contradictions and dangers inherent in all this have been well noted by Janet Daley. Reflecting on the wider social implications of the consecration of the openly gay bishop Gene Robinson in the Diocese of New Hampshire in November 2003, she writes:

> So far, liberalism has [decreed] religious practice, or the belief in moral absolutes...to be an inherently private matter of conscience. You may believe what you like, follow what rules and proscriptions you choose, in the privacy of your own home (or your own mind) but you must make your peace with the secular State. [But] trickier problems...are emerging now as a result of a more doctrinaire form of liberalism which demands not just tolerance, but absolute equivalence between life choices. This liberalism militant wants not mere acceptance of homosexuals by the Church, but a fully-fledged openly homosexual bishop. Its insistence on the strict equality of life choices has had deep repercussions on our public policy and social fabric. Governments no longer feel that they can favour married couples in the tax and benefit system: single parent families, however much they may be proved to be less stable and beneficial to children, must not be discriminated against. Unmarried couples, not to mention same-sex couples, must be given the same legal status as married ones, even though marriage as an institution has shown itself to be the most robust force for community well-being. And when communities fail, because family networks have broken down, the State must step in and take over their responsibilities. Liberalism has pushed its dogma to a kind of logical conclusion. What it has done by abandoning the tactful fudge in favour of aggressive enforcement of its own code is to expose itself to just the kind of rigorous examination that it cannot afford. By insisting on its gay bishop, by demanding not just tolerance but moral equivalence, it does not just risk a backlash. It threatens to destabilize the ethical edifice on which our imperfect, but reasonably benign, social settlement rests.[12]

When faced with this more militant, intrusive, legally-bolstered brand of state control Evangelicals can draw on an honourable heritage of civil critique, and indeed, of civil disobedience. It is worth reviewing this heritage before considering more specifically how we might respond to the trends which Daley describes.

---

[12] Janet Daley, '"Gay" Bishops Threaten our Foundation', *Daily Telegraph*, 6 November 2003.

Reformation and post-Reformation sources

Article 16 of the Augsburg Confession (1530) may have enshrined Martin Luther's doctrine of the state as a 'second kingdom' ordained by God 'for the sake of good order', and may thereby have insisted that the state is not to be 'overthrown'; but even this most magisterial of Reformation texts still admits an exception for cases in which the civil authority actively coerces Christians to sin. In such cases, says the Article, we must do as Peter and the apostles did in Acts 5:29: we must 'obey God rather than man'.[13]

Like Luther, Zwingli and Calvin both insist that the state is a positive divine 'ordinance'. Calvin, in fact, stresses that it is God's 'minister'.[14] Yet as Eberhard Busch has noted, the Reformed theologians adopted a more radical stance than Luther on the *accountability* of the state to Christian standards and values. In the simplest terms, 'Luther tended toward the idea that the government is God's servant *because and in so far as* it is the *government*. Zwingli and Calvin, on the other hand, tended toward the idea that the government is the government *when and in so far as* it is [or functions as] God's *servant.*'[15] So, for example, Calvin expressly refused to identify the state directly and automatically with God's will, 'as if God had made over his right to mortal men, giving them rule over mankind! Or as if earthly power were diminished when it is subjected to its Author!'[16]

While these divergent emphases are detectable in various modern evangelical concepts of church-state relations - with Luther's influence most obvious in Anglican evangelical defences of Establishment and Calvin and Zwingli fuelling the public theologies of Newbigin and a Dutch Reformed school shaped by the thought of Abraham Kuyper[17] - it is probably fair to say

---

[13] 'The Augsburg Confession, 1530: Article 16 - Civil Government', in Charles Villa-Vicencio (ed.), *Between Christ and Caesar: Classic and Contemporary Texts on Church and State* (Grand Rapids: Eerdmans, 1986), 47.

[14] Ulrich Zwingli, *Von göttlicher und menschlicher Gerechtigkeit*, in *Zwingli Haupscriften*, 8 vols., ed. Fritz Blanke, Oskar Farner and Rudolph Pfister (Zurich: Zwingli-Verlag, 1948), 7: 74ff.; John Calvin, *Institutes of the Christian Religion, Volume 2*, ed. John T. McNeill, trans. Ford Lewis Battles (Philadelphia: The Westminster Press, 1960), 4.XX.4, 1489-90.

[15] Eberhard Busch, 'Church and Politics in the Reformed Tradition', in Donald K. McKim (ed.), *Major Themes in the Reformed Tradition*, (Grand Rapids: Eerdmans, 1992), 184.

[16] John Calvin, *Ezechiel und Daniel*, in *Auslegung der Heiligen Schrift*, 9 vols., ed. Otto Weber (Neukirchen: Neukirchener Verlag, 1938), 9: 385.

[17] Paul Avis, *Church, State and Establishment* (London: SPCK, 2001); Wesley Carr, 'Crown and People: Reflections on the Spiritual Dimensions of Establishment', Lecture given at Westminster Abbey, 16 September 2002. Text available online at <

that among western Evangelicals today another, more radical paradigm is gaining most ground. This has its roots not in the magisterial Reformers, but in the Anabaptists, and is closely related to that disavowal of the Constantine which I mentioned earlier.

Anabaptist theology and ethics find seminal expression in the Schleitheim Confession of 1527. Here, the general problem of church-state relations is crystallized in the specific question of whether it is right for a Christian to serve as a magistrate. To this question, for the reasons I have cited, Luther, Calvin and Zwingli would have replied 'Yes'. Schleitheim's clear response, however, is 'No'. The reasons given are as follows

> The government magistracy is according to the flesh, but the Christians' is according to the Spirit; their houses and dwelling remain in this world, but the Christians' are in heaven; the weapons of their conflict and war are carnal and against the flesh only, but the Christians' weapons are spiritual, against the fortification of the devil.[18]

To many twenty-first century Evangelicals steeped in the theology of social involvement this may well seem wildly dualistic - but Anabaptism cannot fairly be accused of 'otherworldliness', if by that is meant a deliberate withdrawal from society and community. Rather, its goal was to constitute the church as an *alternative society* - a *distinctive community* which through separation from the state and its power-structures would free itself to bear witness to that state and, where necessary, oppose it on Christian grounds.

Represented most influentially in modern times by the Americans John Howard Yoder, Walter Wink, James McLendon and Stanley Hauerwas,[19] and in

---

http://www.westminster-abbey.org/event/lecture/archives/020917_jubilee.htm>; John Habgood, *Church and Nation in a Secular Age* (London: SPCK, 1983); David Holloway, *Church and State in the New Millennium* (London: Harper Collins, 2000); Oliver O'Donovan, *The Desire of the Nations: Rediscovering the Roots of Political Theology* (Cambridge: CUP, 1996); Cf. Lesslie Newbigin, *The Gospel in a Pluralist Society* (London: SPCK, 1989); *Truth to Tell: The Gospel as Public Truth* (Grand Rapids: Eerdmans, 1991); Abraham Kuyper, *Lectures on Calvinism* (Grand Rapids: Eerdmans, 1943); Luis E. Lugo (ed.), *Religion, Pluralism, and Public Life: Abraham Kuyper's Legacy for the Twenty-first Century* (Grand Rapids: Eerdmans, 2000); John Bolt, *A Free Church, a Holy Nation: Abraham Kuyper's American Public Theology* (Grand Rapids: Eerdmans, 2001).

[18] 'The Schleitheim Confession', in Villa-Vicencio, *Between Christ and Caesar*, 73.

[19] Yoder, *The Politics of Jesus*; Walter Wink, *Naming the Powers: The Language of Power in the New Testament* (Philadelphia: Fortress Press, 1984); *Unmasking the Powers: The Invisible Forces that Determine Human Existence* (Philadelphia: Fortress Press, 1986); *Engaging the Powers: Discernment and Resistance in a World of*

the UK by Nigel Wright, Stuart Murray Williams and the Anabaptist Network,[20] the influence of this Anabaptist paradigm is shown in the fact that by no means all who propound it are themselves members of historic Anabaptist communities. As articulated in Yoder's now classic treatise *The Politics of Jesus*, this model self-consciously rejects what it sees as the overly compliant orientation of the church towards the state in classical Protestantism.[21] Instead, it advocates renunciation of what Yoder calls the 'interplay of egoisms' so often represented by the state, and most distinctively demonstrates its critical distance from government in its fundamental commitment to pacifism. As Yoder expresses it,

> The place of government in the providential designs of God are [sic] not such that our duty would be simply to do whatever it says ... The claims of Caesar are to be measured by whether what he claims is due to him is part of the obligation to love. Love in turn is...defined by the fact that it does no harm. In this context, it therefore becomes impossible to maintain that [our relationship to the State] can include a moral obligation under certain circumstances to do harm to others at the behest of government.[22]

Now it is significant that Yoder's words here form part of a lengthy discussion of a specific biblical text - a text which, more than any other, has exercised theologians across and beyond the spectrum of Evangelicalism on the questions of whether, when and how a Christian might oppose, protest against and disobey the state. As we have seen, these questions are more than merely hypothetical for British Evangelicals today, and they need to be considered seriously now if we are to prepare for life in a potentially more hostile civic sphere. The text in question is Romans 13:1-7, and no consideration of church-state relations, or parachurch-state relations, can get very far without addressing it. In the New Revised Standard Version, it reads as follows:

> [1] Let every person be subject to the governing authorities; for there is no authority except from God, and those authorities that exist have been instituted by God. [2]Therefore whoever resists authority resists what God has appointed, and those

Domination, Philadelphia: Fortress Press, 1992); James C. McLendon, *Systematic Theology, Vol. 1: Ethics* (Nashville: Abingdon Press, 1986); Stanley Hauerwas, *A Community of Character: Toward a Constructive Christian Social Ethic* (University of Notre Dame Press, 1988); Stanley Hauerwas & William H. Willimon, *Resident Aliens: Life in the Christian Colony* (Abingdon Press, 1989).

[20] Nigel Goring Wright, *Disavowing Constantine: Mission, Church and the Social Order in the Theologies of John Howard Yoder and Jürgen Moltmann*, Carlisle: Paternoster Press, 2000; Stuart Murray (latterly Murray Williams), *Biblical Interpretation in the Anabaptist Tradition* (Ontario: Pandora Press, 2000); Anabaptist Network website: <http://www.anabaptistnetwork.com>

[21] Yoder, *The Politics of Jesus*, 193-94.

[22] Yoder, *The Politics of Jesus*, 208.

who resist will incur judgment. [3] For rulers are not a terror to good conduct, but to bad. Do you wish to have no fear of the authority? Then do what is good, and you will receive its approval; [4] for it is God's servant for your good. But if you do what is wrong, you should be afraid, for the authority does not bear the sword in vain! It is the servant of God to execute wrath on the wrongdoer. [5] Therefore one must be subject, not only because of wrath but also because of conscience. [6] For the same reason you also pay taxes, for the authorities are God's servants, busy with this very thing. [7] Pay to all what is due them - taxes to whom taxes are due, revenue to whom revenue is due, respect to whom respect is due, honour to whom honour is due.

Luther, Calvin and Zwingli's discussions of the state have this text prominently in view, as do all the more recent sources I have cited. It is particularly pertinent for Evangelicals in early twenty-first century Britain, as we contemplate what it might mean to live with integrity in a state whose attitudes, actions and laws might increasingly diverge from our most basic convictions.

More specifically, it will be helpful to examine how Christians on the ground in three especially challenging contexts during the past century interpreted Paul's words to the Romans. I do not pretend that these three examples are exactly comparable to what British Evangelicals might face in the coming years. Indeed, the situations in question are surely much graver than anything we might dare envisage for the UK during our lifetimes. Yet I would suggest that they can still function as case studies for this whole subject – templates from which we can derive certain core principles, even if the precise tactics deployed in each instance may not be so obviously transferable.

The examples in question are: Germany under Nazism, Eastern Europe under Communism, and South Africa under Apartheid. As we consider each in turn, it will be salutary to bear in mind that Hitler rose to power in a highly pluralized, democratic political climate, having exploited the proliferation of parties, and the consequent dissipation of authority, which pertained in the Germany of the 1930s. It will be salutary, too, to bear in mind that Communism was founded on a mass 'democratic' ideal. It will also be worth remembering that Apartheid arose from a devout, biblically literate, but woefully misguided ideal of Christian governance and the godly state.

Romans 13 in cultural and canonical context

In seeking a biblical understanding of church-state relations, we do not come to Scripture in a vacuum. Whether consciously or not, we approach this subject against a tradition of political-philosophical thinking which stretches from

Plato, through Thomas More, Thomas Hobbes and John Locke, to modern scholars such as Kenneth Dyson and Robert Nozick. For our purposes here, however, Peter Goodrich's definition provides a useful signpost. The state, writes Goodrich, may be described as 'The political organization of a body of people for the maintenance of order within its territory by coercion, or, more loosely, the body of people so organized or its territory.'[23] The organizational principle which lies at the heart of this definition goes hand in hand with what we have come to call 'government', while the territorial principle relates closely to the concept 'nationhood'.

Although the biblical narrative does not present anything quite as compressed or refined as this definition, there are a number of texts which could be construed as pointing to the role of the state in the providence God (e.g. Judg. 9; 1 Sam. 7:7-12; 1 Kgs. 12; 21; Lk. 4:6-7; Mk. 1:13ff; Tit. 3:1; 1 Tim. 2:1-2). While it is far from easy to construct a definitive political theology from such references, it does appear that once Israel is constituted as a nation, some fairly consistent principles for governance emerge. These may be identified under the general heading of 'public stewardship'. Furthermore, it is crucial for us to note from the outset that where such principles are flouted, they are seen to warrant legitimate prophetic dissent. Such principles include the fair distribution of wealth (Lev. 19:9-10; 23:22; 25:1ff; Deut. 24:19-22; Prov. 31:8-9; cf. Amos 5:11ff; Isa. 58:6-14), the restraint and just punishment of crime (Ex. 21:12-36; Num. 35:16-34; Deut. 19:1-13; Jos. 20:1-9; cf. Ezk. 18:10ff.) and the protection of aliens (Ex. 12:48-9, 22:21, 23:9; Lev. 19:33-4; Deut. 1:16; 24:14, 17; cf. Ezk. 22:29; Mal. 3:5).

Written against the backdrop of a hostile Roman Empire, the New Testament more consistently addresses the dilemmas faced by believers whose whole value-system may diverge radically from that of their political rulers. Jesus' stark contrast between prevailing Gentile government and the government of God's kingdom (Matt 20:20-5), coupled with his decidedly qualified acknowledgement of Caesar (Mark 12:13ff), and his robust response to Pontius Pilate (Jn 18:33-7), suggest at the very least a cautious and critical view of the state.

Given the 'hermeneutic of suspicion' implicit in such texts, it must be conceded that Paul appears strikingly conservative by comparison (Titus 3:1). He may have suffered under Rome (2 Cor. 11:23), but he also took pride in his Roman citizenship, and was not averse to displaying it as a badge of authenticity (Acts 16:35-40; 22:22-9). Nowhere, however, is this apparent conservatism more apparent, nor more thoroughly expounded, than in Romans

---

[23] Peter Goodrich, 'state, the', in Ted Hoderich (ed.), *The Oxford Companion to Philosophy* (Oxford/New York: Oxford University Press, 1995), 850.

13:1-7.

Exegetical issues

Paul's advice on relating to government and state in Romans 13 has aroused deep passions among biblical critics. J.C. O'Neill wrote in 1975 that 'These seven verses have caused more unhappiness and misery in the Christian East and West than any other seven verses in the New Testament'. Indeed, he refused to believe that they could be Pauline, or even Christian, and attributed them instead to a Stoic source.[24] James Kallas was less dismissive, but still regarded them as an interpolation.[25] On the other hand, after careful consideration, Ernst Käsemann concluded that there was 'no reason to dispute the authenticity of the text'.[26] Käsemann's grounds for this judgment resemble those given by the majority of other commentators who reckon that Paul's words can be fitted logically into the context of the letter:

First, there is the obvious point that Rome was the capital city of the empire, and that Paul would probably have felt a special obligation to comment on the church-state dynamic when addressing the Christians there.[27]

Second, although the 'interpolation' theory is rendered plausible by a tonal link between 12:21 and 13:8, it is just as likely that Paul discusses civil government here precisely to qualify the prohibition on private vengeance expressed in the preceding verses (12:17-21). This is to say, while *individuals* should not 'repay evil for evil', Paul is nonetheless keen to underline the responsibility of *government* for the trial and punishment of crime (especially in vv. 3-4).[28]

Third, Marcus Borg, Everett Harrison and Leon Morris all seriously entertain the idea that Paul is here trying to restrain the radical theocratic tendencies of certain Jews within the Roman congregation. One strand of Israelite tradition had undoubtedly refused to acknowledge *any* pagan ruler (Deut 17:15). Jewish Christians in Rome might have cited recent oppression by the Emperor Claudius as reason enough to adopt such a stance (cf. Acts

---

[24] J.C. O' Neill, *Paul's Letter to the Romans* (Baltimore: Penguin, 1975), 209.

[25] James Kallas, 'Romans 13:1-7: An Interpolation', *New Testament Studies* XI (1964-5), 365-74.

[26] Ernst Käsemann, *Commentary on Romans*. London: SCM, 1980, 351.

[27] Käsemann, 350; C.E.B Cranfield, *A Shorter Commentary on Romans* (Edinburgh: T&T Clark, 1976), 322; Leon Morris, *The Epistle to the Romans* (Grand Rapids: Eerdmans, 1988), 457-58.

[28] On this point see Morris, *The Epistle to the Romans*, 457.

18:2). It might even be that a militant group has adopted a strategy similar to that of the Palestinian Zealots, and that Paul is here seeking to dissuade them from outright revolutionary action against the authorities.[29] It would seem that he does this mainly from a conviction that such action would detract from the church's evangelistic imperative (11:14ff.; cf. 1 Tim 2:1ff.).

Fourth, given Paul's earlier attack on antinomianism (7:7-25 cf. 14:13), and his commitment to structure and stability in the church (1 Cor. 11:3ff), it is not entirely surprising that he might want to extend his defence of 'good order' into the more general realm of state authority.[30]

Fifth, it is conceivable that Paul is providing an extended commentary on the saying of Jesus which would become "Render unto Caesar that which is Caesar's" (Mk. 12:17). The common background of debt and tax (vv 6-7) supports this inference.[31]

These may be sound reasons to take Paul's words seriously within their immediate context, but we still need to consider more specifically how those words might have been intended by Paul, and how they might have been understood by those to whom he was writing. For our purposes, it will suffice to highlight a few core terms - terms which illustrate the main issues arising from the text as a whole.

Key terms in the passage

Everyone (pasa psychē, v.1). There is considerable disagreement among commentators as to how widely the apostle's teaching is meant to be applied. Some see *pasa psychē* here denoting 'all people everywhere' - a reading inferred from the fact that Paul goes on in a universalizing vein to insist that 'there is no authority except that which God has established'.[32] Others confine the meaning of this phrase to 'every believer', given that the principles of submission Paul proceeds to espouse would only have made sense to those who had themselves submitted to Christ and to one another as Christians.[33] Others confine the meaning of the text simply to 'every Christian in Rome', on the

---

[29] Marcus Borg, 'A New Context for Romans XIII', *New Testament Studies*, XIX (1972-3), 205-18; Everett Harrison, *Expositors' Bible Commentary: Romans* (Grand Rapids: Zondervan, 1976), 136. Morris, *The Epistle to the Romans*, 458.

[30] Käsemann, *Commentary on Romans*, 357.

[31] Käsemann, *Commentary on Romans*, 352; Cranfield, *A Shorter Commentary on Romans*, 324.

[32] Morris, *The Epistle to the Romans*, 460.

[33] Harrison, *Expositors' Bible Commentary: Romans*, 36.

grounds that Paul is addressing the very specific and very volatile situation in that city following the Emperor Claudius' persecution.[34]

Submit (hypotassesthō, v1). This is probably the most crucial word in the whole passage. Does submission mean acceptance of every state policy, or is there room for dissent? If dissent is possible, when exactly does it become legitimate? Among all but the most conservative scholars, there is at least agreement that submission must mean more than mere uncritical 'subjection' or 'obedience'. A form of this same verb is used in 1 Corinthians 16:16 and Ephesians 5:21, where it denotes the reciprocal accountability of believers to one another in a Christian fellowship. Obedience, by contrast, cannot be reciprocal! Cranfield thus broadly represents the mainstream when he states that 'Paul is enjoining…no uncritical obedience to whatever command the civil authority may decide to give, but the recognition that one has been placed below the authority of God'. Cranfield goes on to stress that 'the Christian's "subjection" to the authorities is limited to respecting them, obeying them in so far as such obedience does not conflict with God's laws, and seriously and responsibly disobeying them when it does'.[35] This is, of course, extrapolating somewhat from the text itself. Still, most serious critics echo Luther and the Augsburg Confession in citing the obvious Acts 5:29 as corroboration for such a view.[36] Quite *when* or *how* a civil authority might be deemed to have forfeited God's mandate remains, however, a moot point.

Servant (diakonos, v4). The key issue here is whether the interpretative emphasis is placed: a) on the fact that servants are authoritatively *appointed* and *empowered* for certain tasks, or b) whether they are *accountable* and *subject* as servants to the one who engaged them. In either case, Morris is right to infer from Paul that civil authority is delegated by, and secondary to, divine authority.[37] Even so, the distinction remains vital when Christians seek to decide exactly how much a state should be allowed to 'get away with'. If they lean towards interpretation a), they may be more inclined to give the state the benefit of the doubt; if b), they may be inclined to adopt a more consistently critical or 'prophetic' line. Sure enough, Acts 5:29, together with Acts 4:19-20 and (maybe) 1 Peter 2:17b would suggest that the servant state should be challenged when it suppresses the public proclamation of the gospel. But are there not also less blatant reasons for Christians to rebel? Käsemann is right to point out that not even the proclamation issue was an immediate worry for the

---

[34] Cranfield, *A Shorter Commentary on Romans*, 320; Käsemann, *Commentary on Romans*, 355.

[35] Cranfield, *A Shorter Commentary on Romans*, 321.

[36] E.g. Harrison, *Expositors' Bible Commentary: Romans*, 136; Morris, *The Epistle to the Romans*, 462.

[37] Morris, *The Epistle to the Romans*, 463-64.

Romans: Claudius may have left things rather tense, but he had gone, and Nero had not yet come. This may be why Paul so glaringly fails to address 'the exception that the community must not let itself be forced to offend against...its own Christianity'.[38] It is probably also the main reason why Romans 13 has caused so much anxiety and disagreement in the church down to our own day - anxiety and disagreement which are starkly apparent in the three case studies to which we shall now turn.

Paradigmatic applications of the text: three examples

1. The German church under Hitler

The resistance of the Confessing Church to Hitler's regime, and to the so-called 'German Christians' who had colluded with that regime in such vast numbers, is summed up theologically in the famous Barmen Declaration of 1934.[39] By his own admission, the Barmen text was largely the work of Karl Barth.[40] The Declaration itself does not explicitly refer to Romans 13 - but interpretation of Paul's teaching, and critique of its abuse by the German Christians, are implicit throughout. Barth, however, would later publish an extensive reflection on Barmen under the title 'The Christian Community and the Civil Community' (1954).[41] Here he does deal with Romans 13 in some depth.

Echoing the exegetical debate about 'obedience' mentioned above, the Declaration makes it clear from the outset that 'Jesus Christ is the one Word of God whom we have to...trust and obey in life and in death'. It then rejects as a 'false doctrine' the teaching that 'the church could and should recognize as a source of its proclamation, beyond and besides this one Word of God, yet other events, powers, historic figures and truths, as God's revelation'. This, in effect, is a highlighting of Paul's implication in Romans 13:1 that civil authority is derived from, and so subject to, divine authority. Barth's text then cites Matthew 20:25-6 in condemning the planned appointment by the German Christians of 'Reich Bishops' as politico-religious leaders over a new national state church. It goes on to quote 1 Peter 2:17 when declaring as heresy the view that 'beyond its special commission, the church should and could take on the nature, tasks and dignity which belong to the state and thus become itself an organ of the state'.

---

[38] Käsemann, *Commentary on Romans*, 357.
[39] 'The Barmen Declaration', in Clifford Green (ed.) *Karl Barth: Theologian of Freedom*. London: Collins, 1989 pp. 148-51.
[40] Eberhard Busch, *Karl Barth* (London: SCM, 1976), 245.
[41] Karl Barth, 'The Christian Community and the Civil Community', in Green *Karl Barth: Theologian of Freedom*, 265-96.

In his later reflection, Barth sets the radical cadences of Barmen in a fuller context - a context which takes at face value Paul's proposition that the state is established by God to fulfil his purposes. Hence with reference to Rom 13:1b, Barth can insist that 'however much human error and human tyranny may be involved in it, the state is not a product of sin but one of the constants of the divine Providence and government of the world in its action against sin'.[42] The same concept of a godly institution which may fall into sin without becoming *intrinsically* sinful also informs Barth's exposition of the 'servant' motif in verses 4 and 6:

> The activity of the state is, as the apostle stated, a form of divine service. As such it can be perverted just as the divine service of the church itself is not exempt from the possibility of perversion. The state can assume the face and character of Pilate. Even then, however, it still acts in the power which God has given it ("Thou couldst have no power at all against me, if it were not given to you from above", John 19:11).[43]

Barth goes on to argue that the 'rebellion' against government which Paul attacks in Romans 13:3 must be understood to have a corollary in an equivalent sin of Christian 'indifference' towards the state.[44] Very often, Barth implies, it is just such indifference which masquerades as the 'subjection' of Rom 13:1. Where such misplaced piety occurs, it ought to be exposed - even when it appears in the work of a great Reformer:

> Luther's translation [of this verse] speaks of 'being *subject*', which is something dangerously different from what is meant here. The last thing this instruction implies is that the Christian community and the Christian should offer the blindest possible obedience to the civil community and its officials. What is meant (Rom 13:6f) is that Christians should carry out what is required of them for the establishment, preservation and maintenance of the civil community and for the execution of its task...'sub-ordination' means the carrying out of this *co-responsibility* in which Christians apply themselves to this task with non-Christians and submit themselves to the same rule.[45]

In specific terms, Barth links this 'sub-ordinating' co-responsibility to the faculty of 'conscience' invoked by Paul in Romans 13:5. Responsibly submitting one's conscience to the state can include '*reminding* people of God's Kingdom', and this in turn can entail a humble but dynamic *critique* of civil authorities. Hence, 'The Christian community "sub-ordinates" itself to the

---

[42] Barth, 'The Christian Community and the Civil Community', 271.
[43] Barth, 'The Christian Community and the Civil Community', 271.
[44] Barth, 'The Christian Community and the Civil Community', 272.
[45] Barth, 'The Christian Community and the Civil Community', 273.

civil community by making its knowledge of the Lord who is Lord of all its criterion, and *distinguishing* between the just and the unjust state...between government and tyranny; between freedom and anarchy...between the state as described in Rom. 13 and the state as described in Rev. 13.'[46]

In this analysis, Barmen is presented as a faithful outworking of Romans 13, rather than a challenge to its ethos. Barth certainly bears out his Reformation heritage by 'interpreting Scripture with Scripture' in ways similar to those used by the expositors referred to above: his case is carefully constructed with reference to Matthew 22:21, John 18:36 and 19:11, 1 Timothy 2:1-7 and 1 Peter 2:14. More problematically, however, it must be questioned whether his glossing of 'submission' to the state as first 'sub-ordination', then 'co-responsibility', then 'reminding' and finally 'judging' does not read too much systematic theology back into the original text. Certainly, his hermeneutic might at the very least be described as 'canonical' rather than purely exegetical. Even so, the willingness of Barth to expound so difficult a passage so positively in relation to Barmen and so robustly over against Nazism, bears out his commitment to the Reformation imperative of *sola scriptura,* and offers helpful pointers to British Evangelicals today as we seek to develop responsibly biblical paradigms of witness and resistance in the post-Christian public square.

2. *The Russian Baptist churches under Communism*

In 1960-1 a severe rift opened up in the Russian Baptist community as it debated how best to proceed under Soviet Communism. Although some division had already occurred over the issue of state registration, this had not hitherto affected the common view that Baptist children should be raised and educated within the Baptist fold. However, when the official leadership of the All-Union Council of Evangelical Christians and Baptists (AUCECB) succumbed to new government restrictions on private education, the majority of unregistered churches broke away in protest to establish a Council of Reform Baptists. As Michael Bordeaux has observed, 'the AUCECB appeared to have become an instrument of state policies'.[47] With *Perestroika*, the two communions came closer together, but through the 1960s and '70s, their enmity was very bitter indeed.

In 1965, the AUCECB attempted to mend relations with a letter. In this letter, the AUCECB addressed the Organising Committee of the Reform Baptist Council thus: 'We desire to meet with you and talk about the question

---

[46] Barth, 'The Christian Community and the Civil Community', 276.
[47] Michael Bordeaux, *Gorbachev, Glasnost and the Gospel.* (London: Hodder & Stoughton, 1990), 110.

of reconciliation and the future relations between us'. The response of the Reform Baptists to this approach was uncompromising. They refused categorically to meet with the AUCECB, making clear their conviction that it had 'rejected...the basic principles of Evangelical Christian and Baptist teaching'.[48] As these principles are defined in the Reform Baptists' reply, Romans 13 looms large in their argument.

The Reform Baptists begin by asserting that 'the Teaching of Evangelical Christians and Baptists demands complete separation of the church from the state'. As one might imagine, they quote in defence of this position both John 18:36 and Matthew 22:21. Next, however, they tackle Romans 13 head on, adding to it the same kind of caveat articulated by Barth in relation to Barmen:

> We believe that the powers that be are ordained of God (Rom. 13:1-2), and that he gives them authority to protect the good and punish the evildoer (Rom. 13:3-4). We therefore consider that we must needs be unconditionally subject to their laws (Rom. 13:5-7; Tit. 3:1; 1 Pet. 2:13,14,17) *on condition that these do not restrict our free observance of the duties incumbent upon us as Christians* (Mt. 22:21; Acts 4:19-20; 5:29-42).[49]

The reply continues by refuting the AUCECB's use of John 19:11 to defend accommodation with the atheist Soviet state. It deems Christ's declaration that Pilate's power is 'given from above' to be 'irrelevant to this case'. Furthermore, 'Pilate had the power to crucify Christ, but no-one has ever doubted, nor ever will, that Christ was subject to his Heavenly Father alone and did not carry out any orders opposed to his will'.[50] There then follows a scathing dismissal of the registered church's exegesis. 'Unlike Christ who never flinched before Herod and Pilate', it contends, 'you are crudely distorting the meaning of Christ's words in order to justify the way in which you have destroyed the principle of the church's independence.'[51] The 'appeal to Christ' tactic is thus turned back on the AUCECB. Far from properly submitting to the state, the registered Baptists are cast as having 'rebelled against obedience to Christ'. Far from 'sub-ordinating' themselves to civil authorities in the positive Barthian sense, they are said to have 'made a close and unlawful alliance' with demonic authorities - that is, with 'the powers of this world (John 18:36; Acts 4:19; 5:29; James 4:4)'.[52]

---

[48] Cit. Michael Bordeaux, *Protestant Opposition to Soviet Religious Policy* (Basingstoke: Macmillan, 1968), 98.

[49] Bordeaux, Protestant Opposition to Soviet Religious Policy, 100. My emphasis.

[50] Bordeaux, *Protestant Opposition to Soviet Religious Policy*, 100.

[51] Bordeaux, *Protestant Opposition to Soviet Religious Policy*, 100.

[52] Bordeaux, *Protestant Opposition to Soviet Religious Policy*, 101.

Once having invoked the spectre of spiritual warfare, the Reform Baptists move on formally to excommunicate the AUCECB, declaring that 'as a religious organization, it can no longer be renovated nor reformed (Mt. 7:15-19)'. In so far as pastoral concern is maintained, it comes only as a stark warning that nothing less than the eternal destiny of registered Baptists is at stake:

> We sincerely want you to be saved, and we wish to cry out to you: Yakov Ivanovich, Alexander Vasilievich and all who are with you! Run to save your souls! ... Run with repentance to Christ and find a refuge in the shrine of Christ's Church for: 'The great day of the Lord is near, it is near and hasteth greatly...the mighty man shall cry there bitterly![53]

The understandable passion of these words springs from the Reform Baptists' conviction that the Bible speaks unequivocally into the Russian situation, and that they have discerned it aright. It would be hard to doubt their basic convictions, but it cannot be ignored that in the specific case of Romans 13, they had to qualify what Paul specifically told the Romans with a retrospective doctrinal composite of less ambivalent texts. Still, the Russian Baptists of the early Sixties offer a fascinating, if tragic, illustration of the issues we have been exploring. Not least, they offer a solemn reminder that a hostile state can place as much pressure on internal Christian unity as on authentic gospel witness.

3. Evangelicals under Apartheid

In 1986, 132 'concerned Evangelicals' signed a Declaration entitled 'Evangelical Witness in South Africa'.[54] Recognising that evangelical South African Christians had been hampered by innate conservatism and an unhelpful 'theology of the status quo', they denounced Apartheid as heretical, sinful and hypocritical, and called upon their fellow Evangelicals to 'come out boldly and be witnesses of the gospel of salvation, justice and peace in this country without fear'. They went on, 'You have not received the spirit of slavery to fall back into fear (Rom. 8:15) as many have done. We have to take a stand now even if it may mean persecution by earthly systems.' [55]

---

[53] Bordeaux, *Protestant Opposition to Soviet Religious Policy*, 103.
[54] Concerned Evangelicals, *Evangelical Witness in South Africa: A critique of Evangelical Theology and Practice by South African Evangelicals Themselves* (London: Evangelical Alliance (UK)/Oxford: Regnum, 1986).
[55] Concerned Evangelicals, *Evangelical Witness in South Africa*, 37.

In one sense, these concerned Evangelicals were simply following the lead taken by the World Alliance of Reformed Churches, whose 1982 'Resolution on Racism and South Africa' had similarly denounced Apartheid as a heresy.[56] One of the points which distinguishes the Evangelicals' statement, however, is its explicit reflection on Romans 13, and the way in which this passage had been used to reinforce an quietistic 'state theology'. 'Whenever victims of oppression raise their voices or resist the oppression', it observes, 'Romans 13 is thrown in their faces by beneficiaries of these oppressive systems. Romans 13 is used therefore to maintain the status quo, and to make Christians feel guilty when challenging injustices in society.'[57]

The Declaration goes on to identify three faults in this approach to the text. First, it ignores 'the context or background' of Paul's words. Second, 'it is not read to the end to understand the whole message Paul was communicating'. And third, 'no reference is made to other related texts in the Bible'.[58] In other words, the more conservative line criticized by the Concerned Evangelicals bypasses the main interpretative methods we have been examining. Restoring these methods to their rightful place, the same Concerned Evangelicals then offer a succinct application of Paul's words to their own situation:

> Our understanding of Romans 13 is that although governments are 'ordained' by God what these governments *do* is not necessarily from God and at times can be completely opposed to God. And should this happen as it is with racist and apartheid South Africa, we are bound to say with Peter and John that we shall 'obey God rather than man' (Acts 5:29), because it is not right in the sight of God to listen to man rather than to God. 'For we cannot but speak of what we have seen and heard' (Acts 4:19-20). ...No. Romans 13 does not call for blind obedience to all evil systems. It is racist missionaries, colonialists and theologians of the West and their churches who have developed this tradition to maintain Western domination and imperialism. Romans 13 defines the nature of an ordained government that has to be obeyed. It says that governments are not a terror to the people but punish wrongdoers (Rom 13:3-4). The South African regime as we are experiencing it is just the opposite of what Paul said.[59]

The Declaration proceeds to underline that strand of exegesis which sees Paul addressing an incipient antinomianism among the Roman Christians, and suggests that this more immediate context may not be so applicable to South African Evangelicals, whose problem has, if anything, been the opposite one of

---

[56] Alan F. P. Sell, *A Reformed, Evangelical, Catholic Theology* (Grand Rapids: Eerdmans,1991), 233.

[57] Concerned Evangelicals, *Evangelical Witness in South Africa*, 21.

[58] Concerned Evangelicals, *Evangelical Witness in South Africa*, 21.

[59] Concerned Evangelicals, *Evangelical Witness in South Africa*, 21.

excessive conformity and deference to those in authority. This insight underlines the importance of distinguishing that in the biblical text which is directly applicable to a contemporary circumstance, from that which is not. The Concerned Evangelicals then go on to derive a telling cultural critique from their work on the passage:

> It is still strange to us how Evangelicals call for a blind obedience to all governments as a scriptural demand and in the same breath call for the subversion and condemnation of so-called 'communist' governments. If anyone has the right to raise a finger against 'communist' governments, then others must also have the same right of condemning and subverting the racist apartheid regime of South Africa.[60]

Finally, while they identify the right of gospel proclamation as a *sine qua non* of Christian allegiance to the state, the Concerned Evangelicals rightly point out the dangers of defining the gospel in question too narrowly:

> Some enthusiastic missionary evangelists argue...that for the sake of the gospel...we must not interfere with those in power. This position usually means preaching the gospel at the expense of the gospel. It means leaving sin to prevail in a society to be able to preach against sin. What a contradiction![61]

Conclusion

Obviously, we British Evangelicals must hope that our application of Romans 13 during the next few years will remain less urgent than it necessarily became in the three cases analysed here. Yet even as the Evangelical Alliance undertakes the comparatively minor civic critiques and legal protests which I have described, those patterns of biblical dissent worked out by the Confessing Church in Nazi Germany, the Reform Baptists in Communist Russia and the Concerned Evangelicals in Apartheid South Africa should assure us that Paul's injunction to be good 'subjects' cannot be glossed as a prescription for unqualified acquiescence in respect of the state and its works. Granted, it will still be crucial in each instance to discern precisely at which points government will have to be disobeyed, and how; or as Anna Robbins puts it in her paper for this book, to choose which battles to fight. Granted, neither Romans 13 itself nor the case studies I have cited provide us with so specific a set of plans. Yet taken together, they do indicate just how momentous and costly Christian movements for change can be.

---

[60] Concerned Evangelicals, *Evangelical Witness in South Africa*, 22.
[61] Concerned Evangelicals, *Evangelical Witness in South Africa*, 23.

8. Social Transformation as a Missional Imperative: Evangelicals and Development since Lausanne

Joe Kapolyo

Introduction

The reawakening of evangelical social concern in the later part of the twentieth century was marked by two key gatherings: the 1966 World Congress on Evangelism in Berlin and the 1974 International Congress on World Evangelisation in Lausanne. Although the Berlin Congress stoutly reaffirmed evangelism as the 'one task' of the church and gave little time to social issues on its main agenda,[62] speakers like John Stott, Paul Rees and Benjamin Moraes did address the relationship between gospel proclamation and practical service, and the closing statement featured a strong condemnation of racism.[63] As Tim Chester has noted, however, the impact of Berlin in terms of social outreach was felt as much through the various conferences it spawned as in the Congress itself. Regional follow-up meetings in Singapore (1968), Minneapolis and Bogota (1969), and Amsterdam (1971) each worked out a more thoroughgoing commitment to the integration of words and works in the mission of God.[64] This process reached its culmination in Lausanne 1974, the epochal Covenant from which affirmed that 'evangelism and socio-political involvement are both part of our Christian duty', and deemed both alike to be 'necessary expressions of our doctrines of God and man, our love for our neighbour and our obedience to Jesus Christ'.[65]

While the journey from Berlin to Lausanne saw a significant raising of social consciousness among Evangelicals, the determination to keep this linked inextricably with evangelism can to some extent be seen as a reaction to the perceived over-socialization of the gospel by the World Council of Churches (WCC).[66] Since the landmark Edinburgh World Missionary Conference of

---

[62] Carl F.H. Henry and Stanley Mooneyham, *One Race, One Gospel, One Task*, Vol. 1 (Minneapolis: World Wide Publications, 1967), 6.

[63] Henry & Mooneyham, *One Race, One Gospel, One Task,* Vol. 1, 41, 307-8. The closing statement is in Vol. 1, 5.

[64] Timothy Chester, *Awakening to a World of Need: The Recovery of Evangelical Social Concern* (Leicester: IVP, 1993), 30-35.

[65] John Stott (ed.), *Making Christ Known: Historic Mission Documents from the Lausanne Movement, 1974-1989* (Carlisle: Paternoster, 1996), 24.

[66] Stott, *Making Christ Known,* 169.

1910, the ecumenical movement, which consolidated into the WCC in 1948, had committed itself to a programme of action focused increasingly on improving the material conditions of humans at the expense of evangelism. By contrast, in the decades after Edinburgh, Evangelicals had typically seemed content to pay lip service to the very real material needs of those hundreds of millions of people who were 'destitute, lacking the basic necessities for survival', thousands of whom died of starvation every day.[67] By explicitly rejecting this emphasis where Berlin '66 had begun to question it, Lausanne '74 represented a unilateral, distinctively evangelical embrace of the social transformation agenda. In defining this agenda as a legitimate expression of Christian discipleship and doctrine, Lausanne underlined that both the Great Commission (Mt. 28:18-20) and the Great Commandment of Christ (Mt. 22:37-40) demand social responsibility. Hence, too, paragraph 5 of the Covenant introduced what was at the time a novel vocabulary for Evangelicals - the vocabulary of justice and reconciliation, and of liberation from oppressive regimes. On these grounds, it has been said with justification that with Lausanne, 'the evangelical movement reaches a new turning point'.[68]

The full text of paragraph 5 reads as follows:

> We affirm that God is both the Creator and the Judge of all men. We therefore should share his concern for justice and reconciliation throughout human society and for the liberation of men from every kind of oppression. Because mankind is made in the image of God, every person, regardless of race, religion, colour, culture, class, sex or age, has an intrinsic dignity because of which he should be respected and served, not exploited. Here too we express penitence both for our neglect and for having sometimes regarded evangelism and social concern as mutually exclusive. Although reconciliation with man is not reconciliation with God, nor is social action evangelism, nor is political liberation salvation, nevertheless we affirm that evangelism and socio-political involvement are both part of our Christian duty. For both are necessary expressions of our doctrines of God and man, our love for our neighbour and our obedience to Jesus Christ. The message of salvation implies also a message of judgment upon every form of alienation, oppression and discrimination, and we should not be afraid to denounce evil and injustice wherever they exist. When people receive Christ they are born again into his kingdom and must seek not only to exhibit but also to spread its righteousness in the midst of an unrighteous world. The salvation we claim should be transforming us in the totality of our personal and social responsibilities. Faith without works is dead.[69]

---

[67] Stott, *Making Christ Known*, 177.

[68] James A. Scherer, *Gospel, Church and Kingdom: Comparative Studies in World Mission Theology* (Augsburg: Fortress Press, 1987), 173.

[69] Stott, *Making Christ Known*, 24.

After this, Evangelicalism could not easily continue to ignore socio-political action. Although considerable debate would ensue among Evangelicals on the precise nature of the relationship between such action and evangelism, the former was now firmly established on the agenda. Then again, the Covenant is still careful to insist that 'reconciliation with man is not reconciliation with God, nor is social action evangelism, nor is political action salvation', and one senses in this wording a residual suspicion of the socio-political agenda among those who gathered at Lausanne. Evangelicals had not on the whole connected general human activities like work, marriage, parenting, leisure and relaxation to evangelism, and even as the Covenant clearly urged them to do so, it here also acknowledged a widespread fear of going the way of the WCC, and *replacing* evangelism with social action as the basic imperative of mission. To put it in other words, Evangelicals were wary lest a 'preoccupation with social responsibility' might 'blunt' their 'evangelistic zeal'.[70] This theological concern is understandable, but it arises from a distinctly western context. Most of the people who argue over this question of evangelism versus social action have never really had to deal with personal hunger and material need on a daily basis. Also, perhaps, the prevalence of small family units, thoroughgoing individualism and state social security provision have shielded many westerners from hearing or responding to other people's cries of help on account of material indigence. As an African, it seems strange to me that any one should ever have to justify alleviating people's hunger or other forms of deprivation. Of course such action should never be equated with evangelism or mistaken for the total mission of the church. But it is a legitimate Christian ministry in its own right - one which does not need validating in relation to evangelism. It arises out of the nature of God and the nature of human beings in much the same way that evangelism arises out of the nature of God and humans. Perhaps the very classification we use is the problem. We treat social action as separate 'ministry' when in fact it should be a natural outflow of our common humanity, or at any rate an expression of our gratitude for the love which Jesus Christ has demonstrated to us.

Since Lausanne, Evangelicals have continued to seek more clearly to define the relationship between evangelism and social action. One of the most important contributions to this process was The Grand Rapids Report on Evangelism and Social Responsibility (1982). Here, six possible accounts of the relationship were mooted,[71] the last three of which were endorsed:

---

[70] Scherer, *Gospel, Church and Kingdom*, 183.
[71] John R. Reid, 'Evangelism and Social Responsibility', in Edward R. Dayton & Samuel Wilson (eds.), *The Future of World Evangelization: Unreached Peoples '84* (Monrovia, California: MARC, 1984), 75-76.

1. *Social responsibility is a distraction from, or even a betrayal of evangelism. In this case evangelism is seen as the exclusive mission of the church.*

   To hold to this relationship between evangelism and social action would put paid to the claim to be holistic in approach to mission. At the heart of this position is a basic misunderstanding of the nature of God and nature of humanity, social responsibility and even the place and reason for evangelism.

2. *Social responsibility is evangelism. It is argued that it is artificial even to distinguish them since they are so interrelated.*

   This position is an attempt to buy unity by confusing matters. Social responsibility implies taking action to alleviate the sufferings of other human beings. Evangelism at the very least includes an explanation of the gospel with a view to placing before a person the twin choice of accepting Jesus, salvation and eternal life on the one hand and rejecting Jesus, embracing God's condemnation and the consequent consignment to hell. It is undeniable that social action might be the basis of questions asked which might then lead to an evangelistic opportunity. But the two things are not the same.

3. *Social responsibility is a manifestation of evangelism. In its most attractive form it makes the message significantly visible.*

   The first part of the statement is manifestly not true while the second part is true but not as a corollary of the first. It is hard to imagine how social action can be a manifestation of evangelism unless this statement means that those who are evangelized and accept the Lord Jesus see social action as a natural consequence of their new-found faith. But evidently this was not what was intended, as is shown by the next alternative, in which the words 'consequence of evangelism' are used.

4. *Social responsibility is a consequence of evangelism and it results from the teaching the new converts receive.*

   This statement was chosen as one of the three adopted relationships to guide evangelical understanding of social action. But the statement cannot mean that social action is a natural consequence of evangelism. Evangelical negligence and failure in active engagement on social action clearly point away from this solution. But evangelism can be said to be a very sound basis for social action. For all Christian service should stem from our gratitude to God for what he has done for us and should extend to all people in need. This is particularly important in the African Christian context. Africans in general are very generous with hospitality and the support of their extended families. But this generosity is limited to those within the parameters of the extended family. When Africans become Christians they do not naturally become generous to everybody outside of the defined boundaries of the kinship structures. They need to learn that their generosity must now cover people who do not have any natural biological or kinship ties with them.

5. *Social responsibility is a partner to evangelism, and both are expressions of love.*

Certainly one without the other makes Christian mission deficient, just as the Lausanne Covenant declared that a bird with only one wing or a pair of scissors with one blade is deficient.[72] *Kerygma* and *diakonia* go hand in hand. They did in the life of Jesus and the ministries of the Apostles and we must not separate them. Partnership is a good word to express the relationship between evangelism and social responsibility. The one needs the other and is threatened without the other. Evangelism that blocks its ears to the cries of starving humanity is a mockery of the love and sensitivity of the Lord Jesus. On the other hand social action that is blind to the spiritual dimension of humanity is not faithful to the Lord who calls all people to repentance (Mk. 1:15).

6. *Social responsibility is a bridge to evangelism. It is often possible to move from felt needs to the needs of the spirit.*

In the history of Christian mission social action has often been seen as a means to evangelism and discipleship. This was certainly so among the first missionaries to Zambia, some of whom saw the aim of education as getting 'the native really saved and on the Rock, Jesus Christ'. Education was a means to an end, and that end was the salvation of souls.[73] This approach can easily translate into psychological manipulation leading to the hypocrisy of 'rice Christians'.[74] In any case, it is often self-defeating. One has observed in the Zambian situation that many took the education that the missionaries provided but did not necessarily join the church. Yet rightly developed, social action can break down walls of hostility and suspicion and pave the way for meaningful interaction, leading to the conversion of souls. Waldron Scott points out that the most significant church growth in Guatemala took place in the aftermath of the 1976 earthquake, following practical intervention by scores of evangelical relief agencies. The demonstration of love in action broke through barriers of

---

[72] Stott, *Making Christ Known*, 182.
[73] Peter D. Snelson, *Educational Development in Northern Rhodesia 1883-1945* (Lsk: National Educational Company of Zambia, 1974), 99.
[74] Ronald Sider, *Evangelism and Social Action (Guidelines)* (London: Hodder & Stoughton, 1993), 142.

apathy and indifference which one hundred years of preaching had failed to penetrate significantly.[75]

James Scherer comments that the Grand Rapids Report offered a theological solution to a potentially divisive issue, rather than a specific programme of action.[76] Be that as it may, it did lay down clear biblical principles for future action. What, sort of project, then, would reflect such principles?

One good model of present-day evangelical social responsibility is offered by The Micah Network. In September 1999 a small group of evangelical leaders from non-governmental relief and development organizations met in Kuala Lumpur, Malaysia. Here they planned a new international forum which could both strengthen the capacity of participating agencies, and enhance their ability to act collectively in key areas of concern. Recognizing the problem identified by David Hilborn in his paper for this volume - namely, that much otherwise laudable evangelical social engagement has been blunted by its fragmentary, piecemeal nature - the Kuala Lumpur group resolved to create a focus for greater consultation and co-ordination. Soon afterwards, the Colombian theologian Rene Padilla, who with Samuel Escobar had been central in steering the Lausanne Congress towards the social responsibility agenda,[77] agreed to be the Network's President. A Co-ordinating Group was formed, comprising representatives from every continent. The core aims of the Network were defined as a) making a 'biblically shaped response to the needs of the poor and oppressed', b) 'speaking strongly and effectively regarding the…the mission of the church to proclaim and demonstrate the love of Christ to a world in need', and c) 'prophetically calling upon and influencing the leaders and decision-makers of societies to maintain the rights of the poor and oppressed and rescue the weak and needy.' Since its formation, the Micah Network has organized regional workshops on achieving best practice in delivering relief, held consultations on terrorism and peacemaking after 11 September 2001, on globalization and the poor, and on Christian management. It has also done much to refine the emphases of Lausanne and Grand Rapids in a significant Declaration on Integral Mission. This text defines integral mission as 'holistic transformation' which is advanced by 'the proclamation and demonstration of the gospel'. It continues as follows:

It is not simply that evangelism and social involvement are to be done alongside each other. Rather, in integral mission our proclamation has social consequences

---

[75] Waldron Scott, 'Mercy and Social Transformation', in Vinay Samuel & Christopher Sugden (eds.). *The Church in Response to Human Need* (Grand Rapids and Oxford: Eerdmans and Regnum Books, 1987), 206-217.

[76] Scherer, *Gospel, Church and Kingdom*, 182.

[77] Chester, *Awakening to a World of Need*, 73-78.

as we call people to love and repentance in all areas of life. And our social involvement has evangelistic consequences as we bear witness to the transforming grace of Jesus Christ. If we ignore the world we betray the word of God which sends us out to serve the world. If we ignore the word of God we have nothing to bring to the world. Justice and justification by faith, worship and political action, the spiritual and the material, personal change and structural change belong together. As in the life of Jesus, being, doing and saying are at the heart of our integral task.[78]

For me there are two points that make this project attractive. First, the name Micah holds before us a biblical mirror showing why we get involved with the needy. Micah, after all, presents a searing prophetic account of social injustice in Judah prior to the reforms of Hezekiah. Micah's analysis is that of a prophet who hailed from the relatively impoverished rural fringes of Jewish society (Micah 1:1). He offers a penetrating description of the empty ritualism, corruption, greed, injustice and other social ills of the day, especially as they affected the small towns and villages of Judah. As such, he provides a grid through which Christians today might attempt to deal authentically with the inequality, exploitation and misery of so many in our own world.

As Christians, we need to be reminded time and again that we engage in relief and development work not primarily out of pity, guilt, love, duty or even need itself, but out of obedience to God. Our commitment to the poor arises from our commitment to God. Second, that commitment reflects God's own involvement in human affairs. At the heart of God's work in the world is his desire to move the poor from the margins of human society, where they are often downtrodden and denied justice, to a central place among his people - a place where they can play a significant role in the advancement of his kingdom. The Bible is full of stories of people like Moses, born to a refugee family, destitute and under threat of infanticide at birth; Rahab, a poor prostitute (Josh. 2:14-21; 6:22-23; Mt. 1:5); Ruth, a poor foreign widow (Ruth 1:1-17; 4:13-22); Hanna, a poor barren woman (1 Sam. 1:1-2:11); David, an unimpressive sibling (1 Sam. 16:1-13); the disciples of Jesus, a motley crowd lacking the normal attributes of the elite of Jesus' day (Acts 4:13); the weak and foolish of the Corinthian church (1 Cor. 1:26-31), and so on. All these people show us what God can do when he takes hold of the poor and sets them free to work according to his plan and purpose. In fact, it is true to say that real progress in the proclamation of the gospel occurs when the poor make the gospel their own. The Micah Network is relatively new and has a long way to go in bearing fruit in line with its early promise, but it does seem to have recognized these vital priorities, and as such, deserves support and prayer.

---

[78] For the full text of the Declaration and other information about the Micah Network, see its website at http://www.micahnetwork.org

Missiological models and the problem of development

Our consideration of missiological models for social transformation would be remiss if it did not acknowledge the enterprise of development aid as practised by both secular and Christian agencies.

A good western friend of mine once visited my family's home in Ndola, Zambia. During her stay she was introduced to a social transformation programme called The Alpha Foundation Trust, which was run by a young, single Zambian woman. The Trust was devoted to alleviating the terrible social conditions under which orphans lived in the particular shanty compound where this woman worked. Some of these conditions, which included the dispossession of widows and ravages of the Aids pandemic, were captured on video. My western visitor reacted to the video by getting a copy so that she could present the needs of the children involved to Tearfund - a leading evangelical relief agency based in the United Kingdom. My reaction was one of anger! That video captured for me the key flaws in many popular western Christian programmes of social transformation. Many such programmes, based as they are on an essentially secular western worldview which James Ferguson has described as a 'linear metanarrative of emergence and progress', seem to me inadvertently to feed on 'underdevelopment'.[79] Indeed, I would go as far as to state that they contribute to, if not actively promote, 'underdevelopment'.

Development programmes breed underdevelopment

A clear example of the way in which development programmes assume and even create underdevelopment comes from the early days of the mining industry which grew up on the Copperbelt of Zambia in the 1890s. Up to that point, most Zambians led subsistent rural lives, outside the money economy. They lived off the land they owned under a system of customary land tenure, and were more or less self-sufficient. The economy did include some trade, and surpluses occurred in domestic implements like hoes, spears, and in other consumables such as bark-cloth and salt. Although standards of trade were quite low, as far we can tell the communities did not suffer desperately from famine, unemployment and grinding poverty. The only form of tax was *Umulasa* and *Umutulo.* Umulasa was the mutually acceptable arrangement under which subjects cultivated a chief's gardens without payment, in return for his leadership and protection in times of hostility. Similarly, at harvest, subjects

---

[79] James Ferguson, *Expectations of Modernity* (Berkeley: University of California Press, 1999), 16.

donated to the king a portion of their crop yield (Umutulo) as a mark of respect and gratitude for the chief's wisdom, leadership and support in times of hardship and war, as well as in acknowledgement that he or she was the supreme owner of the land.

The Zambian 'Industrial Revolution' came with the discovery of large underground copper deposits. Initially these deposits were uneconomical, since no technology existed to extract them cheaply. For some time, both Katanga and South African deposits had proved more viable. Until the beginning of the First World War, American copper proved adequate to meet the demands of the growing military industry. But the War accelerated the development of new technologies, and fresh demand for copper came from emergent automotive industries, from new electricity generating bodies, from communications networks, and elsewhere. Soon, demand began to outstrip supply, and this problem led directly to intensive mining of the Copperbelt of Zambia. By 1925 this new industry was in full swing, funded by both American money and British and South African capital. The extraction of rich copper ores demanded an army of cheap labourers. But most Zambians were neither interested nor available. Hence, the British South Africa Company (BSAC) undertook to create such an army of its own. This it did by resolving 'to turn villagers into wage-workers, to separate men from their wives, families, cattle, rivers and hunting grounds'.[80] Various measures were then enacted in support of this plan.

First, monetary tax was imposed upon a society which did not deal in money. British Colonial and BSAC officials registered everybody in the villages and collected taxes. Those who could not pay were sent off to work for government in a range of Public Works projects. This demand forced men to leave their villages for periods of up to eighteen months at time, to go in search of work so that they could earn enough to pay the offending tax. This became an annual pilgrimage for most men. Later on, many would settle in the urban centres for periods of up twenty years, after which they were pensioned off back to their villages of origin. (Since Zambia gained independence in 1964, the necessity to return to the village of origin has not applied in quite the same way.) In the period 1931–32, the government raised £148,000 - a sixth of its total revenue - from African Taxes alone. Most Africans were paid at the rate of 15 shillings a month (20 shillings = one pound sterling). The unfairness of this system was borne out by the fact that expatriate workers were not required to pay taxes as long as they were married, had two children and earned less than £96 a month!

---

[80] H.J. Simons, 'Zambia's Urban Situation', in Ben Turok (ed.), *Development in Zambia* (Zed Press: London, 1979), 5.

Second, various methods of labour recruitment were deployed, including forced deportations for jobless youth. Right up to the early 1960s, the police regularly raided African homes in search of unemployed young men who were then sent off to work in mines outside the country, either in Zimbabwe or South Africa. By 1920 50,000 wage earners had left the borders of Zambia in search of work. Ten years later the number had risen to 113,000, including some 78,000 employed within Zambia on the so-called 'Line of Rail'.

Third, the authorities systematically killed off locally produced crafts in favour of imports. On the agricultural front, the big mining concerns were not encouraged to buy produce from villagers; instead they were enticed to purchase maize produced by expatriate commercial farmers. Import substitution was reversed, causing the local economy to become almost totally dependent on imports of goods, services and foodstuffs - a switch which further impoverished local skills in crafts and agriculture. The first wave of globalization distorted the political and economic independence of the tribes and their communities. The colonists imposed both political and economic structures which served the interests of their native countries.[81] The monopolies which resulted also meant that the village wage earner could not dictate conditions for the sale of his labour. These were imposed on him by the employers. The migrant system of labour of the early years meant that the mining companies did not bear the full social cost of their operations. Instead, these considerable costs were borne by old people and women left in the villages. So slowly the active labour force was taken out of those villages, thus killing off any prospect that they might benefit from developments in the mining towns. There was an obscene transfer of value from countries like Zambia to metropolitan states in South Africa, Europe and America.

In the video referred to above, I saw a man putting three children to bed. The bed was a bare earthen floor with nothing to protect the children from the cold of the earth. There was not even a piece of cloth or a reed mat. A family which displays to the public that level of personal poverty has lost a natural sense of Zambian pride and shame. A dehumanizing process has stripped it of self-worth and dignity, in exchange for a hope that some kind western donor will keep the flow of easy money running. This mentality will not create an environment through which poverty will be seriously addressed, either at the personal or community level. The double tragedy is that while the woman will sink into greater depths of destitution and indignity, those who manage the process intended to bring development to her will actually benefit from her dehumanized state. As this episode illustrates, while seeking to alleviate

---

[81] Werner Biermann, 1979, 'The development of underdevelopment: the historic perspective', in B. Turok (ed.), *Development in Zambia* (Zed Press: London, 1979), 128-34.

poverty, we must beware of trampling on the essential worth that God has vested in all human beings through the bestowal of his image (Gen. 1:26-27).

The developed get more developed through development programmes

The second flaw, which is really a corollary to the first, is that the main development which takes place almost invariably does so in the persons who are the 'developers', and in the developed economies they represent, rather than among those they ostensibly seek to develop. We must applaud the excellent work of western relief agencies in responding to crises arising from famine, disease or natural disaster. But development is very different issue from relief work.

An instructive example of the process to which I am referring may be drawn from the world of secular international development. It is anecdotal, but hardly atypical. In the mid-1980s, a small Zambian international airport needed some major repairs to its infrastructure. The national civil aviation authority sourced some much-needed funds from the then European Economic Community (EEC). The total amounted to six million US dollars. If it had been made directly available, this sum would have been adequate for the work. However, the project did not come to fruition because the conditions attached made the whole scheme unworkable. The EEC slapped a million-dollar commission on the project because the money had come through their good offices. Next, they insisted that all the technical experts and equipment needed for the work should be provided by EEC member countries. This accounted for four million dollars. One million was then left for the purchase of local labour and construction materials. Evidently, according to the local Civil Aviation representatives, this was not going to be enough for the work. The airport manager at the time related all this to me, and while there may be another story to tell, the sorts of strictures to which he bore witness are very commonly applied in the global South.

If the airport project had gone ahead with all these restrictive conditions, it would at have at best resulted in a partial refurbishment. Perhaps this would have been better than nothing, but within a few years far more money would have had to be spent on the same project. What did not seem in doubt was that five million dollars would have been spent in the EEC generating jobs, equipping engineers and giving them invaluable overseas experience in construction work. The benefits to the local airport would have been minimal - mere crumbs under the table by comparison with the benefits of the project to the EEC, its economies and citizenry.

Another example may be cited from the world of social anthropology. Since the First World War social scientists have created an industry out of studying exotic peoples. While living among the Trobriand Islanders between 1915 and 1918, the Polish academic Bronislaw Malinoski developed 'participant observation' as the key method for anthropological studies. Since then an army of researchers have 'invaded' just about every people group and studied them. Scholars like Godfrey Wilson, Elizabeth Colson, Mary Douglas, Audrey Richards, Max Gluckmann and J. C. Mitchell followed Malinowski's lead, immersing themselves for extended periods in the language, culture and rituals of various traditional people-groups before returning to their countries and sponsoring institutions to write up and publish their research. As such, they turned their experiences and reflections into marketable commodities, gaining scholarly recognition and, no doubt, the material rewards which go with it. In this sense, they came to own academic 'property' rights over the people they had studied.

Although participant-observation is avowedly non-interventionist, and although anthropologists generally eschew the promotion of social transformation projects, their academic endeavours are disproportionately weighted in their own favour, at the expense of the very people whose beliefs and behaviour-patterns form the basis of their new found knowledge, and from whom they receive hospitality. True development is this scenario takes place among the 'developers'. The underdeveloped are needed as fodder for this process to work.

Now lest it be thought that evangelical development agencies are immune from the sort of 'secular' exploitation described in these last two examples, a further case study will demonstrate the lines of continuity which can run from the one sphere to the other.

A bishop in an East African diocese undertook to familiarize himself with all the development projects in his bishopric. Without exception, he found only remains of what had once been 'successful' schemes. Ironically, the Non-Governmental Organisation (NGO) set up by the diocese to run these projects was still active, and was continuing to receive funding from foreign development agencies. Local NGOs are not passive conduits for channeling funds to projects. They are organisms, which live off the same development money. In time they grow and can siphon off large quantities of resources to maintain certain 'professional' infrastructures for the management of the projects. In this case, the real development takes place not within the project itself, but at the level of the NGO. It is the operatives in the latter who understand government legislation, who can process the many complicated forms issued by government departments, and who therefore benefit most from any transformation which might take place. It is their children, unlike the children in the communities where the photographs for 'sponsor a child' campaigns are taken, who go to good schools and prepare for a better future. There is something in the way that development models are conceived which seems to favour the developers and their agents against the people for whom the programmes are devised. It may well be that one of the failures of the whole social transformation agenda lies in the fact that the intended recipients of transformation more commonly appear to be its objects than its subjects. Especially when focused on societies riddled with gross inequalities, development aid will often only really benefit those who control and the structures through which the aid is given.[82]

It is important to reiterate here the distinction I have already drawn, between development and emergency aid. I would include in the latter category all medical work, whether of the mission hospital type (with the possible exception of training institutions), or of the Medicine Without Frontiers type. To a lesser extent I would also include elementary education in a context where there is no established curriculum and the likelihood of progress beyond primary level is negligible. It is in these situations that aid has been most successful, but it needs to be stressed that the projects in question have characteristically been short term, and have rarely led on to sustainable development.

Development proper is people not programmes

It really makes little difference whether a programme is presented as 'top down' or 'bottom up'; it is still a programme, and as such will most probably have been conceived far away from the people who are supposed to gain from it.

Some years ago I watched the film *Mr. Holland's Opus*.[83] In Stephen Herek's movie the eponymous lead, played by Richard Dreyfuss, sets out to write the symphony to end all symphonies. He hopes that this will make him rich, respected and famous. In the meantime, while waiting for inspiration, Mr. Holland takes on a day job teaching music in a High School. He turns out, in fact, to be a very successful teacher. He is able to inspire otherwise hopeless students, not only teaching them music, but giving them a reason to live. The years go by. Mr. Holland gets more and more involved in the school, and in the lives of the young people he tutors. The symphony, however, remains elusive, and unfinished. One day without warning he is declared redundant. He is by

---

[82] M.R. Matthews, 'The Implications of Western Theologies of Development for Third World Countries and Churches', in Ronald Sider (ed.) *Evangelicals and Development, Towards a Theology of Social Change* (Carlisle: Paternoster Press, 1981), 89-101.
[83] Cinema release: Hollywood Pictures, 1995. (Video, 1996; DVD, 2000).

now past middle age. He has spent the best years of his life giving himself wholly to the school and its pupils, and now finds himself surplus to requirements. It is a bitter blow. He has failed to achieve his intended magisterial opus. However, a secret farewell is arranged with the collusion of his wife. Here, many generations of his students turn up. Each has a story of real success to tell. One is a Chief of Police, another a Head of a School, still another a State Governor. As he hears these stories, Holland realizes that these testimonies are, in fact, his great work, his legacy. Development should be focused on people for their own sake, on empowering people to run programmes of their own devising. It is about helping to supply the tools and skills with which people can organize their own lives successfully.

Imagine for a while that the church is a development project. The Lord Jesus Christ was the initiator of the project. He did not tell his disciples how to build local congregations. Instead he poured his life into twelve unpromising men and then trusted them to make vital decisions about how their lives and congregations should be run. That development project is still going strong all over the world. For three years they had witnessed his teaching and his miraculous works. Then he commissioned them to take responsibility for hands-on mission across the world. And effectively, at the ascension, he left them to it. Of course, he promised his continuing presence through the Holy Spirit in all they would do (Mt. 28:16-20), but the extent of his delegation and trust was awesome nonetheless. The apostle Paul was similarly committed to investing in people such as Luke, Timothy, and Titus. He could describe Timothy as one who knew 'all about my teaching, my way of life, my purpose, faith, patience, love, endurance, persecutions, sufferings...' (2 Tim. 3:10). Timothy served under Paul, had been taught by Paul, and had been sent by Paul on mission. In the end, though, Paul gave him charge of the church at Ephesus.

One modern missional model that seems to come close to this biblical pattern is what I will call the Stottian model, after the work done by John Stott in establishing, promoting and developing with others the Evangelical Literature Trust, the London Institute for Contemporary Christianity and the Langham Partnership. The focus of these ventures is to give individual people in less affluent regions the opportunity through reading and study to develop in such a way that they manage their own affairs. There are many Churches and Christian organizations all over the Third World which owe their vision to the work under God of this one man, John Stott. His commitment to and shaping of these projects provide a model not only for long-term leadership development programmes, but for other shorter-term initiatives, too. Such commitment and organisation will be crucial in the century ahead if evangelical efforts at social transformation are to have any lasting effect, and if they are to avoid the self-serving tendencies that I have described here.

The Temple Addresses

The First Temple Address (2001)

Delivered at the Inner Temple Hall, 20th February 2001

James Jones, Bishop of Liverpool

Godly Instincts for Social Change

It is a great honour to be able to associate myself personally with the Evangelical Alliance. I'm conscious that the word 'evangelical' conjures up different images, and that often the media have no understanding whatsoever of its noble heritage. They commonly associate it with tele-evangelists from the other side of the Atlantic. I want to say right from the outset that as a Bishop who sees himself as Bishop within the whole church of God, I nevertheless do take to myself, humbly and proudly, the word evangelical - standing in the tradition of people like Wycliffe and Cranmer and Wilberforce. Wycliffe, who gave his very life for truth. Cranmer, perhaps one of the finest wordsmiths in the English language. Wilberforce, whose reading of the Bible led him radically to change the nature of our society through the abolition of slavery. It is touching that when William Wilberforce was tempted to throw in the towel, a letter from John Wesley, the great champion of personal evangelism, persuaded him that having set his hand to the plough, he should not to look back. It was the greatest privilege for me to be invited to be Bishop of Hull, the very constituency served by Wilberforce. I shall never forget going to Hull with the Archdeacon of the East Riding after my interview with the Archbishop of York. We parked in the centre of the city and I asked, 'What's that statue there?' The Archdeacon said, 'William Wilberforce'. I felt in many ways that I had come home, because since my student days Wilberforce had been a hero to me - someone who took the Bible seriously, and from the Bible shaped a manifesto for serving the community.

Another famous MP for Hull is John Prescott. We asked Mr. Prescott if he would come and open a drop-in centre for young people. We had taken the old boiler out of the basement of one of our churches and turned it into a safe place where young people could come off the street, find information about drugs and sex, and spend time among caring, responsible adults. The idea was that Mr. Prescott would cut the tape and that I'd say a few prayers. It was just before the 1997 election, a Saturday, and the church was packed. I met him at the door and we went up the aisle together. Now by his own confession John Prescott is an agnostic, but he was delighted to come and say how much he appreciated the community values of the church. Half way up the aisle, his mobile phone started ringing. Tony Blair's office wanted a conversation between Mr Prescott and Mr Blair. So he shouted down the phone, 'Tell Blair I'm just going into church with the Bishop of Hull to say some prayers'! Apparently Tony Blair had to sit down and have a cup of tea. He didn't know New Labour had gone quite that far!

I am optimistic about the future of the church. I am optimistic about the mission of God, and for this reason: St. Paul said to the philosophers in Athens, '"From one ancestor God made all nations to inhabit the whole earth, and he allotted the times of their existence and the boundaries of the places where they would live, so that they would search for God and perhaps grope for him and find him – though indeed he is not far from each one of us. For 'in him we live and move and have our being' as even some of your own poets have said."' (Acts 17:26-28). I am optimistic because I believe that within every human being there are three basic instincts: the spiritual, the moral and the social. And I believe that into each of these three instincts, the Christian faith continues to speak powerfully and in a transforming way. We need to realize that Christianity was born in a world just as pluralistic as the world in which we now live. We must not be defeatist, nor allow defeatist talk to make us pessimistic about the future of the mission of God. It is, after all, God's mission, and it is God who has made us spiritual, moral and social beings. I would like to highlight some aspects of these three instincts.

When I was Vicar of Emmanuel Church, South Croydon, the church had the vision to appoint a full-time Youth Minister. They were privileged to have the resources to do that. One of the first things the Youth Minister did was to conduct a survey of the religious and moral attitudes of young people between the ages of 14 to 18 who did not go to church. One of the questions was 'When did you last pray? Last year? Last month? Last week?' Over 60% of these unchurched young people said they had prayed in the previous week. Of course, they didn't find church relevant, but what the survey demonstrated is that they were spiritual people.

I was telling this later, after I became a Bishop, to a well-known broadsheet journalist, who was rather dismissive: 'Oh yes, but what did they pray for?' To which I replied, 'What do *you* pray for?' Your wife gets cancer: of course you start praying. You're about to be made redundant: of course you start praying. Our prayers are no different from the prayers of young people. They see their parents about to split: of course they start praying. They find themselves going into an exam for which they haven't done enough work: of course they start praying. And the amazing grace of God is that though it might take disaster to drive us towards him, he's not like the famous politician who tells us to get on our bike. He doesn't say 'Well, you had no time for me before, so I've got no time for you now'. The amazing grace of God is shown in that whenever such crisis moments come to any of us, at any age, he effectively says, 'I've been waiting for this moment all your life." The truth is there is barely a single person on the face of this earth who does not at some stage in his or her life find themselves praying.

Not only is there a spiritual instinct in us all, there is a moral instinct. I want to challenge those people who cave in too quickly to the post-modernist critique of society, saying that we can no longer speak about absolute values. That simply is not my experience. It may be true of the chattering classes of Hampstead and Islington, but it is not true of the people that I share my life with as Bishop of Liverpool. People have a profound sense of right and wrong. During Lent last year, as part of our millennium celebrations, I went to every deanery in the diocese of Liverpool, and in each deanery I asked the head of the local secondary school if I could come in and meet with the sixth form, and if they would invite other sixth forms in the deanery. The sound of the doors being flung open was deafening. I said I wanted to listen to young people, to hear about their aspirations and their fears for the future. I wanted to tell them of the relevance of Jesus Christ, 2000 years on. In some places up to 250 young people came along. We produced three short video clips: one on the future of the planet, one on relationships, and one on the spiritual quest, to help stimulate the discussion.

In every venue, I said to the young people, 'On a scale of 0 to 10, how worried are you about the future of the planet? 0 is not worried at all, 10 is very worried. Place yourself on the scale of 0 to 10. Now please would you put your hand up if you have placed yourself between 5 to 10.' This is not an exaggeration: in every single venue, 100% of the hands went up. I then said, 'On a scale of 0 to 10, do you think we ought' - note the moral word – 'do you think we ought to do something about the future of the planet? 0 is don't bother, 10 is yes, we really ought to. If you placed yourself between 5 to 10, please you put your hand up.' 99% of all the hands were raised.

It is absolutely not true to say that relativism rules in our culture. As far as the environment is concerned, young people believe there is a moral imperative (in Kantian terms, a categorical imperative) - that we *ought* to care for the planet. That's why I'm so glad to see that the church is now taking this issue seriously: if we want to find a moral bridge between us, the gospel, and young people today, we need to rediscover the environment.

But for us, the protection of the planet isn't just speaking against the desecration of the earth as a crime against humanity and its future; to desecrate the planet ultimately is blasphemy, because as Colossians 1 tells us, it was made by Christ, and for Christ, and therefore to desecrate it is not just a crime against humanity, but an offence against God.

If we observe our society over the last 25 years, clearly its sexual mores have changed. That mustn't lead us to think that somehow it's now a sea of relativism. That's just not so. The biggest example of the world's behaving as if there were an absolute morality was when the world community united and forced a sovereign nation to change its internal structure - namely South Africa and apartheid. Did you ever hear anybody in that context say that morality was all relative? That it was all the product of social conditioning? That whether or not you thought blacks and whites were equal simply depended on how you were brought up? Of course you didn't: there wasn't much relativism in that debate. People said apartheid was wrong: not relatively wrong, but absolutely wrong. That was why the world community acted, and forced a sovereign nation to change its internal structures. What the world was doing was intuiting this absolute value. It is the church's calling to help people trace back a link from their intuition to the God who has spoken in creation, in history, through the prophets, and supremely through the person and teaching of Jesus Christ. There was no relativism there, the world was right, as it intuited an absolute value, that all men and women, and children and young people, are equal in the sight of God, regardless of creed, race or colour.

There's a wonderful story about Nelson Mandela on the last day of his state visit, sitting next to Her Majesty in the royal box at the Royal Albert Hall. All the dancers, actors, musicians, and singers came onto the stage for the final reprise, with glorious African music vibrating and throbbing through the arena. The audience all stood up and began to boogie to the music. Not to be left out, and even though he was sitting next to Her Majesty, Nelson Mandela stood too, and began to boogie away. I heard it described on the radio, and the reporter said, 'Then the Queen stood and swayed gently.' A wonderful picture of Nelson Mandela at the very heart of the establishment that had been party to his oppression, breathing new life into it. But what had unlocked the door of his cell? It was the world intuiting an absolute moral value, that all men are equal in the sight of God, regardless of their colour or creed. There was and is a moral instinct.

I sense this moral instinct is at work when people are thinking about their children's education. That is why a million children in this country are educated in Church of England schools. That is why they are queuing up, why I have to spend so much time writing to people who have been disappointed because they can't get their children into a church school. What's driving them? Yes, the schools' performance is good; their academic results are good. But there's something more that people are seeking. They are looking for the moral formation of their young people. They want that Christian ethos; they want an ethical dimension within education. I trained as a teacher myself; I did my PGCE in 1970. If you had told anybody in 1970 that 30 years later the church would be offered an even greater stake in state education, nobody would have believed you. They would have laughed you out of the tutorial. We are at a unique and I believe a providential moment in our social history. The political parties, and the present government in particular, are opening the door for the church to be even more involved in education. I'm not a pessimist. I long to see Christians with sensitivity, compassion and conviction, taking those opportunities. There's a moral as well as a spiritual instinct, and it is clearly evident in our society.

Thirdly, the social instinct. Sociologists tell us that the future is relational; that people are impatient with institutions; that they're more interested in relationships. I believe this gives the church a golden opportunity. Because what lies at the heart of the church is an experience, a personal relationship with God through Jesus Christ, mediated by word and sacrament and expressed through service in the community. What characterizes the church is belonging. The church is one of the few organisations left where people meet across social barriers. I know it's fashionable to knock synods, but in the diocesan synods you find the rural, the urban and the suburban, all coming together, telling their stories and listening to one other. The church has a presence in every community. The bank may have retreated; the post office may have gone; the surgery may not be there any more; even the pub may be closing; but the church is still there. That is why the church has a unique authority to speak about where comfortable and uncomfortable Britain is today. I hope not arrogantly, I hope sensitively, but we are there.

It's been good to see politicians recognize the churches' unique experience, and welcome the church and groups like the Church Urban Fund as partners in the renewal of our communities. But what makes renewal happen? When I think of renewal I think of Jesus outside Jerusalem, weeping and saying, 'If only you knew the things that make for peace' (Lk. 19:42). There have been countless government programmes for regeneration, but I'm still hearing that sigh: 'If only you knew those things that make for peace'. I'm hearing it because the regeneration of our communities - urban, rural and suburban - has got to be more than economic, more than the fabric, more than the material; it has to be spiritual and social and moral. For what is at stake in the end, is men, women, young people and children taking responsibility for one another, caring for one another. There is an ethical and a spiritual dimension to that renewal. And if we don't see that, we will forever be hoping that another government will find some magical recipe for regeneration, and the spiral of degeneration will continue.

I believe passionately in the value of the family to the social cohesion of our society. It is lamentable that no politicians, of any party, have fully recognized the importance of reinforcing the very relationship in which children are nurtured. We have not yet grasped the nettle of strengthening the institution of the family, for the sake of the children. Many children are deprived of parental nurture, in some cases not just for one generation, but for two and three generations. I believe it is an absolute priority that public policy in this area be reviewed urgently. I believe it's important for politicians to listen to pastors, and to address some of the things they hear.

Finally, one of the most pressing issues in modern society is the nature of leadership. There is a crisis of leadership in the modern world. Despite being quite a widely travelled person, I have never yet met a member of a focus group! I have to believe they exist, but I've never had the privilege of meeting one. So who is shaping public policy? Is it formulated according to the lowest common denominator? Serious problems are arising from the fact that private life is being divorced from public office. Private life becomes a legitimate subject of public interest when you stand for public office, because to stand for public office is an invitation to be trusted. So if you have proved untrustworthy - in the community, in business, in the family - that does reflect your fitness to represent others in the civic sphere. There are many and complex reasons for the cynicism about politicians today, but one of the factors is this: the more you divorce private life from public office, the more cynical the public becomes, because they think that you're on the make and you're just there to feather your own nest. I believe we need a debate about the nature of leadership in the modern world.

Leadership is about vision. We need a vision not of goals and objectives. This is the difference between the gospel message entrusted to the church, and most modern-day management-speak. In the Bible, vision is not primarily about goals and strategies. It is about God. We need an articulation of social policy that is theologically rooted in our understanding of God – a God of justice, and of mercy. A just society is a hard place for sinners. We need a society of justice and of mercy, modelled on the very character of God. So I long to see God raise up, in our generation or maybe the next, a new Wilberforce, who can set before us a vision of society which is indeed motivated by moral, spiritual and social instincts - a vision that both connects with humanity and transcends it. A vision of a society restored to the image and the vision of God.

The Second Temple Address (2002)

Delivered at the Inner Temple Hall, 27th June 2002

Jim Wallis

Christian Values and the Three Poverties

I like the old story of the Anglican ordinand worrying about his first Eucharist. He was anxious that in the liturgy he would get his parts wrong, that the congregation would get their parts wrong, that the whole thing would fall apart, and that he'd be thought a failure as a priest. So he approached the altar very nervously on that first day, and just panicked when he realized that the microphone had gone dead. As the people sat and waited, he tapped the microphone frantically, saying, 'something is wrong with this thing.' The congregation duly replied, 'And also with you.'

I think of that story now because something indeed is wrong in our world when phenomenal wealth exists alongside death-dealing poverty. The recent G8 meetings revealed that half the population of sub-Saharan Africa lives on less than one pound per day, fully one third of all its people are malnourished, and 25 million now have HIV/AIDS. But perhaps the deepest poverty is a poverty of values that, among other things, allows us to tolerate such disparities.

There's a lot of talk where I come from, in the USA, about the Faith-Based Initiative. It's a big issue for The White House, for Democrats and Republicans. I teach at Harvard part-time, and even up there most of us didn't know that we were FBOs – Faith-Based Organisations – until a couple of years ago. We were just church folks in the streets, in the trenches. Now, according to the President, we're FBOs. So we've had these conversations with him and others. But my notion of it all doesn't really derive from the halls of power, or from academia, as important as those places are. It derives, rather, from an invitation I received a couple of years ago, from the inmates at Sing Sing Prison, in upstate New York. The inmates there said, 'Would you come and speak to us'? I thought this was a good idea, so I wrote back and told them I would. 'When would you like me to come?' I asked. They said: 'We're free most nights, we're kind of a captive audience!' The prison officials were very generous: they gave us a room in the bowels of the prison, way back underneath, and 75 men and I spent about four hours together. I'll never forget what one of them said that night. He said: 'All of us are from about four or five neighbourhoods in New York City, the whole prison, just about five neighbourhoods. It's like a train begins in my neighbourhood and that train ends up here, at Sing Sing Prison.' 'When I get out,' he said, 'I want to go back and stop that train.'

That inmate had a conversion inside the walls of Sing Sing. Two years later, I was in New York City speaking at a town meeting, and guess who was up front? That young brother was leading a town meeting in New York City. Last month we honoured him at a banquet in Washington DC with what is known as the Amos Award - a way of recognizing those from humble beginnings, sheep and goat herders, who become prophets of justice. When those on the very bottom of society can have that kind of faith - a faith to stop trains or move mountains - well, that's what I call a faith-based initiative.

I want to speak to you about what I'm calling the Three Poverties: material, spiritual and civic. These poverties have become so debilitating that they threaten the very essence of our democracy. I've been working to overcome poverty for many years and I've realized that I haven't understood this deeply enough. We are used to hearing about one aspect of poverty - that reflected in those G8 facts - but these three poverties together represent something much deeper and broader - something we have to understand in a more theological way.

Probably nothing I do on the road has as much impact as my recitation of the great Mahatma Gandhi's 'seven deadly sins'. They speak right to the heart of the values question for me, and your current focus on values in the Evangelical Alliance UK brought them back to my mind. There is such a powerful reaction every time I cite these that I thought I should do so here. They were the key maxims which Gandhi used when instructing his young converts at the Ashram. The 'seven deadly sins' are:

1. Politics without principle
2. Wealth without work
3. Commerce without morality
4. Pleasure without conscience
5. Education without character
6. Science without humanity
7. Worship without sacrifice

Gandhi's diagnosis speaks powerfully to our own values crisis in the USA. Our economy is booming, but how happy is life behind America's gated communities? The poor aren't the only ones worried about their kids today; the affluent are worried as well, about the consequences of their own values showing up in their kids. It is no longer just the children of inner-city folk from my neighbourhood who are now erupting in violence. We've had that reputation for years. It's now kids from middle-class, white, affluent communities responding in horrific ways to their own disappointments and anger.

Many people still want to underestimate or minimize the first of the Three Poverties - namely, the problem of material poverty. They want to blame the poor themselves for their predicament. The systematic causes of such material poverty, and the moral indifference of the affluent towards it, are not popular subjects. Yet all our major religious traditions focus on how we treat those who are poor. The prophets are absolutely clear on this. The test of a nation's integrity or righteousness, as they would say, is neither our GNP nor our military firepower, but how we treat the poorest and most vulnerable in our midst.

At a deeper level, a materialistic society fails to recognize the second Poverty - that is, the problem of its own spiritual poverty. The fact that all our anxious striving has impoverished our souls is a spiritual reality that we are still not quite ready to face. Yet at some deep level I think we know it's true. I'm taking our spiritual poverty much more seriously than I used to. In battling to get the richest nations on earth to address their own poverty and the appalling inequalities in the world, I think I have often underestimated the spiritual consequences of the nervous and shallow existences of so many people in the west. They find themselves trapped, unable to respond to a call for justice. The result is a life without a deep sense of meaning or purpose - one that feels empty.

I have also come to believe that the breakdown of our public life can also be understood as a third form of poverty - a civic poverty. This is manifested in various ways. It is seen in the rapid decline of citizen participation and involvement in politics, with voting figures plummeting and people feeling that there's nothing worth voting for, that it makes no difference, that they're not represented, that no one is speaking for them. It is seen in political debate that descends too often into a battle of extremes, with the media presenting politics as a new form of entertainment. It is seen when political leaders in Washington DC and around the world take a problem and now no longer even seek a solution, but simply find someone else to blame for it. Our political cycle is: name a problem, pin it on someone, take a poll, have an election and see whose spin has won. We never get back to solving the problem. This is what I mean by civic poverty.

Material poverty is the exclusion of marginalized people, those who are the most vulnerable of God's children. The Torah, the New Testament, the Koran - all make it clear that the treatment of the other is the test of true faith. The whole picture is very stark indeed: you know it, I won't labour it. You have more conversation in this nation about the facts than we do in ours. You know that 30,000 children die each day from easily prevented hunger and the diseases related to it. Here's a fact to ponder: by the end of our evening, more children will have died of preventable causes than all those who perished in the Twin Towers on September 11th 2001.

Certain contrasts always strike me. The United Nations Human Development report estimates that basic education for all would cost $6 billion a year, yet $8 billion is spent annually on cosmetics in the United States. Installation of water and basic sanitation for all would cost $9 billion; $11 billion is spent annually on ice cream in Europe. Basic health care and nutrition would cost $13 billion; $17 billion a year is spent on pet food in Europe and the United States. $35 billion is spent on business entertainment in Japan, $50 billion on cigarettes in Europe, $105 billion on alcoholic drinks in Europe, $400 billion on narcotic drugs around the world, and $780 billion on the world's militaries.

You probably didn't expect any reference tonight to Biblical archaeology, but something from this field has challenged me recently, and I'm still wrestling with it. When archaeologists dig down into the ruins of ancient Israel they find houses and artefacts of life from certain periods that show a relative equality between the people: dwellings of more or less the same size and so on. During these periods there were no prophets: no Amos, no Isaiah, no Jeremiah. Yet during other periods, such as the 8th century, the houses were large and the shacks small, and the instruments of life show a great disparity between people - and it was at these times that the prophets thundered with the judgement and justice of God.

The biblical ethic doesn't idealize poverty, and it doesn't even mind prosperity as long as we prosper together, as long as some aren't left behind. You are blessed, I think, to have a Prime Minister and a Chancellor of the Exchequer, Tony Blair and Gordon Brown, who are raising these issues - a 'Marshall Plan' of aid to developing countries in order to accomplish the ambitious goals of the UN's Millennium Summit. I was over here for meetings with some of your church leaders and government people. When I came home, I was in a discussion the next week with chief staff representatives, Democrats and Republicans in the US Senate - the ones who are running the offices of the most powerful people in my nation. I mentioned the Millennium Summit goals for 2015 to cut global poverty in half, reduce infant mortality by two-thirds, and make primary education available to all children. These top Senate staff said to me, 'Millennium goals? 2015?' It's not even a conversation in the United States. Most journalists, too, would be ignorant of the Millennium Summit goals. Yet this is a conversation that God understands.

And it is a conversation which is tied to our spiritual poverty. I think there's pressure on the affluent - with two parents working full time there's the poverty of time. There's no time any more for children, for family, for marriage, for church, for community. We're in a relentless cycle, under relentless pressure. It never ends. Descartes said, 'I think, therefore I am'. We might well say, 'I shop, therefore I am.' There is no time. It's all spent in work and consumption, and both are increasingly meaningless to us. So we lead lives that are full of anxiety, alienation, stress and emptiness.

I was looking at some figures that you gave me, some of your social and demographic data. The juvenile crime rate in the 1940s was only a third of what it is now according to a consumer analysis group survey. Philip Burley of the Variety Club said that crime seems to be the new form of illness in children, for which we're going to need complex social solutions. Jan Walsh, head of the CA group said, 'I believe that commercial society is a root cause. There's a much greater emphasis on what we possess today. From the earliest age, through TV adverts and peer pressure, children are persuaded that they must possess all kinds of things. It is now a very basic fact of a young person's life that they must have the right trainers on their feet and the right logos on their bags and kids are winding up getting killed for their jackets.' That is spiritual poverty.

Jesus' first temptation, while fasting in the desert, was to turn stones into bread. Here was the temptation of the easy answer, the quick fix, the instant solution. Why deny yourself anything? You can have it all and you can have it now! This is the ethos of modern advertising. That was the tempter's promise, and it has taken root in our consumer culture. Jesus responds to the economic temptation in the desert by asserting, "One does not live by bread alone." Bread is not bad; on the contrary, it is good. Jesus liked events like the one we are enjoying tonight, but bread is not all there is. Too much security is as dangerous as too little. Jesus advises his followers to resist the temptations of the easy life, to be more modest and patient, to simplify their lives, and to replace anxious striving with prayerful trust.

Then there is our civic poverty. I know public officials, members of Congress, whom I respect greatly. Like many of your own MPs, some of whom are here tonight, they are dedicated and deeply committed. But when blame takes precedence over solutions, when politics becomes the clash of opposing opinions, when the media polarizes discussion, our problems will only be compounded. We recently had a religious broadcasters' convention – for all the television preachers in town. I got a call from a network and they said 'We've heard that Jesus once got really mad and knocked over a bunch of tables or something at a convention.' 'Well, sort of, but it was in the Temple, and they were money-changers,' I replied. 'Great,' he said. "That's what we have in mind. We'd like to film you walking into the convention centre with all of those right wing preachers and we'd like you to look really mad. And we'll film all that and then you walk up to the table of (and I won't name his name) and you probably shouldn't knock over his table, but just argue with him. We've already worked it all out with him and he thinks it's a really cool idea!" This is the media's idea of dialogue!

Listening to both sides, you would think we are being forced to choose between promoting family values or creating good jobs, between protecting the sacredness of life or defending the rights of women, between expanding economic opportunity or securing economic justice, between holding the entertainment industry accountable for its moral values or pressing large corporations to be responsible to their workers and communities, between upholding personal responsibility or working for racial equality. You would think that these things are mutually exclusive, when most of us would support them all. This is civic poverty.

I believe spiritual renewal will supply the energy for justice. Faith and spirituality will become the most powerful forces for social justice at the beginning of a new millennium. Some would think that a bold and even unbelievable statement, given the common perception of religion today and the inward preoccupation of much contemporary spirituality. Religion has been regarded as a mostly private affair, even a very reactionary influence. And much of the resurgence of spirituality we've seen over the last several years has been commercialized into a self-help movement. But I think there's a return to the spiritual power of faith. Virtually every single social movement that has made a difference in this world, from antislavery and child labour reform to women's suffrage, has had a spiritual foundation and a spiritual dynamic. History is changed by social movements with spiritual foundations. Spiritual principles and values have been at the centre of almost every positive cultural, social, political and economic change.

I believe in the linkage of faith and justice, and I see a hunger for spirituality way beyond the churches. For me, this vision is so beautifully put in Isaiah 58. I teach all the time, I'm on campuses almost every week. And I love what's happening among young people in my country. They're volunteering; they're mentoring inner city kids; they're working in soup kitchens; they're building houses for homeless people; they're in the Middle East right now, in the most dangerous towns and communities; they're in South Africa, often in daunting and dangerous circumstances. And I say, Why? Why are you volunteering in ways that are more than is necessary for a balanced résumé? And time and again I hear two words: meaning and connection. These young people are looking for meaning, and they're looking for connection. In doing so, they're stumbling on the wisdom of Isaiah. Isaiah says, 'Is this not the fast that I choose: to break the bonds of injustice and let the oppressed go free? Is it not to share your bread with the hungry, and to bring the homeless poor into your house, when you see the naked to cover them, and not to hide yourself from your own flesh?' (58:6-7). That part I always knew: it was a social justice text. I had it down, I memorized it - but I missed this next part: 'Then *your* light shall break forth like the dawn, and *your* healing shall spring up speedily' (58:8). Not just *their* healing - not just the healing of those poor unfortunate folks who are being helped. *You* - who have bread to share and houses to shelter others - *your* healing is also at stake in all of this. There is a profound point here for our present-day western self-help culture: the path to genuine healing and self-fulfilment is the journey that connects us to other people, and especially to the poor and the marginalized.

How often have you heard people say: 'I want to get involved in some kind of service, but first I have to get my own life together'? Isaiah emphasizes that if you do that, you may never get your life together. It could be a trap. He says: 'If you want to get your life together you've got to make this connection.' Today, bookstores have all manner of volumes on healing and prosperity, balance and wholeness. It's a multi-million dollar industry. But Isaiah says: 'save your money. You want healing? Make the connection between self-help and helping others.' In Isaiah's vision, we all get healed. Here is the link between personal and social healing. Here is the cure for material poverty, and for spiritual poverty. They both get healed in the same movement. It's not just some people doing good for others. It's a transaction, a transformation, a new relationship, that if lifted to a new scale could change everything about our societies.

Isaiah also speaks to our civic poverty. His prophecies challenge those who would point the finger, who would denounce evil but not tackle it, who would blame and posture rather than solve problems. He insists: 'You rather must be called 'the repairer of the breach' and 'the restorer of streets to live in.' (58:12). I love the description of what is promised here. It would whet the appetite of any self-help enthusiast:

> If you offer your food to the hungry and satisfy the needs of the afflicted, then your light shall rise in the darkness and your gloom be like the noonday. The Lord will guide you continually and satisfy your needs in parched places, and make your bones strong, and you shall be like a watered garden, like a spring of waters whose waters never fail' (58:10).

This Isaiah vision is a vision for our time. A vision for changing the world. Not a utopian vision. Utopian visions have been part of our problem. But how do we change our neighbourhoods, our schools, our congregations, our workplaces? All over the world churches have the chance to be the leaders here, but not unless we come together.

Faith communities offer a sense of meaning, purpose and moral value that is increasingly missing in society. Faith communities can speak directly to the deep spiritual hunger so many people feel. Faith communities are best situated to speak to the moral and spiritual impoverishment of the society, which others seem to accept as inevitable. They can help re-establish a sense of ethics and values. Faith communities offer people practical opportunities to love their neighbour, serve their community, contribute to a larger purpose and sacrifice, to something worth believing in. The time is ripe for a new spiritual movement to address these Three Poverties I have identified.

I'll close with this story and a metaphor. Call to Renewal is one of the Sojourners' key initiatives.[1] I got the idea for it in an unusual setting. I was at a Gang Peace Summit in Kansas City. We had 125 gang leaders from 25 cities around the country. Crips and Bloods, Vice Lords, Latin Kings, Cobras, Gangster Disciples (that's my favourite: Gangster Disciples out of Chicago, 50,000 GDs; now they call themselves the Growth and Development group). There we were, 125 gangsters, and on Sunday morning at St. Stephen's - a large Black Baptist church where we held this thing - they were there in the congregation alongside all the folks. They sat with their tattoos, baseball caps and baggy pants, body armour everywhere, and Revd Mac Charles-Jones, 300 lbs of Baptist preacher, did an altar call. Now I don't know if altar calls are in your tradition, but they're in my tradition. He preached the Prodigal Son. "Young man, Jewish man's in the hog pen. If you're a Jewish boy and you're in the hog pen, you're on the bottom. In the text it says the young man came to himself: he didn't hear a radio message or a tract, he just came to himself. And he got up and he walked home and his father's waiting, looking - he's been waiting many days. He's waiting and looking and he sees his son, and the son sees his father. The son gets his story together and he says, 'sorry dad, I

---

[1] Call to Renewal was formed in 1995 when Jim Wallis envisioned a movement to overcome poverty and dismantle racism in the United States. The epiphany he describes here resulted in a rededication of Sojourners, the organization he serves as Executive Director from its base in Washington DC. It also led to a founding document, *A Cry for Renewal: Biblical Faith and Spiritual Politics*, which was endorsed by nearly 100 religious leaders. Jim Wallis currently serves as Convener of Call to Renewal. For the full text of *A Cry for Renewal* and other information about the Movement to Overcome Poverty, see http://www.calltorenewal.com

squandered the inheritance, I blew it, but now I want to be one of your servants', and he doesn't even get his story out. His father says, 'My son who was lost is found, he was dead and now he's alive.' And he has a party." And Mac, standing there looking like God, this big Black preacher, said to those gangsters, "Get out of the hog pen, come home, the church is waiting. We're going to have a party."

Now altar calls are a dangerous thing. You give the invitation and there's that long silence. How many verses of *Just as I Am* can you sing? Well, we sang five and finally two young men, a Crip and a Blood, stood up and walked to the front. They had been trying to kill each other for a year in a drug war. And in that pulpit they dropped their gang colours. A blue kerchief and a red kerchief, signifying the gangs they belong to. They dropped their colours in the pulpit. You can be killed for that. And they said, 'From now on we walk the same road together.' There wasn't a dry eye in the place.

My tears came when I realized if Crips and the Bloods could do this, why can't Evangelicals, Lutherans, Catholics, Protestants, black and white churches? Why can't these faith communities make more effort to walk the same road? I can say this: I'm a Pastor. In my country at least, churches have acted like gangs. Turf territory. Grievances, grudges, all that paraphernalia. We have differences - real differences, important differences. But on this issue of poverty it seemed time to come together. So we put a call out, and now we have a table and all the church gangs are there. The Catholic Bishops Conference – they're a large gang in our country, chapters all over the place. All the denominations are there. World Vision is there, and World Relief is there. We have a National Association of Evangelicals; we also have a National Council of Churches. This is the only table they sit at together. They've been like the Crips and the Bloods, those two. So I put a Mennonite between them every time, to make sure nothing goes wrong! That kind of coming together is essential for any success in leadership.

And I want just to say what leadership is. Leadership is what I said to 2,000 low income people who came to Washington two weeks ago to speak to their members of Congress about what poor people needed in our new social policy. They were people not used to getting heard. But these 2,000 people felt strongly. I could sense the energy in the room. It was on the Mall, a big tent. And I said to them, 'Let me tell you how to recognize a member of Congress. You're here to speak to them. They're the ones walking around with their fingers in the air, and they're often wet fingers because they lick them and put them in the air to see which way the wind is blowing.'

We make the mistake of thinking that we change a nation by replacing one wet-fingered politician with another. While there are dedicated elected officials, most of them do have their fingers in the wind. And if you want to change a nation, as Martin Luther King knew and as Gandhi knew, you don't just need to change elected officials with fingers in the air; you need to change the wind. Changing the wind is our vocation. When the wind changes it is amazing how quickly the political leaders begin to move in a different direction.

Your focus this year in the Evangelical Alliance UK is on values. Values must be fought for, but at the risk of seeming heretical I wouldn't say that the real battle in our time is between so-called sacred and secular values. I know that's what many people think. But I believe that the more pressing battle is a battle between cynicism and hope. Who will have the hope to believe what I have envisaged - that neighbourhoods and lives and families and nations can be changed in this way? Even Christian folk, even the politically correct folk, even the justice folk, can fall prey to a cynicism which doesn't really believe that it can happen. They still think the right things, believe the right things and say the right things, but they hedge their bets because they've lost faith that it can ever truly be delivered.

Hebrews 12:1 says that faith is 'the substance of things hoped for and the evidence of things not seen.' The world is waiting for a people who will offer the value of hope. Hope that change is possible. Hope that inspires them to bet their lives on such change. My own paraphrase of Hebrews 12:1 is this:

Hope is believing in spite of the evidence, and then watching the evidence change.

It is both a statement of faith and a practical vision to transform the world.

The Third Temple Address (2003)

Delivered at One George Street, Westminster, 24th November 2003

Lord George Carey

Recovering Hope

The Evangelical Alliance represents a significant proportion of Christians in the UK, and it is so good that under Joel Edwards' leadership as General Director it has become increasingly determined to make an evangelical contribution to social thought and action. I am therefore delighted to have this opportunity to reflect on that contribution by addressing your main theme and key value for this year: the value of hope.

Hope is a nebulous word and perhaps the only way to get a handle on it is by way of stories.

Stan is a new friend of mine. I met him in North Carolina just recently. He had been a successful businessman with what he thought was a happy marriage. His job was well paid, but in his view not quite well enough. He was a clever businessman and very shortly he started to cut corners and began to embezzle. One day he was caught and everything fell apart. He was sent to prison but far, far worse was that all that he valued, he lost. His wife left him, taking the children; he lost his home; he lost everything. In prison he started to think seriously about suicide. There seemed no way out. After three years, he was sent to a more relaxed prison and part of his rehabilitation was time in a black urban community. That is where he met Marcia. Marcia, a little black girl of 3, entranced him with her smile. She had no mother and father but when Frank visited her she would beam and hold him tight. He began to visit her several times a week and it started to change him. One day he said to the woman in charge of the baby unit: 'Marcia has started to give me reasons for living. Her radiant smile has given me hope for myself and for the human race.' The woman gave him a strange look and said: 'That's odd. You see, Marcia only began smiling when you met her for the first time and gave her a hug.' Two people in need of love and hope, and both supplied it to the other. Stan has since put his life together and has helped Marcia to get adopted.

Hope may be a nebulous word, but this does not mean that it lacks meaning and direction.

Think of the damage you would do to a child if you said to her or him continuously: "You are hopeless. I can do nothing for you. Hopeless and helpless." Yet there are many people in our society and our world who not only feel hopeless, but are continually told that they are hopeless. During my time as Archbishop of Canterbury I went into many seemingly hopeless situations. I think of Rwanda. My wife Eileen and I were among the very first western leaders to visit that country after the genocide in April 1994 which cost some 800,000 lives. We visited makeshift orphanages where hundreds of lost boys and girls had nothing on which to build a future. I remember thinking that I had nowhere seen a more hopeless situation. Then the Minister for the Interior gave Eileen a photo of three young children, none of them older than five, picking at a hillside with hoes in order to sow seed. Its message was simple - hope may be found in the most unexpected place.

I recall a refugee camp outside Khartoum where I met lovely young Dinka girl with two babies at her breast. She cried to me across barbed wire: 'Help me to get back to my people!' Her despair was palpable. There was nothing I could do to bring hope to her.

But hopeless situations are not simply abroad - they are here with us in Britain, too, and hopelessness creates a dreadful fruit. Hopelessness creates a culture of despair and futility. As the Mexican writer Pedro Casaldaliga wrote from his situation: 'If you take away people's hope you have taken everything away'. When hope dies, everything else dies too. Another writer, Jürgen Moltmann, argues from his experience of returning as a POW to post-war Germany, 'If there is positive hope, we invest in the future. If there is no hope anymore, we incur debts.' Are we really surprised to find young people on some of our housing estates lacking hope when they start to believe that they really are the bottom of the heap and the chips are stacked against them?

But hopelessness also creates a culture of cynicism and world-weariness. I remember when I was a prison chaplain - years ago I must add, but I doubt if the prison service has transformed that much to make the story irrelevant - I met a young man who was in for a succession of minor crimes. The puzzle was that he was quite bright and really could do much better for himself. I decided to spend more time with him. I found an able young man who had already given up. He told me that he had sought job after job, but because he had a record he was rejected again and again. He then made a revealing observation: 'I came to the point when nothing made any difference to me.' That was when he decided to work the system and wreak as much havoc as he could. The breakthrough came when it dawned on him that the social workers, the teachers and the chaplain actually did believe in his abilities and he had worthwhile reasons to live. He flowered when he began to rise above cynicism to belief, and hope in a future began to develop. It is no accident that in Dante's great allegorical poem *The Divine Comedy*, there is an inscription above the entrance to hell which reads: 'Abandon all hope, you who enter here.' To be without hope is to be in a place of hell.

How then do we replace hopelessness by hope?

First, hope must have a content. I agree that the hope of a lottery win probably keeps a lot of people going, but the chances of winning are very slim indeed. I am assuming that hope for most of us has to have a moral, purposeful basis, so that we hope for something which is worthwhile and which makes a difference to others.

I rather wonder what politicians hope for and what values they reach towards. It is sad that politicians get such a low score when trust is assessed. It clashes with my knowledge of them because the ones I know - and I know quite a few - are people with high ideals and great compassion. Could it be that because politicians are human, too, the ideals which drove them to seek political office are gradually eroded by frustration and dimmed by a thousand disappointments? If that is so, do we not want politicians to regain their hope that things can be different?

I can think of no better example of hope in the political sphere than the great Martin Luther King Jnr. He was a not in the first instance a politician, but he acted politically. He was first and foremost a Baptist preacher and would have felt very much at home with us this evening. I never met him, but through his writings I feel I have known him for a very long time. I have stood under that great statue of Abraham Lincoln, on the very spot where Martin Luther King gave that life changing speech: '"So I say to you, my friends, that even though we must face the difficulties of today and tomorrow, I still have a dream. It is a dream deeply rooted in the American dream that one day this nation will rise up and live out the true meaning off its creed - 'We hold these truths to be self evident, that all men are created equal.'"' They were electrifying words when first spoken, and even now they excite. His dream captured the hopes of millions of Americans and his actions gave that dream substance.

So, unrepentantly, I want to encourage our politicians and opinion formers to start dreaming of new possibilities, and then start on the lengthy process of making them a reality. It is not for me to outline a political charter for a nation, but I rather think that Martin Luther King's approach might have taken this form:

A great nation needs moral values to guide it.
A great nation needs a just legal system to shape it.
A great nation requires an intelligent and educated people to own it.
A great nation must give a bias to the poor and the most vulnerable.
A great nation must give hope to all its citizens.

This kind of vision offers a substantive, inspiring model with which to improve the health of all citizens; to give the education system the resources it needs to make a difference; to strengthen family life; to fight the gun culture in our urban cities; to provide hope for young people who have already concluded that there is nothing to hope for.

I believe President Clinton was referring to such hope when during his time in office he went to the church in Tennessee where Martin Luther King had preached his last sermon before his death. There, President Clinton said: 'Unless we reach deep inside to the values, the spirit, the soul and the truth of human nature, none of the other things we seek to do will ever take us where we need to go.' The key phrase for me here is *the things we seek to do*. 'They won't happen', President Clinton was saying, 'unless that hope is harnessed to the things we most deeply care about.' And each one of his hearers in that church would have known exactly what he meant by 'values'. They would have been Christian values, but not exclusive to Christians: the importance of human freedom for all, dignity, tolerance, goodness, kindness, love, respect, honesty, courage and faith.

I am aware that politicians and others are beginning to focus attention on encouraging more people to vote at the next general election, following the all-time low of 59% in 2001. But, with respect, finding more convenient ways of voting will not address the more urgent questions. Why have people lost interest? Why does politics turn many off? Is it an issue of trust or boredom? Could it be that they do not see a connection between Westminster and their daily lives? If so, the challenge to our political leaders, if they believe themselves to be hope-bringers as I know many do, is to clarify their objectives and their vision. They must focus on those things that are most important to the people they serve – putting community and family values at the heart of policy; promoting justice, equality and fairness for all; passing good laws that protect us from ourselves, as well as those who exploit us.

My second point is that genuine hope overcomes cynicism. I am proud to be British and I cherish our culture, our history and our values. But I can't help but compare Britain unfavourably with America in one particular way: as a people, we British are a more cynical, more cold and more jaundiced than our American counterparts. I have often wondered why this should be. Is it the result of a history and experience that has taught us to distrust until we are quite sure, and to keep ourselves emotionally disengaged in the process? Perhaps this is part of it.

Yet the American spirit attracts me. Americans are more open than we are, more innocent, more trusting and, therefore, more hopeful. Whereas we are tempted to doubt whether a project could succeed, the American spirit is likely to consider that everything can be done, and they will allocate sufficient resources to finish the job. We can learn from that. We are an adaptable and resourceful people, too. Our contribution to the human family is second to none, and we can be rightly proud of all that British people have achieved.

But from where does cynicism originate? Clearly from a variety of sources, not least in feelings of being let down by others - society, employers, schools, churches, and even homes. Wherever cynicism is found, a culture is created which saps the human spirit and doses every good intention with disparagement and contempt. The media has a significant role to play in challenging this mood of cynicism, and perhaps it could pay attention to the way news gets reported. Indeed, it has a major role to play in resisting the drift into a climate of negative criticism, endless carping and constant blaming. Some journalists might reply that it is not their job to moralize or preach. I accept that. But no function is ever value-free. No written article is ever objective. We impose our own way of looking at life whatever we write. It is a half-truth to say that the media simply reflect society's mores and interests - they also influence our habits and attitudes more profoundly than most people realize. The press has the power not merely reflect existing concerns, but to shape future lives and careers.

Take for example the pressure on Iain Duncan Smith that led to his replacement by Michael Howard as Conservative Party leader. Without getting into 'pros and cons' of the leadership tussle itself, the evidence suggests that media pressure played a significant role in his departure. News, in other words, is not merely about external events; it is also constructed and defined by editors and journalists.

Let me give an illustration from my experience as Archbishop. Over the Spring Bank holiday of 1999, I arranged a remarkable youth event in London. Five thousand young people between 16 and 23 came to Lambeth Palace for a programme called 'Time of Our Lives'. It was good news about the church and its engagement in the lives of intelligent young people. They had a terrific time, at a rock concert in the Albert Hall, and in over 100 seminars at Parliament, at Lambeth Palace and elsewhere. Yet despite our efforts to get some news of this in our national press, little or nothing was reported. Why? Because on the very first evening a bomb planted in a Soho pub killed nearly 20 people, and that became the focus of media coverage. One can understand that that horrible event was bound to make front-page news. The irony was, as we found out much later, that the perpetrator of that dreadful deed was a young man in the same age bracket as the 5000 fine youngsters who had come together to learn, study, pray and celebrate. Good news didn't make it that weekend.

'For most folk', said Gloria Borger, Contributing Editor at the US News and World Report, 'no news is good news. For the press, good news is not news.'

Think of the Church of England and the recent debate about the consecration of the actively gay priest Gene Robinson as Bishop of New Hampshire. It would appear from the media that the Church of England is obsessed with sex, and particularly with homosexuality. Yet it was not very long ago that we launched a programme called 'Restoring Hope in Our Church'. The campaign video showed the Church of England in good heart, with much to encourage us. I am not denying that the controversy surrounding Gene Robinson's appointment is important - of course it is. This is a tremendously painful time for the Anglican Communion world wide and there are good, conscientious people are on both sides of the divide. Judging from the coverage, however, it would appear that this is the *only* issue that matters for Anglicans, and it is not: in fact, it is not even the most important matter. Far more important is the mission of the church, and it is sad that in the current controversy, really hopeful stories of mission have been obscured. So I do want to encourage the media to find ways of being 'hope-bringers', and this must involve some challenging of editors to tell stories which show the better side of human nature - fun stories, stories of courage and heroism. Stories like that of recovered heart bypass patient Sir Ranulph Fiennes and his recent completion of six marathons in a week. Stories of faith, courage and goodness. I resist the retort that it would make news 'dull'. That depends on the way it is written up, and I don't believe the British are lacking in ability and imagination!

Allow me to add two very recent pieces of excellent news that are foretastes of what I would like to see. First, the Children in Need Appeal by the BBC, which brings fun and moral earnestness together in a remarkable partnership. It can't be done every week, of course, but it shows the spirit of enterprise linked with a determination to share hope with disadvantaged children. Second, the England Rugby Union team's success in wining World Cup. What a terrific victory, and what a wonderful final! May that trigger a huge wave of pride, and inspire greater success, both on and off the sporting field.

Finally: how do we create a more hopeful, positive and forward-looking society?

I am not among those who gripe on about a collapsing western civilization and a disintegrating society. For one thing, I don't think such notions are true.

The vast majority of our contemporaries are good, decent people, often more profoundly influenced by Christian values than they know. It is important to inculcate a sense of pride in the nation and to encourage a culture of gratitude for all we have been given. Yet even if you share that optimistic view you will agree with me that there is still much to be done. Let me sketch out some of the challenges:

1.   We must seek to harness the idealism of young people. I think of a girl of a 13 who moved with her family to a small village near Hereford and because there was no youth club there, started one herself. Her energy helped transform the local church into a serving community for young and old alike. I think, too, of the young student Lydia Nash, who won £16,000 on the TV quiz show *Who Wants to be a Millionaire* and immediately gave it to a Christian orphanage in Thailand. If the future belongs to the young, we must allow them to give back hope to despairing communities.

2.   We should celebrate the many good things going on in all our voluntary societies and encourage all people to look beyond their own interests to those of others. The church has good news to share in this regard. Statistics reveal that an encouraging proportion of practising Christians are to be found as volunteers.

3.   Since the atrocities of Sept 11th 2001, minority groups in our society have felt vulnerable and fearful. How might we reach across the cultural and religious divides to become a people who hope together? I think of Muslim communities in this country who are the first to get criticized when evil people commit terrorist acts in the name of Islam. We should side with them, and assure them that they have a rightful place in our society. I think of the Jewish community in our land, so fearful after the terrible bombing of synagogues in Istanbul. We must side with them in fighting anti-Semitism and protecting their right to live and worship in safety. Minority communities have much to offer in encouraging hope in their communities and in us all, for the good of the United Kingdom as a whole.

All that I have said here is really about 'rebinding' our country to the values that have worked so richly for us in the past, as a means of encouraging a hope for the future which will transcend the feelings of cynicism and despair that hold us back. 'Rebinding' in fact is an interesting word because it comes from the Latin word 'religio', from which our English term 'religion' originates. True religion is always hopeful – looking for new possibilities and fresh points of renewal. Hope, of course, is a word deeply imbedded in the Christian faith and rooted in the resurrection. Christians, of all people, should be hopeful people, committed to bringing a message of hope to all.

And where true hope flourishes, a good nation becomes great.

Afterword

Transforming Britain: A Christian Vision for the 21st Century

Martyn Eden

The case for uniting to change Britain

As several of the papers in this volume attest, the last few decades have seen rapid change affecting many aspects of life in Britain. Much of this change has been welcome. Since the Second World War, our society has benefited from numerous advances in technology and medical science, and many of us have enjoyed the comparative prosperity which such advances have brought. But not all the changes which have occurred during this time have been for the better. It has been a period of serious family and community breakdown. It has brought us close to the point at which human beings may be cloned from the cells of aborted foetuses. With scientific sophistication have come ever more sophisticated weapons of mass destruction. Technological innovation and mass production have been accompanied by greater greenhouse emissions. The affluence of the west has not spread decisively to the two-thirds world, where thousands each day still die from famine and curable disease.

As ever, there is something at the heart of our society and our world that is out of step with the intentions of our Creator. It has been like this ever since Adam and Eve disobeyed God, but the consequences have became significantly more damaging as one millennium has given way to another. As Callum Brown has noted, from the 1960s 'British people re-imagined themselves in ways no longer Christian – a moral turn which abruptly undermined virtually all the protocols of moral identity.'[1] There are certain key forces which have contributed to this moral turn.

First, Britain has become increasingly individualistic. Whether the focus is on work, shopping, relationships or even religion, the dominant attitude is that 'it must fit me'.[2] Rising divorce rates and a significant extension of the time

---

[1] Callum Brown, *The Death of Christian Britain* (London: Routledge, 2001), 14-15.

[2] Michael Moynagh, *Changing World, Changing Church* (Eastbourne: Monarch, 2001), 18-34. See also John Drane, *The McDonaldization of the Church: Spirituality, Creativity and the Future of the Church* (London: Darton, Longman & Todd, 2000), 20-28. For an

people live alone before marriage - both in themselves markers of individualism - have helped virtually to double the proportion of lone person households, from 17% in 1971 to 31% in 2001.[3] One major corollary of such individualism is consumerism. Indeed, the exaltation of the self is experienced most blatantly in the shopping malls which have become the materialist cathedrals of our age. As Don Slater has observed, when the core values of a culture come to derive from consumption rather than the other way around, as has happened in present-day Britain, 'all social relations, activities and objects can in principle be exchanged as commodities', and this in turn effects 'one of the most profound secularizations' that can take place.[4] Or as Rodney Clapp puts it, in contemporary western culture, 'heaven is a vast supermarket; hell is a corner shop stocking only one brand of aspirin or toilet paper, or more significantly, only one brand of religion, morality or marriage.'[5] One of the political campaigns which the Evangelical Alliance has critiqued recently - the move to allow transsexual people legally to change their gender from the one in which they were born and to record this on a new birth certificate - can be seen as a radical manifestation of such individualism and consumerism. It privileges self-image and self-definition over given facts and historical events, and redefines personhood as a 'brand choice', realized in the consumption of hormone injections and plastic surgery.

It is but a short step from individualism to relativism. There is little place in contemporary culture for absolutes; everyone does what is right in their own eyes. The long-standing moral consensus, rooted in the Judeo-Christian heritage, is disintegrating. As Patricia Morgan of the Institute of Economic Affairs has noted, we have entered a world in which yesterday's immoralities have become today's family forms.[6] Not only are seven times more marriages dissolved today than in 1961, with divorce rates climbing above 40%; cohabitation outside wedlock has doubled in the last 20 years alone, as has the proportion of lone parent households. In addition, one child in every four now experiences the trauma of family breakdown.[7] Of course, the actual phenomenon of family breakdown is not new; as Morgan points out, however,

---

analysis of the socio-political shifts which ushered in this new spirit of individualism, see Will Hutton, *The State We're In* (London: Vintage, 1995), 27-29.

[3] Source: Central Statistical Office, *Social Trends: 1996 Edition*, London: HMSO, 50-51; 'Percentage living alone, by age and sex: Living in Britain' at http://www.statistics.gov.uk/STATBASE (accessed December 2003)

[4] Don Slater, Consumer Culture and Modernity (Cambridge: Polity Press, 1997), 27.

[5] Don Slater, Consumer Culture and Modernity (Cambridge: Polity Press, 1997), 27.

[6] Patricia Morgan, *Farewell to the Family? Family Breakdown in Britain and the USA*, (London: Civitas: Institute for the Study of Civil Society, 1995).

[7] Source: Central Statistical Office, *Social Trends: 1996 Edition*, London: HMSO, 1996, 54, 57-59.

what has changed is the scale on which it is occurring, and the widespread claim that it is actually 'nothing to worry about'.[8]

Relativism in turn spawns pluralism. Post-modern tolerance typically allows everyone to believe in whatever deity or deities they choose, so long as they keep it to themselves. It is this model of religious privatization which drives those now campaigning for the abolition of church schools and religious assemblies. It also serves as the justification given by some local authorities for not funding Christian projects from the public purse. As David Hilborn suggests in his paper for this volume, if carried to more extreme lengths, it could result in the curtailment of open-air evangelism, and not least mission among people of other faiths.

In broad terms, there are three possible responses to the trends I have outlined. Evangelicals can accommodate to them. We can retreat from them into a religious ghetto. Or we can engage in a constructive counter-cultural movement. Accommodation and retreat are not options for Christians. Jesus called his disciples to be different from the world, as different as light is from the dark (Mt. 5:14-16). Indeed, the consistent message of the entire Bible is that God's people are to be holy, set apart for his service. What Jesus adds is the calling for God's people to penetrate society like salt rubbed into fish or meat as a preservative, to slow down decay and give them flavour (Mt. 5:13).[9] We have to be different and remain different from the world in order to make a difference in it. Those who acquiesce in a God-free culture neglect this vital differentiation, and those who retreat into a ghetto abandon it. The remaining option, recognized by a growing number of Christians, is to unite to change our nation and its culture.

How realistic is this idea? Well, as much of the material in this book attests, it is a biblical idea, and if we are Evangelicals committed to the divine authority and inspiration of the Bible, we ought to trust in its realism on this as on other aspects of mission. Furthermore, as the various historical and sociological analyses offered in this book suggest, even quite small groups of Christians can make a substantial difference if they are committed enough. As John Wolffe has helpfully shown, while their social contexts contrasted significantly from our own, there are still instructive lessons to be drawn today from the methods adopted by William Wilberforce and the Clapham Sect, and, a generation later, Lord Shaftesbury.

Further still, we sense the hand of God uniting us to change our society. Since 2002 the Evangelical Alliance has been in strategic conversation with

---

[8] Morgan, *Farewell to the Family?*
[9] Cf. John R.W. Stott, *Christian Counter-Culture* (Leicester: IVP, 1978), 57-68.

five major Christian organisations, all of whom have all felt called to the same vision: the Bible Society, CARE, Tear Fund, the London Institute for Contemporary Christianity and the Relationship Foundation. So too have Gerald Coates and the Round Table Group that he convenes, and the Clapham Connection chaired by Clifford Hill. There is also a cross-party group of MPs who support the idea. We believe the convergence of such a diverse collection of individuals and organisations on this vision to be the work of the Holy Spirit.

Finally we can learn from the impact made by various social groups and movements over the past century which have either been non-religious in ethos or else only partly Christian in their composition. The Suffragettes, the American Civil Rights Movement, the Green Movement, and, in our own time, the gay movement are examples of successful change-makers who began on the margins of their culture, but whose ideas entered the mainstream of social and political life thanks to the dedication of their leaders, the incisiveness of their strategy and the persistence of their campaigning. We may not like what some of these movements have achieved, but we cannot deny that they have influenced public opinion and civic policy in substantive ways. The American sociologist Robert Bellah suggests that 'The quality of a culture may be changed when 2 per cent of its people have a new vision.'[10] Derek Tidball has wisely added that this will happen only when the 2% act concertedly on that vision.[11] It is time for us Christians to take this challenge seriously and begin to make a difference, trusting in the wisdom and power of the Holy Spirit.

What is the vision?

The movement for change that the Evangelical Alliance and its partners feel called to help build is rooted in a contemporary understanding of the Kingdom of God at work in society. It is a movement of people coming to faith in Jesus Christ, integrating that faith into every dimension of their lives, and working together to transform society so that it matches more closely God's design and intentions. It is a nation-wide movement of people prepared to be agents for change in every sector of society. In particular, agents for change will seek to influence the key change drivers in our culture: the worlds of education, politics, the media and the arts, business and the professions. More than anything, it is a vision of all God's people honouring the Lordship of Christ wherever we have an opportunity to do so - at work, at home, at play, as well as at church, just as the early church did. If Brennan Manning was right that 'the

---

[10] Robert Bellah, 'Civil Religion: The Sacred and the Political in American Life' (A Conversation with Sam Keen)', *Psychology Today*, 9/8, January 1976, 58-65.
[11] Derek Tidball, on the Evangelical Alliance video *Introducing a Movement for Change* (London: Evangelical Alliance, 2003).

greatest single cause of atheism is Christians who acknowledge Jesus with their lips then walk out the door and deny Him by their lifestyle', we must encourage Christians to be living examples of authentic Christianity. In our pluralistic culture, where everything is an option, authenticity will be central to effective mission.

Anyone wary that this might be nothing more than a recycled 'social gospel' need not fear this model of Evangelicals uniting to change society. The emphasis on authentic Christian discipleship which I have described presupposes personal conversion. Moreover, the stress placed on Christians being front-line missionaries in the work place, media, politics, education and the arts, is yet another expression of commitment to evangelism, tailored to fit contemporary British culture and society. If people will not come to church to hear the gospel preached, we have to live it and share it wherever we have opportunities. The work place, where many Christians spend a large part of their time and develop relationships of trust, has to offer one of those opportunities.

The role of the local church in all this is crucial. Changing our society and its culture will be no easy task, but God gives us the power both to be different and to make a difference. By their teaching, prayer life and pastoral support, churches will equip and mobilize a generation of Christian disciples to develop a Christian counter-culture. Of course, not all churches are as outward looking as this scenario requires. They can be very focused on their own ministries and meetings rather than on releasing members to fulfil a Christian ministry in the wider community. This is why the Evangelical Alliance collaborated in March 2003 with Mark Greene of the London Institute for Contemporary Christianity in the publication of *Imagine*, a challenging essay about how Britain will be won for Christ. Our aim was to trigger a debate within the church, and it is gratifying to report that this debate is being carried forward in a series of meetings with key church leaders, evangelists, publishers, college principals and others. Additionally, the Alliance's Church Life team has begun to accept invitations from local churches to help them review their mission strategies. We call this our Changemakers programme, and it is being presented as a means to helping churches turn inside out in order to turn the world upside down.

The Evangelical Alliance has also now carried out a major survey of the caring activities of churches and Christian groups in British cities, assessing their form and impact. This has revealed just how significant a contribution these faith-based projects are making to their communities. We may hear a lot today about declining church attendance; but much less widely reported are the positive roles many churches are playing in this area. The Government has acknowledged the value of faith-based schools, but they could equally well recognize the contributions made by faith-based organisations which care for people with disabilities or those with drug and alcohol problems, for the homeless and for many other client groups who are ignored and neglected in our self-centred society. Our survey has found that 29 per cent of Christians and 40 per cent of churches are involved in some form of voluntary, caring activity. It is clear from the research that it is their Christian faith that motivates those who provide this compassionate service. This is a huge encouragement for us as we advocate a movement for Christian social transformation. It tells us that we are not starting from scratch: Christian agents for change are already at work.

The challenge, then, for those seeking to build a Movement for Change is threefold. We have to encourage one another and ensure that we retain our Christian distinctiveness. We have to work together where appropriate, rather than compete or build private empires. And we have to ensure that the wider society understands what the Christian community is giving, and what it has to do with Jesus Christ.

In his paper on Evangelicals and the state, David Hilborn alludes to one important issue on which Evangelicals have recently found themselves seeking to make a difference in the public square - namely, in relation to new employment legislation passed by the Westminster Parliament in June 2003. Some background detail on this is instructive with respect to the vision I have been setting out here. The European Union began to talk about outlawing discrimination as far back as 1999. Soon afterwards, the Evangelical Alliance began to work with colleagues in the European Evangelical Alliance and in CARE to lobby the European Commission and Parliament. This process continued for the next two years. Our goal was to ensure that the provisions to block religious discrimination did not prevent religious organisations from employing people of their own faith community, in order that they might preserve their distinctive ethos. The Whitehall Department responsible for employment did not really understand the issues, but asked us to work with them. With a lot of help from the Irish Government we managed to achieve most of our objectives. After the 2001 General Election, the European Directive had to be incorporated into British law and the legislation team again asked us to work with them. Following more complicated negotiation, the Government recognized our case, drafted the legislation accordingly, and carried it through both Houses of Parliament. The fact that a coalition of unions has subsequently appealed against this legislation, and that as I write we are having to co-sponsor a defence of it in the High Court, only confirms that lasting Christian influence in the public arena is likely to become harder-won as the new century progresses.

No doubt Evangelicals do need to recognize that as a minority group in our society we no longer have a moral right to impose our values and beliefs on the majority. Yet this does not mean that we are powerless to make a difference. We can respond constructively when invited to do so, and if we are operating according to God's commands, we can demonstrate that they make sense, thereby potentially persuading policy makers and public opinion-formers that God's ways are good not just for Christians, but for all of society.

Building the movement - the next steps

A number of stepping stones are already in place. In summer 2003 a short video was made to introduce Movement for Change, and copies were supplied to churches and other Christian organisations. A second video is planned for 2004, to make better known some of the hundreds of Christian community projects around the country that are making a positive difference. The objective is to encourage and motivate other Christians to follow their examples and become agents for change in their own communities. As well as this present book, a more popular volume explaining and illustrating Movement for Change is also due, in Autumn 2004.

As this present book went to press, a group of key church leaders met in Westminster to consolidate the network of all those already committed to Movement for Change and its vision of a Christian counter-culture. We listened to God with us and confirmed together that this vision is authentic. Those who attended will be asked to back the creation of a national Forum for Change that will own the movement on behalf of the churches. Funding is being sought to establish a 'think tank', which will ensure that when we go public, our contributions will be based on thorough research, prayer, reflection and debate. Strategic initiatives will be needed to increase Christian influence in education, the media, politics and public policy, the arts, business and the professions, because these are key change drivers in our society. The Clapham Connection is already working with Christian groups in some of the professions - but every salt and light contribution, however local and humble, will have value.

All of this will be shared and owned as widely as possible. It makes no sense to duplicate or compete with existing ministries. All who want to be part of making Britain a more God-honouring society will be welcome. A contemporary movement for change has to be a mass movement of God's people who succeed in persuading many others that the reason for the hope within us is real because it shapes who we are and how we live.

A movement needs people, and not just any people. This movement needs Christians who are serious disciples of Jesus. It requires Christians who are prepared to relate their faith and their relationship with Jesus to every part of their lives, as they seek to meet the needs of Britain's spiritually needy and hungry society. This is a big vision, and it will not be achieved in a short time. It may be necessary to see it unfolding across several generations. Nor will it be cost free. A genuinely Christian Movement for Change will challenge the conventional wisdom of our society. Prophets, after all, are rarely popular.[12] Being different to one's peers and colleagues can be uncomfortable, but it is our calling. The challenge of the apostle Paul remains as pertinent as ever: 'Do not conform any longer to the pattern of this world, but be transformed by the renewing of your mind.' (Rom. 12:2).

Twenty years ago, Tom Sine wrote about God's strategy for changing the world through a 'conspiracy of the insignificant'.[13] Nothing in the intervening years has diminished the relevance of that message. Indeed, it is needed among Christians in Britain now even more than it was then. I pray this book will help to inform that conspiracy, and that Movement for Change as a whole will help to make it a reality.

---

[12] Luke 4:24 (NIV)

[13] Tom Sine, *The Mustard Seed Conspiracy* (Waco, Tx.: Word Books, 1981), 11.